SAINTS AND MONSTERS IN
MEDIEVAL FRENCH AND OCCITAN LITERATURE
SUBLIME AND ABJECT BODIES

LEGENDA

LEGENDA is the Modern Humanities Research Association's book imprint for new research in the Humanities. Founded in 1995 by Malcolm Bowie and others within the University of Oxford, Legenda has always been a collaborative publishing enterprise, directly governed by scholars. The Modern Humanities Research Association (MHRA) joined this collaboration in 1998, became half-owner in 2004, in partnership with Maney Publishing and then Routledge, and has since 2016 been sole owner. Titles range from medieval texts to contemporary cinema and form a widely comparative view of the modern humanities, including works on Arabic, Catalan, English, French, German, Greek, Italian, Portuguese, Russian, Spanish, and Yiddish literature. Editorial boards and committees of more than 60 leading academic specialists work in collaboration with bodies such as the Society for French Studies, the British Comparative Literature Association and the Association of Hispanists of Great Britain & Ireland.

The MHRA encourages and promotes advanced study and research in the field of the modern humanities, especially modern European languages and literature, including English, and also cinema. It aims to break down the barriers between scholars working in different disciplines and to maintain the unity of humanistic scholarship. The Association fulfils this purpose through the publication of journals, bibliographies, monographs, critical editions, and the MHRA Style Guide, and by making grants in support of research. Membership is open to all who work in the Humanities, whether independent or in a University post, and the participation of younger colleagues entering the field is especially welcomed.

ALSO PUBLISHED BY THE ASSOCIATION

Critical Texts
Tudor and Stuart Translations • *New Translations* • *European Translations*
MHRA Library of Medieval Welsh Literature

MHRA Bibliographies
Publications of the Modern Humanities Research Association

The Annual Bibliography of English Language & Literature
Austrian Studies
Modern Language Review
Portuguese Studies
The Slavonic and East European Review
Working Papers in the Humanities
The Yearbook of English Studies

www.mhra.org.uk
www.legendabooks.com

RESEARCH MONOGRAPHS IN FRENCH STUDIES

The *Research Monographs in French Studies* (RMFS) form a separate series within the Legenda programme and are published in association with the Society for French Studies. Individual members of the Society are entitled to purchase all RMFS titles at a discount.

The series seeks to publish the best new work in all areas of the literature, thought, theory, culture, film and language of the French-speaking world. Its distinctiveness lies in the relative brevity of its publications (50,000–60,000 words). As innovation is a priority of the series, volumes should predominantly consist of new material, although, subject to appropriate modification, previously published research may form up to one third of the whole. Proposals may include critical editions as well as critical studies. They should be sent with one or two sample chapters for consideration to Professor Diana Knight, Department of French and Francophone Studies, University of Nottingham, University Park, Nottingham NG7 2RD.

❖

Editorial Committee
Diana Knight, University of Nottingham (General Editor)
Robert Blackwood, University of Liverpool
Jane Gilbert, University College London
Shirley Jordan, Queen Mary, University of London
Neil Kenny, All Souls College, Oxford
Max Silverman, University of Leeds

Advisory Committee
Wendy Ayres-Bennett, Murray Edwards College, Cambridge
Celia Britton, University College London
Ann Jefferson, New College, Oxford
Sarah Kay, New York University
Michael Moriarty, University of Cambridge
Keith Reader, University of Glasgow

PUBLISHED IN THIS SERIES

www.legendabooks.com

Saints and Monsters in
Medieval French and Occitan Literature

Sublime and Abject Bodies

❖

Huw Grange

LEGENDA

Research Monographs in French Studies 53
Modern Humanities Research Association
2017

Published by Legenda
an imprint of the Modern Humanities Research Association
Salisbury House, Station Road, Cambridge CB1 2LA

ISBN 978-1-781884-89-8 (HB)
ISBN 978-1-78188-490-4 (PB)

First published 2017

Copy-Editor: Dr Susan Wharton

CONTENTS

❖

To Mam and Dad

ACKNOWLEDGEMENTS

❖

I've had the good fortune of being surrounded by many more saints than monsters in the course of this project. Much of the research underpinning the book was carried out during my doctoral studies: my thanks to the Arts & Humanities Research Council, Cambridge University's French Department, and St John's College, Cambridge for supporting my Ph.D work. Thanks, too, to my current institution, Jesus College, Oxford.

I am hugely indebted to my doctoral supervisor, Bill Burgwinkle, whose guidance and encouragement have never fallen short of the sublime echelons. Many thanks, too, to Simon Gaunt, Miranda Griffin, Sylvia Huot and Merryn Everitt for reading bits and bobs at the draft stage.

A list of the helpful librarians who facilitated my perusal of manuscripts in the course of this project would be as long as the table of contents for a medieval hagiographical anthology, but the staff of the British Library, Bibliothèque nationale de France, and the Institut de recherches et d'histoire des textes deserve special mention.

Last but not least, I'd like to express a monstrous amount of gratitude to friends, to family, and to Marius, for their love and support.

Note on Quotations

Where I quote directly from medieval manuscripts, scribal abbreviations have been silently expanded, *i/j* and *u/v* have been regularized, and modern capitalization and punctuation have been added. For Old and Middle French lives, final tonic *e* is indicated by *é* (except in *−ee*). Editions of all previously unpublished texts that I examine in detail may be found at <http://www.huwgrange.co.uk>.

All translations of quotations into English are my own, unless otherwise indicated.

H.G., Oxford, January 2017

INTRODUCTION

❖

Holy Comic Books

Stand aside, Batman! Move over, Wonder Woman! Powerful though you are, your super powers are no match for the likes of Sts Francis of Assisi and Joan of Arc! In recent years, several publishing houses, from small companies specializing in the catechism to household names such as Marvel, have brought the heroes and villains of medieval hagiography (the biographies of saints) to the pages of comics.[1] A trend was noted in a 2006 article for the *Sunday Telegraph* by Elizabeth Day: St Francis has been transformed into 'a chisel-jawed man with flowing chestnut-brown locks, rippling muscles and a penchant for "endless parties",' she wryly remarks, apparently assuming that Arcadius Press's portrayal of a medieval saint as a heart-throb blessed with superhuman stamina was an innovation of the twenty-first century.[2]

Had Day been familiar with medieval French and Occitan hagiography, her piece might not have run with the headline 'Holy Comic Books! Saints Are the Latest Superheroes!'. Bodies, of course, should be irrelevant to the biographies of saintly men and women whose minds tend to be fixed upon far more spiritual concerns. And yet vernacular hagiographers communicate this message by bestowing the most extraordinary bodies upon their subjects. Whether they survive barbecuing (like St Lawrence), remain gorgeous despite being whipped and starved (Catherine), look more ursine than human (John Paul), or shed their bodies to become wraith-like shadows (Mary the Egyptian), the exceptional men and women who star as the protagonists of medieval vernacular hagiography are instantly distinguishable from the common herd because of their weird and wonderful bodies. The corporeality of saints was extraordinary long before the advent of comics: in some ways a better title for Day's article would have been 'Superheroes Are the Latest Saints'.

Likewise, centuries before the advent of the Green Goblin, Dr Doom and Magneto, medieval biographers of saints were already pitting their heroes against a range of antagonists no less villainous than these. From the wild beasts that attack St Anthony in the Egyptian desert to the bearded dragon that ingests St Margaret, and from the diabolical pagan who torments St Faith in the eleventh-century Occitan biography to the snake-breathing Saracen giant of the Occitan life of St Honorat, the monstrous creatures of vernacular hagiography stand out from the crowd on account of their terrifying array of physiological, racial and sexual traits (not to mention cultural and moral ones). If hagiography's monsters all bear markers of corporeal difference, however, like comic book villains they are all the more frightening for being irreconcilably different from one another, and for threatening to hybridize, shape-shift or mutate at any moment.

This book is about the extraordinary bodies of medieval French and Occitan saints' lives and their relationships to us in the audience (who, generally speaking, come equipped with rather more ordinary flesh). Hagiography, I would contend, is a particularly fruitful domain for considering corporeality in terms of flesh, collective identity and textual corpus (three sorts of bodies that were intimately connected for medieval thinkers).[3] For biographies of saints are not just entertaining stories that rival those of modern comic books; they claim to provide a material link between protagonist and audience — not unlike holy relics — promising to protect those who find truth in the narrative from all manner of monsters lurking within the confines of the text and beyond.

The earliest surviving literary work in French, generally known as the *Sequence of St Eulalia* (though its liturgical function is by no means certain), provides us with a suitably introductory example of the interconnectedness of hagiography's assorted bodies. These 29 verses in a dialect of *oïl* were added at the back of a manuscript (Valenciennes, BM 150) in the late ninth century, not far (perhaps) from the Germanic-speaking zone.[4] The story they tell is that of Eulalia, a Christian girl from Mérida (in what is today western Spain) who — tradition has it — was martyred for her faith in the late third or early fourth century.

The ninth-century *Sequence* immediately establishes Eulalia's bodily beauty, eclipsed only by her inner beauty (vv. 1–2). No amount of flattery, bribery or torture will persuade her to surrender her soul to the diabolical pagan persecutor Maximian. But so firm is she in her belief — so pure is her soul — that her body does not behave like yours or mine: when Maximian has Eulalia thrown onto a pyre, much to his dismay her flesh refuses to burn: 'Enz enl fou lo getterent com arde tost: | Elle colpes non auret, poro nos coist' (vv. 19–20) ['They threw her into the fire so that she would quickly burn. She was sin-free, so she did not burn.']. Only once the extraordinary intransigence of the girl's seemingly fragile frame is beyond doubt does Eulalia allow the executioner's axe to end her bodily existence. Her soul heads heavenwards in the form of a dove.

The final four verses of the *Sequence* constitute a prayer invoking Eulalia's aid:

> Tuit oram que por nos degnet preier
> Qued auuisset de nos Christus mercit
> Post la mort et a Lui nos laist venir
> Par souue clementia. (vv. 26–29)

> [Let us all pray that she might deign to pray for us, that Christ may have mercy upon us and let us come to Him after death, by his clemency.]

As we read or listen to these lines, we find ourselves subsumed into a fictional 'we'. This collective body imagined through the text needs to be distinguished carefully from the historical 'textual communities' identified by Brian Stock as movements 'based on a literate inner core, a set of written legislation, and a wider, unlettered membership united orally to the same norms'.[5] As some of Stock's own examples show, however, the fictional 'we' of hagiography can make for a powerful rhetorical strategy when it comes to forming and fostering textual communities outside the text. In sum, the exceptional bodies of saints (and, through their interactions, those of their monstrous opponents, too), by figuring the collective body within the text, may play an important role in shaping the identity of audiences beyond it, too.

The collective 'we' of the *Sequence of St Eulalia* is seemingly as intransigent as the fire-proof body upon which it depends. As Kathleen Ashley and Pamela Sheingorn note, however, the emphasis that hagiographers themselves place on similarity and continuity has led modern scholars to presuppose 'an essential identity of a cult and its saint that remains intact over time and space'.[6] Eulalia's *Sequence* may advocate corporeal constancy, but her bodies and texts signified differently to different audiences. Whether deliberately or by accident, fixed hagiographical 'truths' were fixed to meet the expectations and requirements of new audiences: in the transition between one language and another, between one version and the next, and even between one manuscript and another, the saintly and monstrous bodies of medieval hagiography mutate (as it were) in response to various historical, cultural and geographical factors and imperatives.

From the late ninth century, then, we might fast-forward more than half a millennium to a biography of St Eulalia that survives in a paper codex (Paris, BnF, fr. 9759) produced in the Languedoc in the mid-fifteenth century. This anthology is made up of hundreds of hagiographies in Occitan prose translated from the Latin of Jacobus de Voragine's thirteenth-century *Legenda aurea* (a medieval 'bestseller' if ever there was one). Jacobus did not include an entry for Eulalia, but there is one on ff. 205r-206v of this volume. Never having been published, it has thus far received little scholarly attention.

In the late medieval Occitan text — as in the Old French *Sequence* — Eulalia comes equipped with an extraordinary body to match her extraordinary steadfastness of spirit. Her endurance of torture (including, once again, being burned alive) is the stuff of legend, but she does eventually succumb to the corporeal death she longs for, her heaven-bound soul again figured by a dove.

There are, however, some noteworthy differences between the two tales. What distinguishes the saint's body from your flesh or mine here is not so much its flame-retardancy as its insensibility to pain. Eulalia's flesh bears the marks of whipping, hanging and scorching, but she *feels* nothing: as she endures one torment after another she taunts her chief tormentor — here called Dacian — with cries of 'Coma pus turmentada sera, pus ennoblisida sera, per el que ieu los teus turmens no·ls sant!' (f. 205v) ['The more I am tormented, the nobler I shall become, such that I do not feel your torments!']. In the later version, moreover, the devil-serving pagans do not have to wait until Judgment Day to get their comeuppance. Further emphasizing Eulalia's corporeal alterity, the flames intended for her ricochet onto her oppressors and they go up in a puff of smoke as the saint sings a tuneful psalm.

The most obvious difference between the ninth-century *oïl* text and the fifteenth-century *oc* one, however, is a shift in setting. Shortly before the composition of the Old French *Sequence*, the body of a St Eulalia was 'invented' (read: 'discovered') in Barcelona, and the biography of St Eulalia of Mérida has been attached to that holy corpse (now the patron saint of Barcelona) ever since (Berger and Brasseur, pp. 29–30). In the Occitan version Eulalia hails from near Barcelona and meets her death in that very city. And as if to counter objections to the site of her latest tomb the hagiographer dwells on the circumstances of her burial. Dacian has Eulalia's corpse strung up on a cross for the vultures to pick over, but a miraculous mist shrouds the saint, allowing family and friends to bury her in a more fitting fashion (ff. 206r-206v). The life closes with everybody giving thanks for the saint's ongoing protection of her followers. It is not only the community imagined in the text that is tied to Barcelona, however; the inclusion of this Eulalia entry in this volume — also present in several Catalan anthologies — provides a material link between its historical audience in the Languedoc and the Catalan-speaking zone.[7]

Read or listen to one hagiography and we might ask how the bodies of saints and their antagonists differ from each other and, moreover, how they differ from our own, comparatively normal ones. Read or listen to more than one hagiography and we might wonder, as we briefly have with St Eulalia, how holy and unholy bodies change over time and across space to meet the needs and expectations of new audiences. No doubt comic books could inspire similar questions about the corporeality of their heroes and villains (what do *you* think of Batman's latest incarnation?). But when reading or listening to medieval saints' lives the role of the material text in mediating between exceptional bodies and rather average audiences comes to the fore. For when a material object is believed to testify to the truth of the narrative it transmits, comic book tales about life and death become, for their audiences, a matter of life and death.

From the Sublime to the... Abject

One of the ways to tackle some of these questions is to draw on the notion of the 'sublime body' as theorized by contemporary cultural theorist Slavoj Žižek. Mention of the 'sublime' inevitably evokes Kant's *Kritik der Urteilskraft* and his reflections on objects that are not merely beautiful but so far beyond comprehension that they fill the beholder with 'sublime' — that is, morally uplifting — feelings.[8] We might also think of Freud, who, though he does not actually write of the 'sublime' (which Kant called 'das Erhabene'), does elaborate a theory of 'sublimation' ('Sublimerung'). Sublimation, for Freud, is foundational of civilization as we know it: it is the process by which the subject transforms sexual libido into socially sanctioned, non-sexual activities such as artistic and cultural work.[9]

Most obviously, however, Žižek owes his understanding of the 'sublime' to the French psychoanalyst Jacques Lacan. Lacan performs a rapprochement of the Kantian sublime and Freudian sublimation in his Seminar of 1959–60 entitled *L'Éthique de la psychanalyse*.[10] The sublime, for Lacan, lies not on the side of the subject (as it did, say, for Kant), but on the side of the *object*. Sublimation, meanwhile, does not, for Lacan, redirect sexual drives towards another object (as it did for Freud), but alters the function and location of the same object, rendering it aesthetically and ethically 'sublime'. There is nothing intrinsically sublime about a sublime object: its status is determined by its function and location within the topologics of fantasy.

According to Lacan's most famous formulation of sublimation, 'elle élève un objet

[...] à la dignité de la Chose' (*L'Éthique*, p. 133) ['it raises an object [...] to the dignity of the Thing' (*Ethics*, p. 112)]. The 'Chose' in question, which also goes by the Kantian term of 'das Ding an sich' ['the Thing in itself'], refers to the unknowable object that defies symbolization in language and thus belongs, in Lacanian terms, to the realm of the Real. The subject, unable to exist in any meaningful way with the threat of *das Ding* hanging over him, has recourse to sublimation: in a bid to neutralize that threat, he elevates a mundane object to the position of *das Ding*. As Lacan explains, using his pseudo-algebraic symbol for the sublime object (the 'objet *a*'), subjectivity hangs together thanks to the sublime: 'Dans des formes spécifiées historiquement, socialement, les éléments *a*, éléments imaginaires du fantasme, viennent à recouvrir, à leurrer le sujet au point même de *das Ding*' (*L'Éthique*, p. 119) ['In forms that are historically and socially specific, the *a* elements, the imaginary elements of the fantasm come to overlay the subject, to delude it, at the very point of *das Ding*' (*Ethics*, p. 99)].

The examples of figures raised to sublime status cited by Lacan in *L'Éthique de la psychanalyse* are characteristically eclectic, ranging from the eponymous hero of Sophocles's *Antigone* to the victims of heinous crimes imagined in the novels of the Marquis de Sade. But we might dwell for a moment on one of Lacan's historical case studies in particular, since he plucks it from the Middle Ages. Troubadour song, Lacan suggests, provides the perfect example of sublimation:

> Ce que la création de la poésie courtoise tend à faire, c'est à situer, à la place de la Chose, et à cette époque dont les coordonnées historiques nous montrent quelque discord entre les conditions particulièrement sévères de la réalité et certaines exigences du fond, quelque malaise dans la culture. La création de la poésie consiste à poser, selon le mode de la sublimation propre à l'art, un objet que j'appellerai affolant, un partenaire inhumain.
>
> Jamais la Dame n'est qualifiée pour telles de ses vertus réelles et concrètes, pour sa sagesse, sa prudence, voire même sa pertinence. (*L'Éthique*, p. 180)

> [The poetry of courtly love, in effect, tends to locate in the place of the Thing certain discontents of the culture. And it does so at a time when the historical circumstances bear witness to a disparity between the especially harsh conditions of reality and certain fundamental demands. By means of a form of sublimation specific to art, poetic creation consists in positing an object I can only describe as terrifying, an inhuman partner.
>
> The Lady is never characterized for any of her real, concrete virtues, for her wisdom, her prudence, or even her competence. (*Ethics*, p. 150)]

The poet-lover of Occitan lyric takes an object of low status (and it would be difficult to find an object of lower status than woman in misogynistic medieval society, Lacan intimates) and elevates it to the dizzy heights of *das Ding*. The mundane female is uprooted from her earthly existence and made to perform as the idealized demigoddess whom the troubadour addresses as his lady. Were she to return the poet-lover's affections he would never come to any harm, or so the story goes: his sublime object, his sublime 'objet *a*', promises to protect him from all misfortune and act as the ultimate guarantee of his subjectivity. And so courtly love was born.

If it is Lacan who gives the sublime a body (that of the troubadour *domna*), it is Žižek who most systematically situates that body in relation to society at large (a body *qua* body of bodies). Žižek analyses the ideological function of the sublime, most notably in *The Sublime Object of Ideology*, stressing what he would elsewhere call the 'radically *intersubjective* status of *objet a*'.[11] A sublime body, in other words, is not only capable of sustaining an individual's subjectivity; it is capable of sustaining entire totalitarian regimes. Though he draws on Lacan's examples — Antigone, Sadeian victim and courtly lady — Žižek supplements them with all manner of kings and nuns, cartoon characters, and indeed saints.

This motley crew of sublime bodies calls for a typology, which Žižek provides (to a degree) with his discussion of the Lacanian *zone entre-deux-morts* (cf. *L'Éthique*, p. 291). If all sublime bodies inhabit this seemingly uninhabitable symbolic space between 'symbolic' death (death in the eyes of society) and 'real' death (biological death), for Žižek they have not necessarily arrived in the same way. 'In Antigone's case', he suggests, 'her symbolic death, her exclusion from the symbolic community of the city, precedes her actual death and imbues her character with sublime beauty' (*Sublime Object*, p. 135). In contrast, Tom (of Tom and Jerry fame) appears to die at the end of every scene, but that death is never registered symbolically: 'it is as though he possessed another indestructible body' (ibid.).

Žižek's theorization of the sublime has proved fruitful for exploring the curious bodies of vernacular hagiography. In a piece entitled 'The Sublime Body of the Martyr', Sarah Kay observes that medieval French and Occitan biographers of Sts Eulalia, Faith, George, Catherine, Lawrence and Margaret portray the saints' bodies as if they were indestructible, as if they were in possession of a sublime body 'through which the violence addressed to them might become capable of indefinite prolongation'.[12] This, she suggests, make them akin to Antigone or the Sadeian victim:

> The martyr who is burned, broken on wheels, boiled, and yet does not die, possesses a 'sublime body' analogous to that described by the Marquis de Sade, while at the same time supporting an elaborate ideology, as in the *Antigone*. ('Sublime Body', p. 8)

Though not the first to draw parallels between medieval hagiography and modern cartoons, Kay draws on Žižek to make sense of the comparison.[13] Saints, like the cartoon animals cited by Žižek, appear to undergo plenty of real deaths (by all natural laws) while remaining symbolically alive and well. Simund de Fresne's twelfth-century biography of St George, in particular, features what she calls a 'Tom and Jerry plot' ('Sublime Body', p. 13).

With the sublime teetering on the ridiculous, we might turn now to a second (but by no means unrelated) conceptual framework for tackling the weird and wonderful bodies of vernacular hagiography. The notion of the 'abject' is most closely associated with Julia Kristeva's 1980 essay, *Pouvoirs de l'horreur*.[14] Drawing most notably on Mary Douglas's anthropological study of dirt as a by-product of cleanliness, Kristeva puts dirt into Lacanian object relations.[15] In the opening lines of *Pouvoirs* she provides a negative definition of 'dirt', here rebaptized as 'the abject':

L'abject n'est pas un ob-jet en face de moi, que je nomme ou que j'imagine. Il n'est pas non plus cet ob-jeu, petit « *a* » fuyant indéfiniment dans la quête systématique du désir. L'abject n'est pas mon corrélat qui, m'offrant un appui sur quelqu'un ou quelque chose d'autre, me permettrait d'être, plus ou moins détachée et autonome. De l'objet, l'abject n'a qu'une qualité — celle de s'opposer à *je*. Mais si l'objet, en s'opposant, m'équilibre dans la trame fragile d'un désir de sens qui, en fait, m'homologue, indéfiniment, infiniment à lui, au contraire, l'*abject*, objet chu, est radicalement un exclu et me tire vers là où le sens s'effondre. (*Pouvoirs*, p. 9)

[The abject is not an ob-ject facing me, which I name or imagine. Nor is it an ob-jest, an otherness ceaselessly fleeing in a systematic quest of desire. What is abject is not my correlative, which, providing me with someone or something else as support, would allow me to be more or less detached and autonomous. The abject has only one quality of the object — that of being opposed to I. If the object, however, through its opposition, settles me within the fragile texture of a desire for meaning, which, as a matter of fact, makes me ceaselessly and infinitely homologous to it, what is *abject*, on the contrary, the jettisoned object, is radically excluded and draws me towards the place where meaning collapses. (*Powers*, pp. 1–2)]

The abject, then, is neither subject nor object. Nor is it to be conflated with the sublime 'objet *a*', and yet it can, from the above, be understood as its mirror image. If the sublime object shields the subject from *das Ding* ('m'offrant un appui'), the abject is the object that lets *das Ding* in, allowing it to destroy subjectivity: 'l'abject [...] me tire vers là où le sens s'effondre'.

Just as there was nothing inherently dirty about Douglas's dirt, there is nothing inherently abject about Kristeva's abject. It is an ordinary object rendered extraordinary by finding itself in the wrong place at the wrong time:

Ce n'est donc pas l'absence de propreté ou de santé qui rend abject, mais ce qui perturbe une identité, un système, un ordre. Ce qui ne respecte pas les limites, les places, les règles. L'entre-deux, l'ambigu, le mixte. Le traître, le menteur, le criminel à bonne conscience, le violeur sans vergogne, le tueur qui prétend sauver... (*Pouvoirs*, p. 12)

[It is thus not lack of cleanliness or health that causes abjection but what disturbs identity, system, order. What does not respect borders, positions, rules. The in-between, the ambiguous, the composite. The traitor, the liar, the criminal with a good conscience, the shameless rapist, the killer who claims he is a savior... (*Powers*, p. 4)]

The abject is produced by an arbitrarily drawn line. It is an object that, true to its etymology, has been cast down, ab-jected; hence Kristeva's reference to an 'objet chu' (*Pouvoirs*, p. 9).

This logic of casting out an object is fundamental, Kristeva argues, to the foundation and consolidation of subjectivity on (at least) three distinct levels. Firstly, abjection plays a role in a child's thetic development, that is, in the initial, pre-linguistic acquisition of a tentative sense of self: by casting aside the maternal breast (both physically and mentally) the infant is able to establish a clean and proper self. The self does not remain clean and proper for long, however, since the Kristevan subject is always 'in process' ('en procès'). Primary abjection of the maternal body gives way to secondary abjection, which sees ontological limits continue to be mapped onto the body. In secondary abjection, the objects perceived to lie at the threshold separating the 'clean and proper' body from the outside world (excrement, saliva, vomit, and so forth) are cast aside to mark a rigid boundary between self and other. They must be cast aside again and again, moreover, if subjectivity is to be preserved.

The logic of abjection, finally, can also be observed at a collective level, threshold bodies such as traitors, liars and strangers cast out of the community (body of bodies) to preserve group identity (*Pouvoirs*, p. 12). Kristeva's oscillation between *psyche* and *polis* in this way is not uncontroversial. Winfried Menninghaus, for example, laments what he perceives as the hijacking of the psychoanalytic 'abject' by minority groups and the transformation of abjection into 'eine einfache Fabel von Repression und Befreiung' ['a simple fable of repression and liberation'].[16]

Kristeva's concept of the abject has been hijacked — if this is the right word — by scholars of vernacular hagiography in two ways. Firstly, since the early 1990s the bodies of late medieval female mystics have been interpreted through the lens of abjection. Both Martha Reineke and Gail Ashton, for example, draw on Kristeva to examine the ways in which mystics gain mastery over their bodies through mortification, and the role this plays in community formation. Emma Campbell, similarly, links the abjection of the bodies of repentant harlots such as Mary the Egyptian to the emergence of collective identity imagined through the hagiographical text.[17]

The second application of Kristevan terminology to vernacular hagiography was pioneered by Robert Mills. Abject anti-bodies — those 'bodies and identities which readers are ultimately asked to reject' — loom large in saints' lives, he suggests, and violent acts committed against them promote community formation.[18] For Mills it is not only the saint who can possess an abject body; the saint can be a foil for inflicting abjection upon a wide range of iniquitous others.

If the Žižekian sublime and the Kristevan abject have proved useful conceptual frameworks for reading medieval saints' lives, it is not only because they draw attention to the discursive production of the body but because they situate extraordinary bodies in relation to the body *qua* body of bodies. The sublime body, for Žižek and other like-minded Lacanians, acts as the guarantor of the individual's subjectivity but must nonetheless be socially sanctioned (in the sense of approved): it is simultaneously the part-object expected to preserve bodily integrity and/or the other that promises to oversee the solidarity of the collective body. Kristeva's abject, meanwhile, whether or not it threatens the individual body or the collective body of bodies, must be socially sanctioned in a different sense (that is, penalized): it is the part-object that undermines bodily integrity and/or the social minority that menaces the cohesiveness of society. Critics have not always approved of the perceived 'universalizing' tendencies of Žižek's and Kristeva's work, which — admittedly — does not always move from *psyche* to *polis* as gracefully as it might.[19] And yet when we turn to medieval saints' lives, struggling perhaps to make sense of monsters-within that rapidly mutate into monsters-without (or vice versa), it is an attention to extimacy, to the conjunction of interior and exterior, that may enable the most productive readings.

One of my aims here is to draw on medieval literature to probe and go beyond our present understanding of the 'sublime' and the 'abject'. This is not as incongruous as it might initially sound, since Kristeva (who dons her medievalist hat in *Pouvoirs de l'horreur* to cite saints as prime examples of the abject, p. 13) and even Žižek (who mentions saints as paradigmatic of the sublime in *The Sublime Object of Ideology*, p. 116) theorize with hagiography, at least at times, in mind. More specifically, I shall build upon those few theorists who have attempted to relate the sublime and the abject in Lacanian topologics. Little scholarly consensus has been reached so far. Elizabeth Grosz, for instance, employs the sublime 'objet *a*' as another name for the abject.[20] Hanjo Berressem, on the other hand, suggests that the abject and the sublime occupy diametrically opposite positions in Lacanian thought.[21] Vernacular hagiography, with its holy and unholy bodies that are often opposed yet sometimes uncannily similar (or even physically conjoined), is fertile terrain for examining how sublime and abject may be linked.

Though not always avoiding the snares of essentialism, Žižek and Kristeva insist that their sublime and abject bodies are discursive productions. If we are to understand the saints and monsters of medieval French and Occitan hagiography as culturally contingent, we need to go beyond modern editions (where these exist) to situate saints' lives more surely in their manuscript contexts (a second aim of this book). The non-essentialism preached (if not always practised) by Žižek and Kristeva finds an unlikely ally, I would contend, in the mobility of the medieval text — in *mouvance*.

Outline of Chapters

Previous scholars who have explored the holy and unholy bodies of hagiography in relation to the sublime or abject have chiefly drawn upon editions of Middle English and pre-1300 Anglo-Norman lives in verse. While there is some overlap between this corpus and my own, I extend it in several directions (including language, mode, time and space). This, then, is a study of manuscript versions — for the most part hitherto unpublished — of medieval French and Occitan biographies in verse and prose of four saints. Two of these saints (Sts Margaret and George) were venerated right across Latin Christendom, while the cults of the other two (Sts Honorat and Enimia) were localized primarily to what is now the South of France. My selection is thematic: all four were celebrated in the later centuries of the Middle Ages for vanquishing dragons (though employing rather different techniques, from praying for tidal waves to bursting out of the beast's belly). Described by Debra Higgs Strickland as 'the all-purpose medieval symbol of evil', dragons were nonetheless over-determined creatures, able to represent one pole of a binary and its opposite, agents of God and not just of Satan.[22] Hagiography's very own 'harbingers of category crisis', they are apt beasts for considering sublime and abject relations.[23]

Each of the four chapters that follow focuses on the French and/or Occitan biographies of a particular dragon-dispatching saint and advances a specific theoretical point in relation to Žižek's elaboration of the sublime and Kristeva's elaboration of the abject. Though not always the simplest of tasks (given the state of scholarship), I seek to place lives in the context of their Latin sources ('an indispensable step in the critical appraisal', for Duncan Robertson).[24] Unlike Robertson (*Medieval Saints' Lives*, p. 26), however, I also believe it is important to place multiple lives in their various codicological contexts, considering the clues manuscript material provides about production and medieval provenance.

I begin in Chapter 1 with the many lives of St Margaret of Antioch, a virgin martyr whose successful 'delivery' from the belly of a dragon seems to have earned her the role of patroness of childbirth in the later Middle Ages. Taking my cue from Kay's reading of the twelfth-century Norman life of St Margaret by Wace, I examine the construction of the Žižekian sublime body, here in relation to the Kristevan abject and taking a selection of French and Occitan biographies of Margaret as my corpus. The transformation that Margaret's body undergoes in these stories — from frail, mutilated torture-victim to rubbery, cartoon-like martyr — varies quite considerably among vernacular lives, pointing to a constellation of anxieties about the gender and agency of both ordinary and extraordinary bodies. Rather than assuming that Margaret's role as patron of expectant mothers was empowering for women — as many modern readers have done — I draw on Judith Butler's critique in *Gender Trouble* of Kristeva's recuperation of the abject maternal body in the 'semiotic' to consider how medieval hagiographers naturalize maternity.

In Chapter 2 I turn to the French and Occitan lives of St George of Cappadocia, whose fame as a dragon-slayer is largely due to the astonishing success of the thirteenth-century anthology of Latin saints' lives known as the *Legenda aurea*. If Chapter 1 focussed on the relationship between the sublime and the abject, here it is chiefly the relationship between abjects and objects that concerns me. Central to my discussion is the emblematic figure of the 'stranger' in Kristeva's *Étrangers à nous-mêmes*, which I read in the light of her earlier *Pouvoirs de l'horreur* and postmodern theorizations of community (Derrida, Nancy, Agamben). Some of the French and Occitan versions of the George and the Dragon legend — several of the ones considered here are unpublished — cast pagan strangers as abject creatures to be annihilated (building communities within and outside of the text upon abjection), while others can be understood to cast them as objects to be converted (building communities upon assimilation). I also consider how these two principles of community formation come together when one French version of the story is 'Englished' in William Caxton's *Golden Legende*.

The main protagonist of Chapter 3 is St Honorat, who — legend has it — founded the island-monastery of Lérins off the Provençal coast by slaying the twin dragons Leri and Rins. His thirteenth-century Latin biography and the version it inspired in Occitan verse by Raimon Feraut (*c.* 1300) have faced harsh criticism (to put it mildly) from modern readers for their perceived anachronisms. Some of these anachronisms, however, might be better understood as 'asynchronies', the clashing of multiple time zones (e.g. temporal and spiritual) that Carolyn Dinshaw studies in *How Soon is Now?* and that seems to affect saints and monsters in particular. Drawing on recent thinking in queer studies concerning temporality, I argue that the queer genealogies attached to sublime and abject bodies in lives of St Honorat function to 'straighten out' ancestral genealogies in the temporal sphere (both within the text and outside of it). Particular attention here is given to the Hungarian royal ancestry that is conferred upon Honorat in the Occitan biography, a kinship that the saint at once rejects and endorses.

If temporality is the thematic glue of Chapter 3, Chapter 4 dwells on/in space, in relation to the Latin and Occitan lives of St Enimia. A Merovingian princess, Enimia rejects the Frankish court, as symbolized by her abandonment of ostentatious dress, her wilful acquisition of leprosy, and her departure for the 'wilderness' of the Tarn Gorges. Drawing upon the Lacanian notion of the *zone entre-deux-morts* — the space supposedly beyond representation where sublime and abject creatures eke out their impossible existences — I examine Enimia's biographies to map the cultural contigency of such zones. More specifically, after Judith Butler and Slavoj Žižek, I examine the transformational potential of these symbolic spaces. If that potential is severely restricted in the Latin lives, it is fully realized in the Occitan biography by Bertran de Marselha: as Bertran has it, Enimia makes the unliveable Tarn Gorges liveable, founding a community in stark opposition to 'France'.

In the second decade of the twenty-first century, tales of saints battling dragons are not related as often as they once were. Seldom have the attempts by Marvel Comics and others to bring hagiography to the pages of comic books proved commercially viable; rarely have they run for more than a matter of months. And yet we need only look to the superheroes of print and visual media — some of whom burst from monstrous bellies, suffer debilitating diseases or fly to their supporters' rescue, like medieval hagiography's saints — to realize that sublime and abject bodies are as varied and variable as ever. Let's look at why that variation and variability mattered in the Middle Ages.

Notes to the Introduction

1. DC Comics, Marvel Comics, Arcadius Press and Pauline Press have all brought out series featuring Christian saints in recent years. Most were quickly discontinued.
2. Elizabeth Day, 'Holy Comic Books! Saints Are the Latest Superheroes!', *Sunday Telegraph* 26 March 2006, <http://telegraph.co.uk/news/uknews/1513978/Holy-comic-books-saints-are-the-latest-superheroes.html> [accessed 29 September 2015].
3. As Sheila Delany writes, 'the metaphoricity of body was so basic, ubiquitous, and unquestioned a paradigm as to constitute what Medvedev and Bakhtin call an "ideologeme"'. See her *Impolitic Bodies: Poetry, Saints, and Society in Fifteenth-Century England: The Work of Osbern Bokenham* (Oxford: Oxford University Press, 1998), p. 26.
4. For an edition of the *Sequence* and a description of the unique manuscript, see Roger Berger and Annette Brasseur (eds), *Les Séquences de sainte Eulalie* (Geneva: Droz, 2004). Subsequent references in parentheses are to this edition.
5. Brian Stock, *The Implications of Literacy: Written Language and Models of Interpretation in the Eleventh and Twelfth Centuries* (Princeton: Princeton University Press, 1983), p. 238.
6. Kathleen Ashley and Pamela Sheingorn, 'The Translations of Foy: Bodies, Texts, and Places',

in *The Medieval Translator / Traduire au Moyen Âge*, 5, ed. by Roger Ellis and René Tixier (Turnhout: Brepols, 1996), pp. 29–49 (p. 31).

7. On Catalan recensions of the *Legenda aurea* that include a life of St Eulalia, see Charlotte S. Maneikis Kniazzeh and E. J. Neugaard (eds), *Vides de sants rosselloneses*, Publicacions de la Fundació Salvador Vives Casajuana, 48, 3 vols (Barcelona: Dalmau, 1977).

8. Immanuel Kant, *Kritik der Urteilskraft*, ed. by Karl Vorländer, 6th edn (Leipzig: Meiner, 1948).

9. Sigmund Freud, *Das Unbehagen in der Kultur* (Vienna: Internationaler psychoanalytischer Verlag, 1930).

10. Jacques Lacan, *Le Séminaire. Livre 7: L'Éthique de la psychanalyse, 1959–1960*, ed. by Jacques-Alain Miller (Paris: Seuil, 1986). Translations of quotations are taken from Jacques Lacan, *The Seminar of Jacques Lacan. Book 7: The Ethics of Psychoanalysis, 1959–1960*, ed. by Jacques-Alain Miller, trans. by Dennis Porter (London: Tavistock/Routledge, 1992).

11. See Slavoj Žižek, *The Sublime Object of Ideology* (London: Verso, 1989); and *The Metastases of Enjoyment: Six Essays on Woman and Causality* (London: Verso, 1994), p. 179.

12. Sarah Kay, 'The Sublime Body of the Martyr: Violence in Early Romance Saints' Lives', in *Violence in Medieval Society*, ed. by Richard W. Kaeuper (Woodbridge: Boydell, 2000), pp. 3–20 (p. 8). This essay appeared in revised form in 'The Sublime Body: The "Zone between the Two Deaths," Belief, and Enjoyment in Hagiography, the *Romans antiques*, and *Cligés*', in Sarah Kay, *Courtly Contradictions: The Emergence of the Literary Object in the Twelfth Century* (Stanford: Stanford University Press, 2001), pp. 216–58.

13. Duncan Robertson alludes to the 'cartoon-like presentations' of saints' bodies in *The Medieval Saints' Lives: Spiritual Renewal and Old French Literature* (Lexington: French Forum, 1995), p. 69. Sheila Delany, similarly, compares them to Roadrunner (*Impolitic Bodies*, p. 71).

14. Julia Kristeva, *Pouvoirs de l'horreur: essai sur l'abjection* (Paris: Seuil, 1980). Translations of quotations are taken from Julia Kristeva, *Powers of Horror: An Essay on Abjection*, trans. by Leon S. Roudiez (New York: Columbia University Press, 1982).

15. Mary Douglas, *Purity and Danger: An Analysis of Concepts of Pollution and Taboo* (London: Routledge & Kegan Paul, 1966)

16. Winfried Menninghaus, *Ekel: Theorie und Geschichte einer starken Empfindung* (Frankfurt a. M.: Suhrkamp, 1999), p. 555.

17. See Martha J. Reineke, '"This Is My Body": Reflections on Abjection, Anorexia, and Medieval Women Mystics', *Journal of the American Academy of Religion*, 58 (1990), 245–65; Gail Ashton, *The Generation of Identity in Late Medieval Hagiography: Speaking the Saint*, Routledge Research in Medieval Studies, 1 (London: Routledge, 2000), pp. 140–45; and Emma Campbell, *Medieval Saints' Lives: The Gift, Kinship and Community in Old French Hagiography*, Gallica, 12 (Cambridge: Brewer, 2008), esp. pp. 213–22.

18. Robert Mills, 'Violence, Community and the Materialisation of Belief', in *A Companion to Middle English Hagiography*, ed. by Sarah Salih (Woodbridge: Brewer, 2006), pp. 87–103 (p. 94). See also Robert Mills, *Suspended Animation: Pain, Pleasure and Punishment in Medieval Culture* (London: Reaktion, 2005), esp. pp. 106–44.

19. See, for example, the catalogue of criticism levelled against Kristeva detailed in Kelly Oliver, *Reading Kristeva: Unravelling the Double-Bind* (Bloomington: Indiana University Press, 1993), pp. 1–2; and, in relation to Žižek, Robert Samuels, 'Žižek's Rhetorical Matrix: The Symptomatic Enjoyment of Postmodern Academic Writing', *JAC*, 22 (2002), 327–54.

20. Elizabeth Grosz, *Volatile Bodies: Toward a Corporeal Feminism* (Bloomington: Indiana University Press, 1994), p. 81.

21. Hanjo Berressem, 'On the Matter of Abjection', in *The Abject of Desire: The Aestheticization of the Unaesthetic in Contemporary Literature and Culture*, ed. by Konstanze Kutzbach and Monika Mueller, Gender in Modern Culture, 9 (Amsterdam: Rodopi, 2007), pp. 19–48 (p. 22).

22. Debra Higgs Strickland, *Saracens, Demons, and Jews: Making Monsters in Medieval Art* (Princeton: Princeton University Press, 2003), p. 177.

23. That monsters plunge categories into crisis is one of the theses of Jeffrey Jerome Cohen in 'Monster Culture (Seven Theses)', in *Monster Theory: Reading Culture*, ed. by Cohen (Minneapolis: University of Minnesota Press, 1996), pp. 3–25 (p. 6).

24. Duncan Robertson, 'Authority and Anonymity: The Twelfth-Century French Life of St. Mary the Egyptian', in *Translatio studii: Essays by his Students in Honor of Karl D. Uitti for his Sixty-Fifth Birthday*, ed. by Renate Blumenfeld-Kosinski et al., Faux titre, 179 (Amsterdam: Rodopi, 2000), pp. 245–59 (p. 247).

CHAPTER 1

❖

St Margaret of Antioch and her Sublime/Abject Bodies

Memoria S. Margaritae, saeculo XIII in Calendario romano ascripta, deletur, quia Acta S. Margaritae, vel Marinae, omnino sunt fabulosa.[1]

[The commemoration of St Margaret, added to the Roman Calendar in the thirteenth century, is deleted, because the Acts of St Margaret, or Marina, are fabulous in every way.]

With these words the Council Fathers at Vatican II resolved to forget St Margaret of Antioch. The report issued in 1969 justifying the demotion of Margaret's cult may not say so explicitly, but there can be little doubt that it had something to do with one of the more fabulous episodes of her medieval biography: the one which sees Margaret burst out of the belly of a dragon called Rufo.

We might wonder how Margaret and Rufo retained their official position in the Church calendar for so long. Some scholars point to the gullibility of medieval audiences when accounting for the longevity of Margaret's cult (although the Middle Ages knew their sceptics, too). Others restrict credulousness to the *merveilleux*-loving masses. But no discussion of St Margaret is complete without mention of her role as pan-European patroness of childbirth and a quip about how 'ironic' or 'surprising' it is that pre-modern folk should have elected an adolescent virgin to the role.[2]

These scholarly discourses that in one way or another 'other' the Middle Ages endure in part because we have tended to restrict ourselves to a small selection of published lives of St Margaret. Yet we know from the extant texts and the nature of their supports that medieval biographies of St Margaret functioned as contact relics, their material presence promising to ward off demons, prevent house fires, and — most famously of all — safely deliver babies.[3] For many in the Middle Ages, Margaret's biography was fabulous without being the stuff of fables: by no means frivolous, it was raw, corporeal, *touch*.

If ever there was a saint's life in need of studying in its manuscript context, then, it is that of St Margaret. And as for the Vatican's mid-twentieth-century attempt to delete all memory of the saint (a threat often wielded by her persecutors in medieval biographies), medieval readers, listeners, viewers — and *touchers* — would no doubt have laughed at such efforts; so engrained was her story in haptic memory.

The 'Mombritius' Margaret: A New Eve

One of the texts read by Sarah Kay in her discussions of holy bodies in 'The Sublime Body of the Virgin Martyr' is the Old French life of St Margaret by the twelfth-century Jersey-born chronicler Wace.[4] Several of the points made by Kay in respect of Wace's version of the Margaret story are of relevance here.

Firstly, Kay notes that the virgin martyr's body resists the dual threats of rape and conversion at the hands of her pagan persecutors: the saint's stand against unwanted sex is conflated with her stand against idolatry, producing an 'ideologized' body. Rufo's attack constitutes another attempted rape/conversion, but the sexual metaphor changes when Margaret is miraculously 'reborn' from her monstrous aggressor.[5] Secondly, Kay observes that Margaret wishes to suffer torture and death just as much as her tormentor wishes to inflict them, rendering persecutor and persecuted the 'ideal couple' ('Sublime Body', p. 10). Finally — and here we come to the crux of Kay's argument — torment is said to exile Margaret to a Lacanian *zone entre-deux-morts*, 'for although this initial "death" of the saint is enacted and embraced, it fails to "take" and the saint lives on' (ibid., p. 11).

The contradictions that Kay highlights here are based on her reading of one of the medieval lives of St Margaret (among lives of other saints). But as Kay herself notes, in the reworked version of this essay, sublime bodies are 'historically and culturally determined' (*Courtly Contradictions*, p. 216). My intention in this chapter, then, is to explore the varied responses of French and Occitan hagiographers to a saint who, contradictorily, seeks the destruction of her indestructible body and is 'reborn' from the body of her alleged rapist.

It will first be instructive to turn to the most influential Latin account of Margaret's martyrdom (Bibliothecha hagiographica latina [hereafter BHL] 5303), dubbed the 'Mombritius' version because it was published (in one of its recensions) by the Italian humanist Bonino Mombrizio in the late fifteenth century.[6] The Mombritius version is deemed the principal source for most of the extant French and Occitan lives of St Margaret, Wace's included (see Appendix). In the absence of a critical edition of the Mombritius text, however, or a comprehensive study of the other Latin versions of Margaret's biography that circulated in the Middle Ages, we would be wise to treat this assumption with a degree of caution. Our understanding of the transmission of vernacular lives is hampered by our lack of understanding of their Latin sources.

According to the Mombritius tradition, Margaret is the daughter of a pagan patriarch who is raised by a Christian nurse outside the city of Antioch. She embraces Christianity from an early age. A beautiful specimen she may be, but appreciation of bodily beauty is primarily a pagan vice in this tale. One day, a wicked pagan prefect by the name of Olybrius spies Margaret as she is tending sheep in the fields. Overcome by her beauty, he desires nothing more than to make her his wife or concubine. When Margaret refuses to yield to his twin demands for sex and conversion, the tyrant submits her to two rounds of torture, whips and nails tearing at her flesh (pp. 2–20).

The first time Margaret's naked flesh feels the effects of Olybrius's torture instruments, pagan onlookers are horrified at the destruction wrought upon her body (p. 14). She has no choice but to yield to the tyrant's demands, they advise. But Margaret rebukes them, claiming that by relinquishing her body her soul will soon be heading heavenwards. With the next round of torture, even the most ardent pagan voyeurs have to divert their gaze because the bloodshed is so copious. The favourite refrain of the virgin martyr rings out loud and clear as Margaret claims 'carnem meam tradidi in tormentis ut anima mea coronata sit in celis' (p. 20) ['I have handed over my flesh to torments so that my soul may be crowned in heaven'].

The opposition between pagan appreciation of bodily beauty and Christian repudiation, however, is not entirely clear-cut in the Mombritius tradition. Margaret begs for protection not only for her soul but for her body, too. By this I do not simply mean that the saint asks for her *virginity* to be protected, that curious conflation of sexual and religious identity, or — as Emma Campbell has sensibly put it — that 'condition of physical and spiritual wholeness maintained through the refusal of human material and social structures' (*Medieval Saints' Lives*, p. 56). Margaret does indeed long for her body to be protected from 'pollution' when Olybrius poses a sexual threat (p. 8). But she also asks God to heal the injuries she suffers during her first round of torture (p. 14). And during round two she is desperate for her virginity and indeed her *life* (which surely some members of the audience would have taken to mean her biological one) to be spared (pp. 16–18). Some attempt, then, is made to ideologize the saint's body as a symbol of the soul in the opening episodes of the Mombritius version of the life, as per Kay's reading of the biography by Wace. But, to begin with at least, that attempt is unsuccessful. And as for persecutor and persecuted constituting the perfect match, Margaret seems to harbour some serious doubts about their relationship.

Things get worse before they get better. Margaret's body (or what remains of it) is thrown into prison, where she comes face to face with Rufo the Dragon. Though she herself has asked God for this confrontation with her 'enemy' and though she prays for protection from harm, Margaret nonetheless seems to be in serious trouble in the Mombritius tradition, turning green, collapsing to the ground, her bones 'crushed' by mortal dread. The dragon wastes no time in swallowing her whole (pp. 23–24). At this point in the narrative, then, Margaret's body seems to have more in common with the Kristevan abject than with the Žižekian sublime. Fortunately, however, Margaret is able to make the sign of the cross, and this reified symbol expands to such a great size that the monster's belly bursts. She emerges from her ordeal completely unscathed ('dolorem nullum habebat in se', p. 25 ['she herself had no pain']). And from this moment on we find a sublime body akin to the one observed by Kay in Wace's Margaret life.

With the dragon dispatched, an anthropomorphic devil appears and reveals that he had sent Rufo, his brother, to steal her virginity and eradicate her beauty. Margaret, no longer the victim of violence, deflects the physical torment she was supposed to suffer onto the devil, pinning him to the floor with such aggression that one of his eyes pops out. One one-sided theological discussion later and the saint concludes her argument by cracking open the ground and sending the demon back to hell (pp. 28–39).

Beelzebub the Devil is particularly peeved in the Mombritius life to have been beaten by a girl (pp. 34–35), encouraging audiences to consider to what extent and in what ways Margaret can be said to transgress her gender here. In the Mombritius biography she is presented not as Jerome's prelapsarian virago — full of manly virtue — but as a *new* Eve. If, according to Genesis 3, Eve's punishment for eating forbidden fruit is to stamp on serpents and have them snap at her heels, to bring forth children in sorrow, and to be ruled by her man, then Margaret makes for an unruly daughter of Eve: she stamps so hard that the devil-serpents can no longer snap back, she herself is 'brought forth' precisely without sorrow, and she defies all earthly men while submitting wholeheartedly to her spiritual betrothed, Christ. Margaret may be no ordinary woman in Mombritius, but there is nothing to suggest that her gender transgression masculinizes her here.

As she is dragged out of jail, Margaret seals her body by making that sign once again (the verb is *consignare*, p. 39 ['to seal/sign']). Her bodily experience of the next two rounds of torture is rather different from that of the two pre-Rufo rounds. Olybrius has her strung up and orders her flesh to be burned with torches. But Margaret reinterprets her torment, shifting it from a corporeal to a spiritual plane. Olybrius's fire will be God's flames and, rather than destroy her flesh, they will purge her body of sin ('Ure, Domine, renes meos et cor meum ut in me non sit iniquitas', p. 41 ['Burn, Lord, my kidneys and my heart so that there is no iniquity left in me!']). Next, Olybrius tries to drown her, but the pagan tyrant's torture vat is re-symbolized as God's baptismal font: 'Fiat michi hec aqua fons baptismatis indeficiens' (p. 42) ['Make this water a perfect baptismal font for me!']. Margaret may have said that Olybrius could take her body, but her sublime frame is now seemingly beyond his clutches.

There is nothing for Olybrius to do except send Margaret to her execution. The pagan henchman nominated for the task recognizes that his victim possesses no ordinary body, granting her time to commend herself to God. Margaret prays on behalf of all those who establish churches or light candles in her name, and for all those who are connected with a hard copy of her biography (readers, listeners, scribes and owners): their sins will be washed away and their children born physically intact. Before long, a heaven-sent dove has confirmed that all relics of her body (textual relics included) will be the site of miracles for the faithful (pp. 45–53). In the Latin Mombritius version, then, the prayer for babies is present, but the prominence accorded to mothers in many vernacular versions of Margaret's life is lacking. As a new Eve, the saint can promise spiritual integrity to her adherents and physical integrity to their children. But she cannot be expected to alter the childbearing lot accorded to other daughters of Eve: yes, the 'born again' Margaret will protect newborns, but the mimetic link here makes the maternal body appear more than a little dragon-like.

When the saint finally earns her martyr's crown, we get a foretaste of Margaret's thaumaturgical exploits at the level of the diegesis as the sick and insane are cured by touching her corpse. Theotimus, the man responsible for encasing her relics in a reliquary is also the man responsible for encasing her life into a written *vita*, giving us hope that Margaret's textual relics will prove similarly efficacious extradiegetically (pp. 53–56). The Mombritius tradition makes it clear that it is possible to interact with the material text in multiple ways. But when listening, men and women are requested to behave like literate little girls: 'et viri et virgines proponite vos velut puelle tenera lectionem legentes' (p. 4) ['both men and maidens, act like fragile little girls reading the narrative']. Such narratorial instruction is sufficiently imprecise, however, to legitimate responding to the story by invoking Margaret (i.e. behaving, like fragile little girls) or by imitating the saint in one way or another (i.e. behaving like one particular fragile little girl did, many years ago).

Rereading the Mombritius Latin version of the life of St Margaret prompts me to wonder where the abject fits into Sarah Kay's reading of the sublime body in Wace's version of the saint's biography. This, in turn, leads to a series of questions about the relationship between sublime and abject bodies. Do the sublime and the abject play complementary roles in identity formation? How and when does an abject body become sublime? Is an abject creature abjectified, or does it abjectify *itself* to become sublime? Is it, in other words, possible to *be* abject? And does it take the sublime body of a virgin to *make* (in the fully constructivist sense of the word) the maternal body the foundational abject *par excellence*?

The examination of French and Occitan lives of St Margaret that follows will suggest that these are some of the questions that interested vernacular hagiographers, even if they did not phrase them as I have here. The fuzzy boundaries between holy and unholy, saint and monster, soul and body, virgin and mother, were constantly being contested in late medieval lives of St Margaret. My readings will, moreover, have the happy corollary of rebutting some of the received ideas about Margaret and her medieval cult — that medieval audiences' understanding of mythological beasts was necessarily naïve, that Rufo the Dragon appealed particularly to the 'common folk', and that it is wryly ironic that the virginal Margaret was solicited as patroness of childbirth. These are assumptions worth challenging: misremembering, after all, is almost as bad as the Vatican's forgetting.

Margaret Meets Olybrius: Abjection and Agency

As the Mombritius version of the life of St Margaret has it, pagans demonstrate an unhealthy obsession with outward appearances, while the saint continually reminds her textual community that inner beauty is far more aesthetically and ethically pleasing. Some vernacular hagiographers lend further weight to the pagans' superficiality. In the Cambridge verse life, for instance, the infidel spectators gawp inanely at Margaret's body instead of taking her sermons to heart. The more she speaks, the more infatuated with her beauty they become: 'Mes cum parole plus, plus sa beauté amerent' (v. 73) ['The more she speaks, the more they adored her beauty'].[7] In the 'Escoutez tuit par tel couvent' version, the young saint's good looks are cited as the only reason that she receives any affection whatsoever from her 'Saracen' mother (vv. 97–100). And the prose renderings of the thirteenth-century *abbreviationes* — that is, of the biographies by Jean de Mailly, Vincent de Beauvais and Jacobus de Voragine — tend to depict Olybrius aghast that someone so pretty could have faith in Christ.[8]

Some vernacular authors, however, redeem Margaret's beautiful body. In the fifteenth-century metrical life edited by Soleil, even the Christians fail to keep their eyes off the teenager. Margaret's much-lauded Christian nurse is particularly attached to her adopted child on account of her beauty (p. 5), and Olybrius is not the only passer-by who gazes at Margaret as she herds sheep in the fields: 'Chascun pour la voir s'arrestoit' (ibid.) ['Everyone would stop to see her']. According to the widely circulating 'Aprés la sainte Passion' version, meanwhile, the saint's physical beauty mirrors her spiritual beauty The initial description of Margaret's attractive body would hardly be out of place in a romance text:

> Vestue estoit moult povrement;
> Mais le cors avoit bel et gent,
> Les yeux vers et clere la face
> Come cele qui de la grace
> De Dieu estoit replenie,
> Que n'avoit d'autre amour envie,
> Fors de la Dieu entierement:
> C'estoit tout son gaegnement,
> Et Dieu estoit sa vesteüre. (vv. 55–63)

[She was dressed very humbly, but her body was fair and attractive, her eyes sparkling and her face radiant, like someone filled with the grace of God who had no desire for any other love but God's alone. That was all her booty, and God was her clothing.]

Margaret owes her fine body and charming face, however, to God, the only courtly lover she will ever need. (Like many vernacular hagiographers, the author casts the saint as a *sponsa Christi* earlier in the narrative than the Latin of the Mombritius tradition does.) And instead of the sumptuous fabrics of courtly life, it is God who constitutes her true 'vesteüre' (v. 63). Olybrius himself fails to understand the reason behind Margaret's beautiful body, paying no attention to her divine attire: 'Ne prinst pas garde au vestement | Mais au cors qu'ele ot bel et gent' (vv. 69–70) ['He took no notice of her clothing, but (only) of her body, which was fair and attractive']. Here, then, appreciation of the saint's good looks is not condemned as a pagan vice: Christians may gaze at Margaret's body, as long as they pay attention to her perfectly complementary spiritual outfit.

The martyr's mantra — that pagan persecutors are welcome to the body but will never get the soul — is present in almost every vernacular rendering of Margaret's biography. And yet some French and Occitan hagiographers are more reluctant than others to give her body away, the saint's ideologized body at times requiring as much protection as the soul it comes to symbolize. In several lives, Margaret prays for protection for body and soul in equal measure.[9] But her protests are perhaps clearest in the Knoll fragment. Here she does not ask for her wounds to be healed or for her life to be spared, as she does in Mombritius; from the outset not a scratch is to be inflicted upon the Knoll Margaret's body: 'Que par ces tormenz depeciez

| Ne seit mi cors, ne afeblez' (p. 415, vv. 33–34) ['Don't let my body be cut up or weakened by these torments'].

Even where Margaret wishes for her body to be kept intact, however, she endures horrendous torments at the hands of the pagans and, according to most hagiographers, suffers terrific pain as a result. There is always plenty of gore, but the blood and guts are exaggerated in some versions. Wace's description of Margaret's entrails hanging out of her stomach is worthy of the *chansons de geste* (vv. 274–78), but the author of the Soleil text tops it with his anatomical description of the saint's bones, nerves, ribs, veins and various other vital organs that are now fully visible (p. 8). As for the Knoll fragment, Margaret ends up receiving rather more than a scratch as not a single scrap of her flesh, even the size of a penny, is said to have been left unscathed (p. 415, vv. 17–20). Sometimes the pain is simply too much for Margaret's fragile frame to bear: in the abbreviated 'D'une vierge lit on' version, she faints and falls to the ground (vv. 20–22), while in the version by Fouque the tormentors unfasten her because she already seems to be dead: 'Ja estoit li cors trespassez, | Et cil la laissierent abatre' (vv. 216–17) ['Her body was already dead, and they let her fall (*or* stopped beating her)'].

Ideologizing Margaret's body or exaggerating her physical torment may heighten the drama of the story, but there are potential pitfalls in casting her as a victim of her pagan adversaries to a greater extent. If Margaret is already seemingly a corpse and both her body and her body *qua* metaphorical soul are already defeated, then there is a real danger of the pagans being handed an early victory, of the saint never reaching sublime status to protect her textual community. Whipped and beaten to shreds, Margaret's body is always abject, but the threat is that it will seem abjectified by the pagans against her will instead of being abjectified by the saint herself.

The question of agency in Kristeva's theorization of abjection is a thorny one. The art historian Hal Foster writes that 'a crucial ambiguity in Kristeva is the slippage between the operation *to abject* and the condition *to be abject*'.[10] While the process of abjectification is foundational of a 'clean and proper self', the (non-) objects that are its by-products are, by definition, deprived of the cleanliness and propriety that characterize subjectivity. In other words, one can be *made* abject, but the condition of *being* abject shouldn't, strictly speaking, be possible.

Insofar as the abject once lay within and will never permanently be outside, abjectification is always disavowed self-abjectification. But in the opening pages of *Pouvoirs de l'horreur*, Kristeva writes of those beings who — impossibly, it should be reiterated — avow their self-abjectification and identify as abject:

> L'abjection de soi serait la forme culminante de cette expérience du sujet auquel est dévoilé que tous ses objets ne reposent que sur la *perte* inaugurale fondant son être propre. Rien de tel que l'abjection de soi pour démontrer que toute abjection est en fait reconnaissance du *manque* fondateur de tout être, sens, langage, désir. (*Pouvoirs*, pp. 12–13)

> [The abjection of self would be the culminating form of that experience of the subject to which it is revealed that all its objects are based merely on the inaugural *loss* that laid the foundations of its own being. There is nothing like the abjection of self to show that all abjection is in fact recognition of the *want* on which any being, meaning, language, or desire is founded. (*Powers*, p. 5)]

The example Kristeva gives of a creature whose self-abjectification leads to *being* abject is (not altogether surprisingly) a Christian saint. In the thirteenth century, Kristeva tells us, St Elizabeth of Hungary sloughed off her royal self and, in the words of St François de Sales, she loved 'l'abjection de soy-mesme' above all else, the ultimate proof of her humility before God (quoted in *Pouvoirs*, p. 13). Self-abjects always attract sceptics: even in St Elizabeth's day there were those who considered her mad for abasing herself under the authority of her famously brutal 'spiritual adviser', Konrad von Marburg.[11] The difference between these competing narratives is important because it is the *self*-abject, with its powers to abjectify others, that is most obviously edged with the sublime. But it is a difference that can nevertheless be bridged easily by an *ex post facto* transfer of agency.

Olybrius gives orders in lives of St Margaret, but it tends to be the saint who ultimately calls the shots. Kay may refer to tormentor and tormented as the 'ideal couple' ('Sublime Body', p. 10), but this is an asymmetrical relationship. Only in the Cambridge verse life, which reports that Olybrius derived pleasure from 'shaming' his victim with horrific torments (vv. 156–58), does his sadism complement Margaret's masochism. Elsewhere, his growing frustration that his torture methods are somehow not resulting in conversion and marriage suggests that he would rather have her alive and pagan than Christian and dead.

After watching Margaret's first round of torture, the spectators, getting more gore than they perhaps bargained for, strongly recommend that she reconsider Olybrius's proposal. According to the Mombritius version, the crushed saint cheerfully explains that she is by no means a victim: bodily torture at the hands of Olybrius is exactly what she wants in order for her soul to reach heaven (pp. 14–16). Some vernacular authors, however, supply another reason here: Margaret desires suffering *in imitatione Christi*.[12] And just as Olybrius misunderstood the nature of Christ's self-sacrifice for humankind — in Mombritius he interprets the Crucifixion as murder at the hands of his 'ancestors' the Jews (p. 10) — so he misunderstands Margaret's wilful martyrdom as a death penalty he must impose (reluctantly) on his victim. Nowhere is Margaret's authority more apparent at this point than in the Florence life in Occitan verse: foreshadowing the final instructions she gives to her executioner, she incites Olybrius to torture her, claiming that he will be damned if he *fails* to torture and kill her: 'Maldig sies tu, si non ho fas!' (v. 420) ['A curse upon you, unless you do it!'].

In most of the French and Occitan lives of St Margaret, then, we are assured that the saint's (self-)abjectified body is not that of a victim. But some hagiographers feel the need to go further still, pre-empting Margaret's bodily transformation in the central dragon episode to cast her as always already sublime. The authors of the Aurillac and Soleil lives make it clear that she is immune to pain even during her initial rounds of torture (v. 49 and p. 9 respectively). It is sometimes the saint's blood that foreshadows the transformation of abjectified flesh into sublime body: it drains from her body pure like the water of a crystal-clear fountain, or else as white as milk (like that of a decapitated martyr).[13] The 'Aprés la sainte Passion' text, meanwhile, prefigures the symbolization of Margaret's torments more typical of the second half of the Mombritius life:

> Cilz martires n'est fors que bains
> Pour espurgier m'ame et mon cors.
> Par cest martire est m'ame hors
> De la paine de mort seconde.
> Par ce serai de pechié monde. (vv. 216–20)

[This torment is nothing but a bath to purge my soul and my body. Thanks to this torment my body is spared the suffering of the second death. Thanks to this, I will be untainted by sin.]

The saint reconfigures her torment as renewed baptism, a chance for her to purge her body and soul of the effects of sin. Thanks to Olybrius — and completely unbeknown to him — she will thus be able to avoid the symbolic 'mort seconde' of hellfire that he, of course, will endure for all eternity. As ever, pagans fail to see beyond the surface.

Margaret Meets a Dragon and a Devil: The Gender of the Sublime

According to the Mombritius version, the corpse-like Margaret makes the sign of the cross and prays for a face-to-face encounter with 'her enemy' as she is thrown into prison. So terrifying is the dragon she finds there, however, that, paralysed with fear, she is gobbled up whole. Some French and Occitan lives take Margaret's paralysis further, recording that she 'forgets herself' or falls to the ground 'as if dead'.[14] The Sloane manuscript provides something of a contrast. Here Margaret shows no fear, and although she ends up on the floor, it is only to form the shape of the cross (v. 326). (One can imagine a doctor reading this text, which is bound with medical treatises, to a woman in labour and suggesting that she have no fear in the face of parturition.) Margaret remains firmly in control, too, in the Cambridge verse life, asking God specifically 'ke li let au dragun devurer' (v. 179) ['that he let the dragon devour her']. But in almost all cases, the saint appears to have got more than she anticipated: having prayed for the chance to vanquish her enemy, she seems unable to put up much of a fight, her fragile frame immediately abjectified when she had claimed to be *self*-abjectifying all along.

Whether or not Margaret herself is represented as being glad to see Rufo the Dragon, clearly some medieval hagiographers were not. Echoing qualms expressed by the Byzantine hagiographer Symeon the Metaphrast, the Dominican anthologists of the thirteenth century were evidently not overly fond of the flesh–and–blood monster of the Mombritius tradition.[15] Jean de Mailly and Vincent de Beauvais tell us from the outset that Rufo is a devil in disguise and in their versions he vanishes into thin air as soon as Margaret makes the sign of the cross. In some Latin versions of the *Legenda aurea*, Jacobus de Voragine gives a similar account, but then provides Mombritius's rather more corporeal version as an alternative:

> Et ecce, draco immanissimus ibidem apparuit. Qui dum eam devoraturus impeteret, signum crucis edidit et ille evanuit, vel, ut alibi legitur, os super caput eius ponens et linguam super calcaneum porrigens ipsam protinus deglutivit, sed dum eam absorbere vellet, signo crucis se munivit et ideo drago virtute crucis crepuit et virgo illesa exivit.[16]

[And lo, a very fearsome dragon appeared in that very place, and as it rushed to devour [Margaret], she made the sign of the cross and it vanished. Or, as is read elsewhere, it placed its mouth on her head and extended its tongue to her heel to swallow her at once, but as it was intending to devour her, she armed herself with the sign of the cross and so the dragon burst by the power of the cross and the virgin emerged unscathed.]

It should be noted that Jacobus's famous instruction to readers to adopt a sceptical attitude towards the corporeal dragon is not always included in Latin manuscripts. It is only where the Dominican's more prosaic account of the dragon episode is missing that we read that 'quod dicitur de draconis devoratione et ipsius crepatione, apocryphum et frivolum reputatur' (I, 692) ['that which is said about the dragon's devouring and its bursting, is considered apocryphal and frivolous']. But whether the Latin text gives a less fabulous alternative or an outright warning, the Rufo of the Latin *Legenda aurea* is regarded with suspicion.

Vernacular hagiographers, it would seem, rarely shared Jacobus's qualms about a corporeal dragon. Few translations and adaptations of Margaret's *Legenda aurea* entry retain both versions of the dragon episode (only French prose versions 12, 14 and 15). And only one vernacular author renders Jacobus's warning that Rufo's antics are reputed to be apocryphal and frivolous (the early rendering here numbered 10, f. 157r). In all other French and Occitan prose versions based on the *Legenda aurea* Rufo gulps down Margaret without attracting narratorial comment. Several manuscripts, moreover, suggest that French and Occitan authors relish the dragon episode. The author of the life in BnF, fr. 15110 (French prose version 8a), for example, deviates from his principal source — Jean de Mailly had omitted the swallowing incident — to ensure that the saint winds up in the monster's belly (f. 160r). In French prose version 2, meanwhile, highly abbreviated overall, Margaret encounters an intriguing additional monster: the black serpent emerges from the corner of the saint's cell gives birth not to Margaret but to a giant devil that in turn swallows and 'gives birth' to the saint (f. 41r).

We should be wary, I think, of assuming that a sceptical attitude towards the *merveilleux* in Margaret lives corresponded to a clerical audience and a less enlightened one to a lay audience. To be sure, the sole manuscript preserving French prose version 15, copied in a monastic scriptorium, is one of the few renderings of the *Legenda aurea* entry to include Jacobus's less fabulous version of the dragon episode, but version 13, bound with the *Miroir des curés* (a basic manual for parish priests) in three manuscripts, omits both Jacobus's toned-down version of the dragon episode and his doubts about a flesh-and-blood Rufo (f. 347r).[17] On the other hand, the metrical lives, which were largely in the hands of layfolk (to judge by extant codices), often embrace the dragon in all its fabulous bodiliness, but some cast the dragon as a diabolical vision from the outset (e.g. Sloane, v. 311), or dispatch Rufo even before he gets a chance to wrap his tongue around the petrified saint (Knoll, p. 416, v. 26). In the York version, moreover, Rufo is not even allowed to go near the saint (v. 185), in accordance with its primary Latin source, the so-called 'Caligula' version (BHL 5306). In sum, the reasons why a vernacular hagiographer might have delighted in or deleted a corporeal dragon — whether or not he found it in his sources, the theological thorniness of Rufo at the time he was writing, the need to tell a good story, and so forth — cannot be boiled down to the laity's fondness for the *merveilleux* and the clergy's criticism thereof.

Once Margaret has dispatched Rufo the Dragon (with or without her hagiographer's help) by making the sign of the cross, her body is transformed. Having wreaked corporeal havoc on her monstrous opponent, Margaret will no longer be forced to wear the badge of the abject, nor will she proudly adopt that of the self-abject; on the contrary, she will be marked as properly sublime. The precise markers of this corporeal transformation, however, are not the same in all of Margaret's French and Occitan biographies.

When Beelzebub arrives in the saint's prison in the Mombritius version he is a prisoner himself (with the shackles to prove it). He makes the mistake of disclosing that he sent Rufo to steal her virginity, prompting the saint to grab him by the hair, throw him to the ground and stamp on his neck with her right foot (p. 28). In some vernacular lives, however, Beelzebub is not quite so feeble: in the York manuscript, for example, he still has every intention of harming the saint (vv. 192–94); for the author of the Additional version, Beelzebub repeats the dragon's futile attempt to devour her and drag her down to hell (vv. 187–92); and in the ubiquitous 'Aprés la sainte Passion' version, he remains bent on avenging Rufo's death (vv. 328–30). In several of these lives (but also in others), Margaret proves an even more fearsome opponent than she does in the Mombritius version. In the 'Aprés la sainte Passion' text, for instance, Margaret is said to thump and punch Beelzebub at breakneck speed (v. 361). The author of the Sloane text, for his part, has Margaret crush him so hard that she almost kills him, causing him to shriek in pain and accuse her of strangling him as well as blinding him (vv. 378–83, 428–29). And the author of French prose version 4 smuggles a broom into the text, a prop that allows him to paint an even more aggressive portrait of the saint: she not only tramples on Beelzebub's head, but '[d]'un balois qu'ele trova deinz la prisoun le bati fortement' (f. 17v) ['she beat him violently with a broom she found in the prison']. The devil here is left cowering in fear, claiming that Margaret is scarier than any of his infernal comrades: 'Plus espaunté sui d'un regard de toun oil ke de touz les diables d'enfern!' (f. 18v) ['I am more fearful of you looking at me than of all the devils of hell!'].[18]

Much has been made in scholarship of Margaret's bellicosity here in relation to gender. Reading a variety of vernacular lives of the saint, Elaine Treharne suggests that Margaret behaves in a 'masculine manner as a *miles Christi*', Jordi Cerdà Subirachs that she is 'capaz de hacer frente como un hombre a los embates del maligno' ['able to face the devil's onslaughts like a man'], Carole Hill that she is now well on the way to becoming a 'spiritual "male"'.[19] In the Mombritius tradition, Beelzebub is physically crushed by a new Eve and emotionally so because she is a girl and, moreover, of pagan descent. In the *Legenda aurea*, moreover, Jacobus de Voragine strengthens the Genesis link by having Margaret exclaim 'Sternere, superbe demon, sub pedibus femine!' (i, 692) ['Be crushed, proud demon, under the feet of a woman!']. But nowhere in vernacular lives is the saint's bellicosity towards the devil explicitly linked to manliness.

In fact, it is striking how few vernacular hagiographers remark upon the gender transgression that accompanies the saint's transformation from abject to sublime. Beelzebub complains solely about Margaret's lineage in about the same number of lives as he complains about both her ancestry and her gender (as per the Latin of Mombritius).[20] And in the fifteenth-century French prose version 17, which takes the *Legenda aurea* as its source, Margaret exclaims that the devil is being flattened not by female feet, but by the genderless feet of a God-made 'creature' (f. 190r). Margaret's newly discovered body promises to benefit all precisely because, in transgressing the gender role it was assigned by Genesis 3, it is able to abjectify the devil without him snapping back. The risk for the medieval hagiographer is that the saint will not only appear powerful *in relation to the devil* but powerful and even imitable *per se*. Anxieties centring around Margaret's belligerence towards the devil no doubt prompted at least some of the saint's biographers in the Middle Ages to omit overt reminders that it is a woman who pins Beelzebub to the floor.

Margaret emerges from her dragon encounter entirely unscathed. It is not just a question of the saint suffering no pain as she bursts forth from Rufo, nor of the dreadful wounds inflicted upon her by Olybrius's henchmen being miraculously healed; the saint is in possession of a new body, the sublime body described by Sarah Kay in her essays on virgin martyrs.[21] Beelzebub the Devil is usually the first to recognize the transformation. According to the Florence Occitan version and the French prose texts 1, 3 and 7, Margaret's body used to be made of earthly stuff — ashes and dust, or as we find in version 3, filth ('fiens', f. 47r). It was a body, the author of version 7 notes, that could hardly withstand a pagan persecutor's torture equipment: as well as being formed from ashes and dust, 'tes cors estoit toz despeciez' (f. 214r) ['your whole body was torn to pieces']. But now Margaret's body has been transformed. The author of French prose version 3 perhaps puts it most vividly:

> Je voi en toi autre forme: dui pié d'or sont coneu en toi, il demostrent le signe Jhesucrist, pour laquel chose li fruiz meürs de joutise et de suavité et plainz de grace est demostrez en toi plus blanz que lais. Ti doit sont signacle Jhesucrist, et de ce signacle as tu occis mon frere Rufin et m'as lié. (f. 47r)

> [I see in you another form. You are seen to have two feet of gold, which reveal the sign of Jesus Christ, so that the ripe fruit of justice and sweetness, full of divine grace, is visible in you, whiter than milk. Your fingers are the sign of the Cross, and with this sign you killed my brother Rufin and bound me.]

Where Margaret lacks her golden feet, the protective sign of the cross marks her with extraordinary beauty. Beelzebub notes it in French prose version 7 (f. 214r), the saint herself in 1 (f. 20r) and 3 (f. 46r), while in 4 it is Olybrius: when the tyrant drags Margaret out of prison to find her 'seine de ses plaies e en merveillouse beauté' ['healed of her wounds and wondrously beautiful'], he wants the guards killed, suspecting them of letting doctors tend to her wounds (ff. 18v-19r).

In the Mombritius version, the final rounds of torture that Margaret suffers are symbolized so that they cleanse her soul instead of mangling her body. Vernacular authors, too, have the saint cry out for Olybrius's fire and water to be transformed into the fire of the Holy Spirit and the waters of renewed baptism.[22] But her body is also marked as freshly sublime in a number of other ways. Where Olybrius's torture equipment has a very real effect on Margaret's flesh, she is nonetheless immune to pain. In the Soleil life, for example, a particularly sadistic tormentor does his utmost to make her shriek in agony, but even the boiling water feels like dew (p. 13). In some versions the saint's body is both fire-resistant and water-repellent. In the York life, for instance, 'n'en fu, n'en ewe, n'out en lui nule blemie' (v. 291) ['neither in the fire nor in the water was there any blemish on her']. In French prose version 4, similarly, Olybrius has Margaret strung up by her hair as his henchmen attempt to extinguish red-hot irons in her spilt blood, but the saint's body, 'vestu de beauté' ['clothed in beauty'], is said to remain whole (f. 19v). In some French and Occitan lives, finally, the torture is postponed indefinitely. In the Troyes copy of the Wace life, for example, the expected symbolization motif is reversed as the saint asks for her body *not* to be cleansed by purgatorial fire (vv. 527–28) — she is, after all, already pure, so the miscopying scribe makes a fair point — and the flames are extinguished by God (vv. 538–40).[23]

Beyond, resistant to, or protected from Olybrius's torments, Margaret's body bears various markers of sublime difference in French and Occitan accounts of her life. In the biographies based on the Dominican *abbreviationes*, this difference is specifically gendered. Here we are told that the saint's spectators were amazed to see a fragile little girl resist such extreme torture.[24] But we need not read Margaret as masculinized here, as some modern readers have done. It is by sticking resolutely to her gender, when Olybrius's torture equipment should erase all markers of her femininity, that she ends up transgressing her gender. The sublime body is gendered and transcends its gender simultaneously.

Final Prayers: Like Mother, Like Daughter

Margaret's body may seemingly be immune to corporeal death, but every *passio* needs a final decapitation scene. The saint's executioner, recognizing the sublime markers on her body, allows her to pray for her textual community. And it is here that she issues her well-known prayer for unborn children. Critical attention has focused on the medieval eccentricity of such prayers. Carole Hill's comments are typical: 'To the modern mind,' she writes, 'it is hard to engage with medieval thinking that made a self-sacrificing adolescent virgin a patron of childbirth'.[25] To my mind, there is a need to recognize (as Jane Tibbetts Schulenburg, for example, does) that Margaret was not the only patron of childbirth in the Middle Ages, and that not all of her fellow protectors were even women, let alone virgins.[26] But we have surely not yet engaged enough — and, yes, it *is* hard — with thinking that placed such weighty responsibility upon 'a self-sacrificing adolescent virgin' like Margaret for successful parturition.

In the Mombritius Latin version (and indeed in several of the vernacular lives that derive from it), Margaret's childbirth prayer is not for the mother, but for the unborn child:

'Et qui fecerit basilicam in nomine meo aut scripserit passionis mee libellum aut emerit de justo labore repleatur Spiritu sancto tuo, et spiritu veritatis, et in domo eius non nascatur claudus fians, nec cecus, nec mutus, neque temptetur a spiritu inmundo, et quod petierit, indulge ei.' (p. 50)

['And whoever founds a church in my name or copies the book of my martyrdom or buys a copy from honest labour, may they be filled with your Holy Spirit, and the spirit of truth, and may no child be born in their home who is lame or blind or dumb, and may they not be tempted by the foul spirit, and whatever they ask, grant it to them.']

Though no explicit link is made in the text, modern commentators routinely see a mimetic connection between Margaret's emergence from the belly of the monster and the unborn child from the mother's womb. 'If not actual hell-mouths,' writes Jocelyn Wogan-Browne, 'female bodies are consigned by this congruence to the role of expendable dragons'.[27] Sarah Salih makes a similar point: 'The dragon can also be read as the sexual female body, opposed in its abjection to the virgin body,' with the saint 'born whole and perfect from the grotesque corpse of the woman'.[28]

Indeed, Margaret's childbirth prayer as presented in Mombritius seems to provide us with a textbook case of Kristevan abjection. The maternal body is the paradigmatic site of abjection for Kristeva in *Pouvoirs de l'horreur*: only by abjectifying the maternal breast, both physically and mentally, can an infant differentiate himself from his mother's body and achieve a fledging, pre-linguistic subjectivity. This primary abjection is conveyed most pithily, however, in Kristeva's *Soleil noir*, where she writes that 'le matricide est notre nécessité vitale' ['matricide is our vital necessity'].[29] And if the unborn child of Margaret's prayers is ever to establish a clean and proper self, he will have to commit matricide just as the saint slew her monstrous mother Rufo.

Matricide may be a necessity for entry into the symbolic realm of language, but Kristeva is also interested in rehabilitating the abject maternal body in her work. Her essay 'Stabat mater' (originally published in 1977 as 'Hérethique de l'amour') gives us two competing discourses on motherhood.[30] In the right-hand column, Kristeva explores how the cult of the Virgin Mary can be understood to cover over the disjunct between the abject maternal body and the Symbolic. Christianity gives us a safely symbolic mother, the Immaculate Conception and Virgin Birth dispensing with messy female jouissance, the silent scene of the *mater dolorosa* depriving all mothers of a voice. The left-hand column of 'Stabat mater', printed in bold type, interrupts this Marian narrative with a 'FLASH' (p. 225). It gives a highly personal account of the narrator's own experience of childbirth, rooted in the body. In contrast to the *symbolic* mother presented on the right, here we find a *semiotic* mother, where the 'semiotic', as elaborated by Kristeva, may be understood as the recovery of the body — and of the maternal body in particular — in the polysemy of poetic language. As elaborated in 'Stabat mater', the semiotic threatens to subvert the Symbolic order from within, although the former is inevitably contained and constrained by the latter.

If a mimetic link between Rufo the Dragon and the mother of Margaret's prayers can be identified in Mombritius, vernacular hagiographers often complicate such direct mimeticism. Some French and Occitan authors do not dress female audience members in compulsory dragon costumes, but instead encourage them to imitate Margaret's virginity. In several cases, the saint prays for virgins to follow in her footsteps (presumably stopping short of martyrdom — she is hazy on the details). Copies of some of these lives, perhaps tellingly, may have been in the hands of nuns during the Middle Ages.[31]

More prevalent disruption to mimeticism in French and Occitan lives of St Margaret, however, comes in the form of attempts to recover the maternal body from Rufo's abjectified carcass. The life by Wace is the earliest to have come down to us that includes a prayer for both mother and baby. Its importance in the tradition warrants lengthy quotation:

> Qui ma vie en cuer lira
> Ou de bon cuer l'escoutera
> Ou qu'il de sa gaaignerie
> Volra avoir la moie aïe,
> Ou qui chapele u qui mostier
> A moi fera edefiier
> U del sien i metra lumiere,
> Oiés, biax Sire, ma proiere:
> Fai lor ce qu'il te proieront
> Qu'il por lor salu requerront.
> Pardon aient de lor pechiés,
> Nes laissiés estre a mort jug[iés],
> Ne naisse ja en lor maison
> Enfés s'a droit termine non.
> Li enfés sain et entier soit,
> Naturalment, si con il doit.
> Se feme est en traval d'enfant
> Et par besoig moi reclamant,
> Biax sire Dex, lor fai aïe,
> Et l'un et l'autre met a vie. (vv. 631–50)

[Whoever reads or hears my life gladly, or wishes to have my help through their earnings, or has a chapel or church built in my name, or who pays for a candle to be placed there, hear, Fair Lord, my prayer (for them): grant them what they ask you for and need for their salvation. May they be forgiven their sins, and not condemned to death, and may no child ever be born in their household except after the full term. May the child be fit and healthy, naturally, as he ought to be. If a woman is in labour and invokes my aid, Fair Lord God, give them help, and let both of them live.]

The miracle of the dragon episode is that Margaret emerged, however frail her body had seemed, without a blemish. Having been transformed from bloody pulp to sublime body, this saint was the ideal candidate to guarantee that babies would be born 'sain et entier' (v. 645). Wace, however, complicates the Mombritius prayer for the unborn infant — perhaps under the influence of the so-called 'Caligula' Latin version — by asking for the mother, too, to be kept alive and well.

Numerous vernacular authors would later make the same move: women in labour who solicit Margaret's support will be comforted in their suffering, they will be kept from peril, and they will emerge from their ordeal, as Margaret herself did, in rude health.[32] They dwell on this slippery word 'delivery': babies will be 'delivered' of mothers, and mothers will be 'delivered' of both their babies and the Genesis-sanctioned trials and tribulations of childbirth.[33] In many cases, the dragon episode is thus re-symbolized, allowing the maternal body to emerge safe and sound from abstracted torments.

Medieval French and Occitan hagiographers, then, tend to multiply mothers: Rufo the Dragon 'gives birth' to Margaret at the level of the narrative and may figure the abject maternal body of the saint's pre-decapitation prayers, but he also comes to represent everything from which mothers and indeed all members of the textual community wish to be 'delivered'. This generation of maternal imagery can prove, frankly, baffling. When Fouque, for example, repeats the saint's own prayer for as yet unborn children at the end of his version of Margaret's biography, we may be left perplexed as to whose 'belly' he is talking about:

> Cil qui lira ceste leçon,
> Diex li doint sa beneïçon.
> Et la pucelle Marguerite,
> Cui passion est ci escrite,
> Proi Damediex, et jor et nuit,
> Qu'il soit garde de tout le fruit
> Qui de son ventre doit issir,
> Et Diex nos puist touz beneïr. (vv. 491–98)

[May God bless him who reads this text. And may Margaret the virgin, whose *passio* is written here, ask God day and night to be the guardian of all the fruit that emerges from her (his?) belly, and may God bless us all.]

It is not clear here to whom the 'fruit' belongs: to the grammatically male reader, to the virgin Margaret, or perhaps even to God himself? All readings are problematic for one reason or another. But the effect of the multiple mothers is akin to that brought about by the left-hand column of Kristeva's 'Stabat mater': the semiotic production and reproduction of meaning disrupts a patriarchal discourse that abjectifies the maternal body and exploits a virgin to cover up the abjectification process.

Insofar as many vernacular lives of St Margaret ostensibly challenge the mimetic link between Rufo the Dragon and the mother of the saint's childbirth prayer they have sometimes been understood by modern commentators as empowering women readers. 'Medieval women,' writes Carole Hill, for instance, 'pragmatically utilised the saint's legend for their own empowerment, especially in times of physical crisis' ('"Here Be Dragons"', p. 109). In a similar vein, Jennifer Borland suggests that Margaret 'demonstrates the potential for both social disruption and transgressive forms of empowerment that may have been especially relevant to audiences of both religious and lay women'.[34] The question is: to what extent does the disruption of a base equation between dragon and mother *empower* women?

It will be useful at this point to turn to Judith Butler's critique of Julia Kristeva's theorization of the semiotic in *Gender Trouble*. Butler cites a long list of problems with Kristeva's work. Two of the most severe — and they are interlinked — might be outlined as follows. Firstly, Butler queries the subversive potential of a semiotic discourse that remains subordinate to the Symbolic: 'If the semiotic promotes the possibility of the subversion, displacement, or disruption of the paternal law, what meanings can those terms have if the Symbolic always reasserts its hegemony?'.[35] Secondly, Kristeva faces charges of essentialism because her elaboration of the semiotic posits a universal maternal body that precedes discourse:

> Whereas Kristeva posits a maternal body prior to discourse that exerts its own causal force in the structure of drives, Foucault would doubtless argue that the discursive production of the maternal body as prediscursive is a tactic in the self-amplification and concealment of those specific power relations by which the trope of the maternal body is produced. In these terms, the maternal body would no longer be understood as the hidden ground of all signification, the tacit cause of all culture. It would be understood, rather, as an effect or consequence of a system of sexuality in which the female body is required to assume maternity as the essence of its self and the law of its desire. (p. 92)

For Butler, maternity — its disruptive (non)-potential included — is naturalized by a paternal law that legislates 'compulsory cultural construction of the female body *as* a maternal body' (p. 90). In Kristeva's (partial) defence, if she undoubtedly posits pre-discursive maternity, guilty as charged, she is also interested in the discursive construction of maternity. In her art-historical essay 'Maternité selon Giovanni Bellini', for example, she is highly critical of a scientific discourse that posits maternity as 'natural'.[36] She regards the maternal body as 'un seuil où s'affrontent « nature » et « culture »' (p. 410) ['a threshold where "nature" and "culture" meet'], and the *guillemets* are there for a reason.

In vernacular lives of St Margaret, the saint typically promises that children will be born 'naturally'. Wace provides an early example — his Margaret claims that a baby will be delivered 'naturalment, si con il doit' (v. 646) ['naturally, as he ought to be'] — but we do not have to look far to find other cases.[37] When asking to what extent women readers may have found empowerment by reading lives of St Margaret, we should also consider how maternity itself is naturalized in these texts. Imitating the saint's virginity may sometimes be proposed as a viable option for members of the female audience, but vocational virginity is always treated as exceptional. Margaret and those who follow in her footsteps transgress their gender not insofar as they are *masculinized* but insofar as they are females on a higher plane. *Imitatio virginis* is not, then, a model for ordinary women precisely because vocational virgins are not ordinary women. The bodies of ordinary women, on the contrary, are inevitably constructed as maternal bodies in vernacular lives of St Margaret. In the childbirth prayer, the categories of 'woman' and 'mother' are conflated: the Aurillac author, for instance, has the saint ask that 'tota bona Christiana | Que ma passio legira | O en escrih la portara, | *Quant sera prenh*, delieurara' (vv. 102–05) ['every good Christian woman who reads my *passio* or holds a written copy, *when she is pregnant*, will deliver (successfully)']. Rufo the Dragon may no longer represent the maternal body, but the maternal body only emerges safe and sound because obstacles to childbirth and to the 'natural' conflation of women and mothers are projected back onto the monster.

Was it possible, then, for a female audience in the Middle Ages to engage with vernacular lives of St Margaret in a way that empowered them within patriarchy? Whatever limited renegotiation of their roles as virgins and mothers was possible, they were surely no more able to escape the Eva/Ave paradigm than Kristeva's semiotic is able to escape the Symbolic. The naturalized role of temporal women remained to bring forth children, though — with Margaret's help — female readers and listeners might have hoped to do so in a little less sorrow. Yet I am less pessimistic in my reading of Margaret's biographies than Butler is in her critique of the semiotic. For every time the roles of the female audience were renegotiated through Margaret's biography — in the unstable transition, that is, from one manuscript to another, from one performance of the text to another, and from one extradiegetic prayer to another — there was an opportunity to glimpse the *ex post facto* naturalization of women's bodies as maternal bodies. And a discourse that flags up the process of naturalization instead of naturalizing itself is the precursor to imagining bodies differently.

Textual Relics and Re-membering

The Council Fathers at Vatican II were not alone in wishing to erase all memory of St Margaret. In the Mombritius tradition an irate Olybrius expresses his intention of going further than corporeal death and inflicting an additional, symbolic death on his victim (making him analogous to Pope Pius in Sade's *Juliette*). Pagan bystanders observe that the tyrant is bent on eradicating all trace of her ('perdere te festinat et delere de terra memoriam tuam', p. 14 ['he hastens to destroy you and to delete your memory from earth']). A little later on, Beelzebub is forced to confess that he sent Rufo in the guise of a dragon, similarly, to erase Margaret's memory from earth ('ut obsorberet et tolleret memoriam tuam de terra', p. 28 ['to gulp down and remove your memory from earth']).

These anti-hagiographers, however, are ultimately thwarted by the hagiographical text itself. When Margaret is decapitated, her body, though biologically dead, continues to bear sublime markers that distinguish it from an abject corpse. In French prose version 19, for instance, milk issues forth from her severed head instead of blood (f. 49v). And in all the vernacular biographies based on the Mombritius version, invalids come from far and wide and are instantly cured of their physical disabilities and diabolical tendencies by touching Margaret. The corporeally and spiritually weak audience at the level of the diegesis provides a model for the corporeally and spiritually weak audience outside of the text, to whom similar miracles have been promised through the saint's future bodies: relics and texts.

Margaret's late medieval lives assimilate the saint's body and the manuscript codices preserving her story. In the first place, the saint herself is a product of a hagiographical narrative: according to Mombritius, she is initially prompted to devote her body to Christ by hearing about Christian martyrs (p. 6). Secondly, the hagiographical text is treated as one of her relics. Theotimus, in almost all the vernacular verse versions of the *passio*, is named as both her undertaker — the man who reattaches her head, embalms her and entombs her — and her biographer. In the Mombritius version and its vernacular offshoots, proximity to a Margaret manuscript and proximity to relics have equal thaumaturgical power when it comes to pardoning sins and banishing demons (pp. 51–52).[38]

Vernacular authors, however, often place greater emphasis on touching the life than on reading it. According to the Troyes copy of Wace, you should not merely invoke Margaret's name (as per Mombritius), but take a copy of the life with you (vv. 651–54). For the Cambridge author, it is not reading or listening that protects you from lightning and fire (as in Mombritius), but the physical presence of the story (vv. 366–68). Women in labour do not necessarily have to read or listen to the text to guarantee a successful delivery: for the 'Aprés la sainte Passion' author, they need only peruse the book or place a copy of the text on their stomach (vv. 534–40).

Disseminating copies of Margaret's life in a bid to preserve her memory (to *remember* her), then, is akin to Theotimus's efforts to reassemble her body, to turn an abject corpse into sublime relics (to *re-member* her). The author of the York life takes full advantage of the scope for paronomasia in deploying Anglo-Norman *membrer* and *remembrer*. In the account of Margaret's upbringing, she is twice described as 'remenbree', that is 'well-known' to the local community and 'remembered' extradiegetically by us thanks to the text (vv. 64 and 80). During her initial rounds of torture she remains 'ben menbree' (v. 136), 'strong' or 'prudent', but also an ironic comment on the corporeal dismembering Olybrius's henchmen are inflicting. Equipped with a sublime body in the second half of the life, she is 'remenbree' during the final round of torture (v. 277), appropriate enough given that the encounter with Rufo has put her back together again. Finally, as she heads towards her place of execution, she is once again said to be 'ben menbree' (v. 335), forever steadfast in faith and steadfast in body (thanks to relics and text), even though her head is about to be severed.

If relics must be believed to have once belonged to Margaret's body to function as a locus of miracle-working, texts that are treated as relics can be produced and reproduced over and over. That is not to say, however, that the same ethic and aesthetic of integrity that governs Margaret's sublime bodies — in life and in death — and promises to govern the bodies of her textual community does not apply to the saint's story. The author of the Soleil version recognizes that his protagonist's biography circulates in multiple versions, with translators adding and omitting material as they see fit:

> Plusieurs en ont fait a leurs guises,
> Et de latin en françois mises.
> Se l'on en oste, l'aultre y met:
> De leur oeuvre ne m'entremet [...]
> Ce que ay escript tient saincte Eglise,
> Et je le tien en toute guise,
> De ceste vierge gracieuse. (p. 17)

[Several have (told Margaret's story) in their own ways, and translated it from Latin to French. If one takes something away, the next adds to it: I won't get involved in their work [...] Holy Church confirms what I have written, and I confirm it in every way, by this virgin full of grace.]

The author here, then, distances himself from other hagiographers, telling us that he has nothing to do with their texts. His version is the definitive one, he implies, because its authority derives from the Church and from Margaret herself. Neither too short, nor too long, its contents are just right. The author of the Toulouse text, meanwhile, is less concerned with the integrity of its contents than with the physical condition of the manuscript. Margaret's textual community should not only keep a copy of the life close to them to prevent sudden death; they need to take special care of it: 'Totz hom que [...] | Belament la gardara | A mort soptana no mora' (vv. 483–86) ['No-one [...] who looks after it properly will die a sudden death'].

Rather than delete these medieval re-rememberings of Margaret's life, kept so well over the centuries that they have survived to the present (miraculously, some might say), I would contend that we should get to know them a little better. That they are 'fabulous' stories, in every sense of the word, is all very well. That they provide a case study in abjectification — revealing how the sublime and the abject throw each other into stark relief and how abjectified and self-abjectified creatures play very different roles — is interesting enough. But most importantly, we should get to know late medieval vernacular lives of St Margaret because, read in their manuscript contexts, they show how sublime and abject bodies are culturally contingent. And as long as critics are *faux*-surprised to find a virgin acting as the patroness of childbirth, when female subjectivity is still to a large extent split by the same binary, we could do with a reminder of that.

Appendix

French and Occitan versions of the life of St Margaret that circulated in the Middle Ages are listed below, classified initially by language and medium (i.e. verse/prose) and subsequently by source and approximate date of composition.

Verse lives in French

[A] Mombritius

Cambridge. Late-twelfth-century Insular version in 69 monorhymed stanzas of between three and nine alexandrines (402 vv.). Cambridge, UL, Ee.vi.11 (saec. xiii), pp. 1–11. Frederic Spencer (ed.), 'The Legend of St. Margaret. ii.', *Modern Language Notes*, 5 (1890), 71–75.

Additional. Thirteenth-century Insular version in 85 monorhymed, decasyllabic quatrains (340 vv.). London, BL, Add. 38664 (saec. xiii^{med}), ff. 1r–3r. Karl Reichl (ed.), 'An Anglo-Norman Legend of Saint Margaret (ms. BM Add. 38664)', *Romania*, 96 (1975), 53–66.

Sloane. Thirteenth-century Insular version (though the sole witness is Picard) in highly irregular couplets (630 vv.). London, BL, Sloane 1611 (saec. xv), ff. 147v–152v. Paul Meyer (ed.), 'Notice du ms. Sloane 1611 du Musée britannique', *Romania*, 40 (1911), 532–58.

Fouque. Mid-thirteenth-century continental version by Fouque in octosyllabic couplets (498 vv.). Paris, BnF, naf 13521 (saec. xiii^{ex}), pp. 37–43. Guido Tammi (ed.), *Due versioni della leggenda di S. Margherita d'Antiochia in versi francesi del medioevo* (Piacenza: Scuola Artigiana del Libro, 1958), pp. 109–36 [from the late MS Paris, BnF, Moreau 1715].

Escotez, tote bone gent. Mid-thirteenth-century Insular version in octosyllabic couplets (478 vv.). Paris, BnF, fr. 19525 (saec. xiii^{med}), ff. 141v-145r. A. Joly (ed.), 'La Vie de sainte Marguerite: poème inédit de Wace', *Mémoires de la Société des antiquaires de Normandie*, 30 (1880), 173–270 (pp. 229–35).

Aprés la sainte Passion. Late-thirteenth-century continental version in octosyllabic couplets (661 vv. in edition). More than 100 witnesses. Joly (ed.), 'Vie de sainte Marguerite', pp. 215–22 [from Paris, BnF, fr. 1555].

Escoutez tuit par tel couvent. Fourteenth-century reworking of 'Aprés la sainte Passion' in octosyllabic couplets (786 vv.). Paris, BnF, naf 6352 (saec. xv), ff. 1r-17v. Tammi (ed.), *Due versioni*, pp. 137–74]

D'une vierge lit on. Abbreviated fifteenth-century continental version in hexasyllabic couplets (72 vv.). Paris, BnF, fr. 1801 (saec. xv), ff. 65v-66r.

[B] Caligula, or Mombritius and Caligula

Wace. Mid-twelfth-century version in octosyllabic couplets by Jersey-born chronicler Wace (716 vv.). Tours, BM 927 (saec. xiii^{med}), ff. 205v-216v; Paris, Bibl. de l'Arsenal 3516 (*c.* 1267), ff. 125r-126v; Troyes, BM 1905 (saec. xiv^{in}), ff. 155v-175v. Wace, *La Vie de sainte Marguerite*, ed. by Hans-Erich Keller, Beihefte zur Zeitschrift für romanische Philologie, 229 (Tübingen: Niemeyer, 1990).

York. Early thirteenth-century Insular version in 68 monorhymed stanzas of between five and nine alexandrines (437 vv.). York, Minster Library, XVI.K.13 (saec. xiv^{in}), ff. 126v-135r. Frederic Spencer (ed.), 'The Legend of St. Margaret. iii.', *Modern Language Notes*, 5 (1890), 107–11.

Knoll. Fragment of a late-thirteenth-century (?) Insular version in octosyllabic couplets (80 vv.). Location of manuscript unknown. Wolfram Zingerle (ed.), 'Zur Margarethen-Legende', *Romanische Forschungen*, 6 (1891), 414–16.

[C] Jacobus de Voragine, *Legenda aurea*, or Mombritius and *Legenda aurea*

Bozon. Early fourteenth-century Insular version in heptasyllabic couplets attributed to Nicholas Bozon (330 vv.). London, BL, Cotton Dom. A.XI (saec. xiv^{med}), ff. 97r-99r. M. Amelia Klenke (ed.), *Three Saints' Lives by Nicholas Bozon* (St. Bonaventure, NY: Franciscan Institute, 1947).

Soleil. Fifteenth-century continental version in octosyllabic couplets (1332 vv.). Location of manuscript unknown. Extracts in Félix Soleil (ed.), *La Vierge Marguerite substituée à la Lucine antique: analyse d'un poème inédit du xve siècle, suivie de la description du manuscrit et de recherches historiques* (Paris: Labitte, 1885).

Verse lives in Occitan

Mombritius

Toulouse. Thirteenth-century version in octosyllabic couplets (570 vv.), also surviving in two Catalan witnesses. Toulouse, BM 1272 (saec. xiv^{med}), ff. 1r-27v. Alfred Jeanroy (ed.), 'Vie provençale de sainte Marguerite d'après les manuscrits de Toulouse et de Madrid', *Annales du Midi*, 11 (1899), 5–55.

Aurillac. Abbreviated thirteenth-century version in octosyllabic couplets (125 vv.). Location of manuscript unknown. Clovis Brunel (ed.), 'Une nouvelle Vie de sainte Marguerite en vers provençaux', *Annales du Midi*, 38 (1926), 385–401.

Florence. Fourteenth-century (?) version in octosyllabic couplets (1543 vv.). Florence, BML, Ashburnham 40a (saec. xiv^{med}), ff. 23r–47r. Vladimir Chichmarev (ed.), 'Vie provençale de sainte Marguerite', *Revue des langues romanes*, 46 (1903), 545–90. Corrections in Giulio Bertoni, 'Sulla Vita provenzale di S. Margherita', *Revue des langues romanes*, 49 (1906), 299–301.

Prose lives in French

[A] Mombritius

1. Paris, Sainte-Geneviève 587 (*c.* 1300), ff. 18v–21v; Chantilly, Bibl. du Château 734 (1312), ff. 328r–331v; Geneva, BG, Com. Lat. 102 (1320s), ff. 337r–340v; Brussels, KBR 9225 (saec. xiv^{in}), ff. 87v–90v; Paris, BnF, fr. 23117 (saec. xiv^{in}), ff. 439v–443r; Paris, BnF, fr. 183 (*c.* 1327), ff. 86v–89v; London, BL, Add. 17275 (saec. xiv^{in-med}), ff. 315r–318v; Paris, Bibl. Mazarine 1716 (saec. xiii^{ex}-xiv^{in}), ff. 327v–332r; Paris, BnF, fr. 413 (*c.* 1400), ff. 412r–415r. Orywall (ed.), pp. 110–22 (from Sainte-Geneviève 587) [Version A].

1a. Expanded version, possibly influenced by the *Legenda aurea*. Paris, BnF, fr. 20042 (1436), ff. 60r–70r.

2. Heavily abbreviated. Paris, BnF, fr. 187 (saec. xiv^{in}), ff. 41r–41v.

3. Paris, BnF, naf 4510 (saec. xiv^{in}), ff. 42r–50v. Orywall (ed.), pp. 123–34 [Version B].

4. Abbreviated version of Insular origin. Copenhagen, KB, Thott 517 4° (saec. xiv^{med}), ff. 10v–22r.

5. Abbreviated. Rouen, BM 1430 (saec. xv), ff. 57v–58v.

6. Oxford, Queen's College 305 (1460s), ff. 306r–339r; London, BL, Add. 41179 (saec. xv^{ex}), ff. 105r–109r.

[B] Latin translation of the Greek *Passio a Theotimo*

7. London, BL, Royal 20.D.VI (saec. xiii^{med}), ff. 220r–221v; Paris, BnF, fr. 412 (1285), ff. 213r–214r; Paris, BnF fr. 411 (saec. xiv), ff. 271r–272v. Orywall (ed.), pp. 135–39 (from fr. 412) [Version C].

[C] Jean de Mailly, *Abbreviatio in gestis et miraculis sanctorum*

8. Paris, BnF, fr. 988 (saec. xiv^{in}), ff. 124v–125v; Epinal, BM 9 (saec. xiv^{in}), ff. 59v–60r; Lille, BM 451 (saec. xiv-xv), ff. 138v–139v. Orywall (ed.), pp. 140–42 (from fr. 988) [Version D].

8a. Related to the above, perhaps reworked with Mombritius. Paris, BnF, fr. 15110 (saec. xiii^{ex}), ff. 160r–160v; Paris, Bibl. de l'Arsenal 570 (saec. xiv^{in}), ff. 183v–185r; Paris, Bibl. de l'Arsenal 3684 (saec. xv^{med}), ff. 76r–77r [Version Dx].

[D] Vincent de Beauvais, *Speculum historiale*

9. A biography of St Margaret is included in Book 14 of Jean de Vignay's translation of the *Speculum historiale* Paris, BnF, naf 15942 (1370s), f. 5r; Paris, BnF, fr. 315 (saec. xiv^{ex}), ff. 320r–321r; Paris, BnF, fr. 313 (1396), ff. 273r–273v; London, BL, Lansdowne 1179 (*c.* 1400), ff. 244r–245r; Paris, BnF, fr. 309 (1455), ff. 233r–234r; Paris, BnF, fr. 51 (1462), f. 103rv; BnF, fr. 324 (saec. xv^{ex}), ff. 106r–107r. Orywall (ed.), pp. 143–45 (from fr. 313) [Version E].

[E] Jacobus de Voragine, *Legenda aurea*

10. Paris, BnF, fr. 20330 (saec. XIII^{ex}), ff. 156v-157v; Le Puy-en-Velay, Bibl. du Grand Séminaire, unnumbered (saec. XIII^{ex}), f. 126rv. Orywall (ed.), pp. 146–48 (from fr. 20330) [Version F].

11. Version dedicated to Béatrice de Bourgogne. Paris, BnF, fr. 23114 (saec. xv^{ex}), f. 183rv. Orywall (ed.), pp. 153–55 [Version H].

12. Jean de Vignay's translation of the Margaret biography survives in dozens of volumes. For a list, see <http://www.arlima.net/no/15>. Orywall (ed.), pp. 149–52 (from Paris, BnF, fr. 241) [Version G].

13. Brussels, KBR 10203 (1385), ff. 98r-100r; Lille, BM 452 (saec. xv), ff. 346r-348v; Paris, Bibl. de l'Institut 12 (saec. xv), vol. II, ff. 82r-83v; Cambrai, BM 812 (saec. xv^{med}), ff. 199r-200r; Cambrai, BM 210 (saec. xv^{ex}), vol. II, ff. 50r-51v; Cambridge, Fitzwilliam Museum, Charles Fairfax Murray 12 (saec. xv^{ex}), ff. 99r-101r.

14. Florence, BML, Med. Pal. 141 (1399), ff. 173v-174r; Kraków, BJ, gall. f° 156 (c. 1440), ff. 184r-185v; Tournai, BV 127 (saec. xv^{med}), ff. 186v-187v.

15. Paris, BnF, fr. 1054 (1450), ff. 195r-197v. Orywall (ed.), p. 156 [Version J].

16. Semur-en-Auxois, BM 38 (saec. xv), ff. 227r-227v. Fragmentary.

17. Tours, BM 1012 (saec. xv), ff. 26r-27v; Paris, BnF, fr. 15475 (saec. xv^{ex}), ff. 189r-190r. Orywall (ed.), pp. 157–60 (from fr. 15475) [Version K].

18. Paris, BnF, naf 4464 (saec. xv^{ex}), ff. 148r-149r.

19. Paris, BnF, fr. 1534 (saec. xv^{ex}), ff. 48v-49v.

20. Perhaps the work of Jeanne de Malone. Fragment. Leiden, BRU, BPL 46A (1477), f. 11r.

Prose lives in Occitan

Jacobus de Voragine, *Legenda aurea*

1. Paris, BnF, fr. 9759 (saec. xv), ff. 176v-178r.

2. Paris, BnF, fr. 24945 (saec. xv), ff. 23r-24r; Paris, BnF, naf 6504 (saec. xv^{med}), ff. 80r-81v. Monika Tausend (ed.), *Die altokzitanische Version B der 'Legenda aurea': ms. Paris, Bibl. nat., n. acq. fr. 6504*, Beihefte zur Zeitschrift für romanische Philologie, 262 (Tübingen: Niemeyer, 1995), pp. 208–10.

Notes to Chapter 1

1. *Calendarium Romanum, ex decreto sacrosancti œcumenici Concilii Vaticani II instauratum* (Vatican: Typis polyglottis Vaticanis, 1969), p. 130.
2. In the wry little prayer addressed to Margaret in Sara Maitland and Wendy Mulford, *Virtuous Magic: Women Saints and their Meanings* (London: Mowbray, 1998), the saint's medieval devotees are opposed to 'we bright children of the Enlightenment [who] have killed and banished the dragons' (p. 284). On a similar note, it is suggested that women readers in the Middle Ages would not have been able to grasp the mimetic link between Rufo the Dragon and the mother of the childbirth prayer in Jean-Pierre Albert, 'Légende de sainte Marguerite: un mythe maïeutique?', *Razo*, 8 (1988), 19–31 (p. 28). On the basis of the known audiences of French and Occitan lives of St Margaret, it might be argued that Wendy Larson is a little quick to oppose clerical and lay milieus in 'The Role of Patronage and Audience in the Cults of Sts Margaret and Marina of Antioch', in *Gender and Holiness: Men, Women and Saints in Late Medieval Europe*, ed. by Samantha J. E. Riches and Sarah Salih, Routledge Studies in Medieval Religion and Culture, 1 (London: Routledge, 2002), pp. 23–35 (esp. p. 30). Karen P. Smith relates Margaret's exploding dragon to

folkloric motifs in 'Serpent-Damsels and Dragon-Slayers: Overlapping Divinities in a Medieval Tradition', in *Christian Demonology and Popular Mythology*, ed. by Gábor Klaniczay and Éva Pócs, Demons, Spirits, Witches, 2 (Budapest: Central European University Press, 2006), pp. 121–38. Recent quips about Margaret's role as patroness of childbirth include Geoffrey Chamberlain's scepticism surrounding the comfort Margaret could have provided during childbirth in *From Witchcraft to Wisdom: A History of Obstetrics and Gynaecology in the British Isles* (London: Royal College of Obstetricians and Gynaecologists, 2007): 'Her skills in childbirth rested on being swallowed and spat out by a dragon. This apparently gave her unrivalled powers of empathy for the process of birth' (p. 26).

3. Margaret's *vita* survives on birthing girdles which would have been wrapped apotropaically around the stomachs of pregnant women. There are two such parchments in the library of the Wellcome Institute (MSS 50834 and 50835). For a discussion of the use of Margaret's story in amulets, see Don C. Skemer, *Binding Words: Textual Amulets in the Middle Ages* (University Park: Pennsylvania State University Press, 2006), pp. 239–46.

4. The edition to which Kay refers is Wace, *La Vie de sainte Marguerite*, ed. by Elizabeth A. Francis, Classiques français du Moyen Âge, 71 (Paris: Champion, 1932), pp. 3–55.

5. See 'Sublime Body', p. 15. Emma Campbell likewise considers the saint's stand as a 'refusal of pagan authority in both religious and sexual terms' in the Wace *Life of St Margaret*, which she reads through the lens of Agamben's biopolitical model of sovereignty in 'Homo Sacer: Power, Life, and the Sexual Body in Old French Saints' Lives', *Exemplaria*, 18 (2006), 233–73 (p. 263).

6. Page numbers in parentheses to the Mombritius text in Paris, BnF, lat. 17002, published in Wace, *Vie*, ed. Francis, pp. 2–56.

7. For verse lives, numbers in parentheses refer to editions cited in the Appendix, except for 'D'une vierge lit on'. Folio numbers are given for all prose lives. See my own editions at <www. huwgrange.co.uk> for 'D'une vierge lit on' and prose lives that were not edited in Ingelore Orywall (ed.), *Die alt- und mittelfranzösischen Prosafassungen der Margaretelegende* ([Bonn]: n. pub., 1968).

8. In the widespread prose version 12, for example, Olybrius is astonished 'que pucelle si bele et si noble ai [sic] dieu crucefié' (f. 160r) ['that such a fair and noble maiden should have a crucified God'].

9. Hagiographers are evidently fond of pairing body and soul in Margaret's prayers for protection. See, for instance, Fouque (vv. 184–86); 'Escotez, tote bone gent' (vv. 61–62); Toulouse (vv. 77–79); and prose versions 3 (f. 43r), 4 (f. 12r), 6 (f. 106r), and 7 (f. 213r).

10. Hal Foster, 'Obscene, Abject, Traumatic', *October*, 78 (1996), 106–24 (p. 114).

11. Kenneth Baxter Wolf, *The Life and Afterlife of St. Elizabeth of Hungary: Testimony from her Canonization Hearings* (Oxford: Oxford University Press, 2011), pp. 204–05.

12. The *imitatio Christi* motif is most clearly expressed in the Florence verse life: 'El sufertet la mort per me | E tu per luy donas la a me. | Per lhuy vuelh que·m dones la mort, | Qu'el me conduga a bon port' (vv. 256–59) ['He suffered death for me, and you give it to me for him. I wish you to give me death for him, so that he may lead me to a safe haven'].

13. For pure blood, see versions 12 (f. 160r) and 14 (f. 184v), and Sloane (vv. 198–200). For white blood, see Fouque (vv. 146–48).

14. For the forgetful Margaret, see 'Escotez, tote bone gent' (v. 227), and prose versions 1 (f. 20r), 3 (f. 45v) and 7 (f. 213v). She is said to look dead in the Florence verse life (v. 527) and prose version 6 (f. 107r).

15. Symeon the Metaphrast suspected the devil himself had intervened in the story. See the Latin translation of his Margaret life by Laurentius Surius, 'Martyrium sanctae et egregiae et curationum virtute praeditae martyris Marinae', in *De probatis sanctorum historiis*, 7 vols (Cologne: Calenium & Quenelios, 1576–1586), iv (1579), pp. 274–84 (p. 274).

16. Jacobus de Voragine, *Legenda aurea: con le miniature dal Codice ambrosiano C 240 Inf*, ed. by Giovanni Paolo Maggioni, trans. by Francesco Stella et al., Edizione nazionale dei testi mediolatini, 20, 2 vols (Florence: Galluzzo, 2007), i, 692.

17. Version 13 was copied with the *Miroir des curés* in Cambrai, BM 210; Paris, Bibl. de l'Institut, 12; and Brussels, KBR 10203.

18. See also the Toulouse Occitan life, in which Beelzebub is also a shivering wreck (vv. 322–23).
19. See Elaine M. Treharne, '"They Shall Not Worship Devils... Which Neither Can See, Nor Hear, Nor Walk": The Sensibility of the Virtues and *The Life of St Margaret*', in *Proceedings of the Patristic, Medieval, and Renaissance Conference*, 15 (1990), pp. 221–36 (p. 224); Jordi Cerdà Subirachs, 'La leyenda de santa Margarita de Antioquía en Cataluña', in *Medioevo y literatura I-IV: Actas del V Congreso de la Asociación Hispánica de Literatura Medieval (Granada, 27 septiembre-1 octubre 1993)*, ed. by Juan Salvador Paredes Núñez, 2 vols (Granada: Universidad de Granada, 1995), II, 23–32 (p. 26); and Carole Hill, '"Here Be Dragons": The Cult of St Margaret of Antioch and Strategies for Survival', in *Art, Faith and Place in East Anglia: From Prehistory to the Present*, ed. by T. A. Heslop, Elizabeth Mellings, and Margit Thøfner (Woodbridge: Boydell, 2012), pp. 105–16 (p. 108).
20. Beelzebub cites being beaten by a child of pagan parents as the sole reason for his distress in York (vv. 202–03), Fouque (vv. 325–26), 'Escotez, tote bone gent' (vv. 295–96), French prose versions 3, 6, 13, and 17, and Occitan prose version 1.
21. There are, however, exceptions. The authors of the Sloane and Toulouse lives note that Margaret does not look especially healthy after her spell in prison and battles with diabolical creatures (v. 443 and vv. 392–94 respectively).
22. See, for example, Cambridge (vv. 285–86), Sloane (vv. 458–60, 478–80), Florence (vv. 1054–1129), and French prose version 6 (f. 108r).
23. In the prose lives based on the *Legenda aurea*, similarly, an earthquake and a little help from a dove save Margaret from drowning. In version 18 the vat crumbles into pieces (f. 149r).
24. Interestingly, Bozon tells us that the onlookers were amazed that anyone, male or female, could resist such torment (vv. 216–18). The author of Occitan prose version 2 suggests that their surprise is due to Margaret's nobility as much to her gender (f. 81r).
25. Carole Hill, *Women and Religion in Late Medieval Norwich* (Woodbridge, Boydell, 2010), p. 61.
26. See Jane Tibbetts Schulenburg, *Forgetful of their Sex: Female Sanctity and Society, 500–1100* (Chicago: University of Chicago Press, 1998), p. 229. Consider also Margaret's prayer in prose version 1, in which she suggests women in labour would invoke God and his 'glorieuse mere' ['glorious mother'] (f. 21r).
27. Jocelyn Wogan-Browne, 'The Apple's Message: Some Post-Conquest Hagiographic Accounts of Textual Transmission', in *Late-Medieval Religious Texts and their Transmission: Essays in Honour of A. I. Doyle*, ed. by A. J. Minnis (Woodbridge: Brewer, 1994), pp. 39–53 (p. 53).
28. Sarah Salih, *Versions of Virginity in Late Medieval England* (Cambridge: Brewer, 2001), pp. 88–89.
29. Julia Kristeva, *Soleil noir: dépression et mélancolie* (Paris: Gallimard, 1987), p. 38.
30. The essay originally appeared as Julia Kristeva, 'Héréthique de l'amour', *Tel Quel*, 74 (1977), 30–49. It was republished as Julia Kristeva, 'Stabat mater', in *Histoires d'amour* (Paris: Denoël, 1983), pp. 225–47. References here are to the latter.
31. Margaret wishes to act as an example to other virgins in Fouque (vv. 189–90), 'Escotez, tote bone gent' (vv. 177–78), Toulouse (vv. 231–32), and French prose versions 1 (f. 19v) and 3 (f. 44v). The unique witness of the Toulouse life in Occitan verse is a candidate for ownership by a house of nuns: the Latin prayer that follows the text appeals for readers to be adorned with 'castitatis floribus' ['the flowers of chastity'].
32. 'Ne la lessez pener,' Margaret instructs in the Cambridge life (v. 352) ['Let her not suffer'], and 'Trespassez les, Sire, de peines e poürs' in the York life (v. 376) ['spare them, Lord, suffering and fear']. May a mother be given speedy 'aligement' ['relief'], we find in French prose version 11 (f. 183v). She will be kept from peril in versions 8 (f. 125v) and 9 (f. 273v), and emerge 'hors de peril' ['out of danger'] and 'saine' ['healthy'] in Soleil (p. 16). Jean de Vignay, in French prose version 12, also has Margaret ask for the mother to be 'toute saine' (f. 160v) ['completely healthy'], while the author of version 18 asks for the child to be born 'en telle maniere qu'il peüst venir a salvacion et les meres relever en bonne sancté' (f. 149r) ['so that he can achieve salvation and mothers recover their good health']. In French prose version 4, finally, neither mother nor baby will be 'failes de corps ne de membre' (f. 20r) ['weak in body or limb'].
33. A mother will deliver her child ('delieurara') in the Aurillac life (v. 105). God will 'deliver' her in 'Escoutez tuit par tel couvent' (v. 646). She will be 'quite et delivre' ['free and delivered'] in the

'Aprés la sainte Passion' life (v. 540), 'delivree sanz peril' ['delivered without danger'] in French prose version **8a** (f. 160v), and 'sans peril delivrees' [without danger delivered] in version **13** (f. 348r). Mothers are to be granted vague 'deliverance' in Additional (v. 307), Sloane (v. 566), and French prose version **19** (f. 49v). Bozon draws a parallel between the mother's body and that of the infant by having Margaret ask that neither be 'encumbered': 'Ne la femme travaylant | Ne seyt encumbré de l'enfant, | Ne lenz ne seyt enfant né | Par le diable encumbré' (vv. 261–64) ['May a woman in labour not be encumbered by their child, nor may a child be born there encumbered by the devil'].

34. Jennifer Borland, 'Violence on Vellum: St Margaret's Transgressive Body and its Audience', in *Representing Medieval Genders and Sexualities in Europe: Construction, Transformation, and Subversion, 600–1530*, ed. by Elizabeth L'Estrange and Alison More (Farnham: Ashgate, 2011), pp. 67–87 (p. 67).

35. Judith Butler, *Gender Trouble: Feminism and the Subversion of Identity* (New York: Routledge, 1990), p. 80.

36. Julia Kristeva, 'Maternité selon Giovanni Bellini', in Kristeva, *Polylogue* (Paris: Seuil, 1977), pp. 409–35.

37. See, for example, Additional (v. 308), Fouque (vv. 421–22), and French prose versions **1** (f. 21r) and **17** (f. 190v).

38. Note that when the author of 'Aprés la sainte Passion' comes to this passage he conflates texts and relics in the phrase 'riens de ma vie' (v. 560).

CHAPTER 2

❖

St George of Cappadocia (and his Dragon):
Strangers and Communities

For several years, Mark Cazalet's Trinity Reredos, installed in Manchester Cathedral's Fraser Chapel in 2001, hadn't proved particularly controversial. It is the left panel of the triptych that has since caught the eye of some (**Figure 2.1**). It depicts a young, black St George wearing an England football shirt and liberating (rather than slaying) a shackled dragon. There is no princess to admire George's heroism here. Dragon and maiden instead appear to have merged into a single figure, the monster's crest evoking lustrous long hair, and its haunches tracing the outline of an audaciously green dress.

In 2011, a street parade was organized for Manchester's St George's Day Festival, complete with two giant puppets *a la catalana* inspired by Cazalet's triptych (one of George, the other of the dragon-princess). Right-wing movements have hijacked St George as a cultural symbol, those in charge suggested (and when the English Defence League add templar crosses to the George flag and spew forth crusade-inspired rhetoric, it is hard to disagree); and it is high time to claim him back. English nationalism should be about 'tolerance and opening up to people', so let multicultural George release us from the shackles of EDL jingoism.[1] The message, of course, was not accepted by all. The *Daily Star* complained that this was yet another example of political correctness gone mad; Nick Griffin, erstwhile leader of the British National Party, posted extracts from the 'hundreds' of letters of complaint he had been forwarded; and Mancunian clergymen started to receive hate mail and abusive phone calls.[2]

With his dragon-princess, Cazalet conflates images of two strange creatures, the pagan princess (in medieval legends usually the *object* of George's proselytizing discourse) and the monster (typically *abjectified* by the saint). Rather than keeping these strangers in chains, he suggests, let's set them free. Only then will we be rid of a particularly nefarious brand of English nationalism; only then will we ourselves be free to build a better community.

This chapter explores the role of strangers in the formation of community in medieval French and Occitan tales of George and the Dragon. With their group prayers that subsume a saint's diegetic and extradiegetic devotees into a single 'textual community', saints' lives make for a fruitful forum for considering how texts promote collective identity. Biographies of St George are perhaps even more

Fig. 2.1. Mark Cazalet's Trinity Reredos, Left Panel (2001)
[Private Collection/Bridgeman Images]

fruitful than most, celebrated as he was right across Christendom (and, syncretized with al-Khiḍr, even beyond), yet also adopted by particular groups (knights, farmers, the English, and so forth) as their patron. Key to my discussion will be Kristeva's notion of the 'stranger', as outlined (chiefly) in *Étrangers à nous-mêmes*, which I will read in the light of her earlier theorization of abjection in *Pouvoirs de l'horreur* and also postmodern attempts (by the likes of Jean-Luc Nancy, Giorgio Agamben and Jacques Derrida) to advance an ethically appropriate concept of 'community'. Strangers are not all the same, medieval lives of St George tell us; the boundary between objects (to be converted) and abjects (to be annihilated) is in flux. And without an awareness of the production of alterity in the stories we tell, as Cazalet's triptych usefully reminds us, we can hardly aspire to a better being-in-common.

Strangers and Communities in Jacobus de Voragine's George and the Dragon

According to the life of St George in Jacobus de Voragine's *Legenda aurea*, as the pagan princess reveals her unhappy fate to the saint, she is cut off in mid-flow, petrified by the sight of a dragon poking its head out of a nearby lake.[3] It might be said that the tale of George and the Dragon itself makes a similarly abrupt entrance into the saint's biography. The story of George's martyrdom, which pits him against a pagan tyrant and his impressive array of torture equipment, circulated on all shores of the Mediterranean in various guises from the fifth century onwards.[4] But it was not until the eleventh or twelfth century that the first written traces of George's encounter with a dragon surfaced. And for the seeker of origins, the evidence is frustratingly inconclusive: manuscripts preserving the tale in Latin, Greek and Georgian are all of a similar date.[5]

An abbreviated account of George and the Dragon was included in Bartholomew of Trent's mid-thirteenth-century anthology of saints' lives, on which Jacobus de Voragine drew to compile his *Legenda aurea* later on in the thirteenth century.[6] The late medieval success of vernacular tales of George's dragon, however, is almost entirely due to Jacobus. In French and Occitan, we find the saint and his monster, as we would expect, in translations of Jacobus's anthology. But his version was so successful that it also wormed its way into accounts of the saint's biography that were not borrowed from the *Legenda aurea*, including metrical versions that seem to have drawn on a bewildering array of sources (see Appendix). Thanks to Jacobus, by the end of the Middle Ages the dragon was really making a splash.

Whatever its precise origins, in the *Legenda aurea* the story of George and the Dragon is attached to the shorter of the two main versions of the saint's *passio* that circulated in Latin Christendom during the later Middle Ages, the one known as *Z* since John Matzke's pioneering work on the medieval legend.[7] Jacobus made little effort to join the dragon miracle and the account of the saint's martyrdom to form a seamless narrative: he stuck the two stories together without so much as a link-word, producing a composite text punctuated by doubts about his sources and scholarly citations from the *praefatio* to the Mass of St George according to the Ambrosian rite.[8] Particularly awkward, I would suggest, is the shift in the depiction of pagans that occurs as George leaves the dragon he slew in Libya to suffer martyrdom somewhere in the Holy Land at the hands of a pagan tyrant.

Initially at least, the pagans of Jacobus's life of St George are objects — human correlates, that is — to be converted. The pagan-populated city of Silena in Libya comes under daily attack from a dragon that lives in a nearby lake. To prevent the monster breathing its pestilential breath over the walls, the Silenians offer a daily tribute of sheep, but before long their livestock reserves are so depleted that they must instead sacrifice their children. When the city's princess is chosen to become dragon-fodder, Silena seems to have reached a point of no return: by immolating the sovereign's child, the representative of a collective future, it has become Georges Bataille's self-condemning community.[9]

Fortunately, however, a stranger from afar (none other than George of Cappadocia) miraculously appears. He pierces the dragon with his lance, throws it to the ground and instructs the maiden to lead the vanquished beast to the city. The citizens of Silena run for their lives (sensibly enough), but George summons them back and — as several modern commentators have noted — issues something of an ultimatum to the crowd: 'Tantummodo in Christum credite et unusquisque vestrum baptizetur et draconem istum occidam!' (I, 442) ['Just believe in Christ and each one of you receive baptism and I shall kill this dragon!].[10] George offers the pagans the chance to convert and have their dragon slain and, while the alternative may not necessarily be stated overtly, it is standing before them in the form of the pestilential dragon that has devoured all their children. Forced to choose between conversion and death, the people of Silena embrace Christianity. Whereupon George whips out his sword and slays the beast (I, 440–44).

For the remainder of the George entry in the *Legenda aurea*, however, pagans are first and foremost abject creatures ripe for annihilation. The tyrannical Dacian, we are told, takes great delight in persecuting Christians. Having taken Palestine by storm as a proto-crusader, George comes to the rescue of his co-religionists. In retaliation, Dacian has him scraped with nails and his broken flesh burned with torches until his entrails are plainly visible. As was the case for St Margaret in Chapter 1, there is initially nothing sublime about the martyr's flesh. But during his subsequent rounds of torture he comes equipped with a body marked in various ways as corporeally different, the sorcerer's poison having no effect, the wheel breaking when it touches the saint's body and the bath of boiling lead pleasingly refreshing. After his holy make-over, George (with a little help from God) is able to abjectify his pagan tormentors, successfully praying for lightning to strike Dacian's priests, temples and idols, whose charred remains are swallowed up by the earth. Dacian himself suffers a similar fate once George has finally been decapitated: on his way home from the place of execution he too is struck down by divine fire (I, 444–46).

The so-called 'Jerusalem' miracle provides a final fantasy of pagan annihilation. Jacobus may leap forward from third-century Romans to the Fatimid occupants of Jerusalem at the end of the eleventh century, but George's impatience with 'pagan' alterity does not subside with time. George is said to have appeared at the Siege of Jerusalem during the First Crusade, leading the Franks over the walls of the occupied city and helping them to slay every single one of its Saracen inhabitants. Once again, then, the saint shows little concern for converting the pagan foe, instead glorying in his enemies' violent destruction (I, 448).[11]

Glossing his biography of St George, Jacobus notes the various strangers in the story. First is the saint himself: in the prologue to his George entry, Jacobus suggests that the saint's name may derive in part from the Greek *gero*, which he translates as 'peregrinus' (I, 440) ['stranger', 'pilgrim']. Next, George encounters strangers on his travels in dragon-infested Libya. Jacobus's three sermons on the topic cast the saint, in Pauline mode, as a *miles Christi*, an allegorical knight equipped with the chainmail of justice, the sword of Logos, the helmet of hope, the shield of faith and the lance of charity.[12] If the dragon (unsurprisingly) is to be understood as the devil (pp. 190–91), George makes for an ideal preacher, wielding the Word of God to rid pagan strangers of their idols and diabolical ways so that they can become rather more like us (pp. 192–93). Appropriately enough, another etymology Jacobus gives for George in the *Legenda aurea* is the Greek *us*, which he renders as 'consiliator', since the saint acted as a 'consiliator in predicatione regni' (I, 440) ['an adviser in preaching the kingdom (of heaven)'].

Medieval *milites Christi*, of course, were not always confined to allegorical battles against spiritual enemies: by the end of the eleventh century, this slipperiest of terms was also being applied to crusader knights fighting 'divinely sanctioned' battles against flesh-and-blood foes. There is nothing conciliatory about George's encounters with strangers in the second part of the life: here he is not a model preacher who overcomes diabolical snares but an exemplary soldier who slaughters human enemies. This warrants another etymology from Jacobus: 'Vel dicitur a *gerar*, quod est sacrum, et *gyon*, quod est luctatio, quasi sacer luctator, quia luctatus est cum dracone et carnifice' (I, 440) ['Or it derives from *gerar*, which is "holy", and *gyon*, which is "fight", and would mean "holy fighter", since he fought with the dragon and the tormentor']. If some strangers are worth saving (by stranger-saints), the radical alterity of others places them beyond redemption.

According to Jacobus, while George was awaiting execution he successfully prayed for all his followers' wishes to be granted (I, 448). Subsuming the saint's supporters — diegetic and extradiegetic, and past, present and future — this rhetorical strategy sustains a fiction that has become known as a 'textual community'. Some of the specificity of this term, which Brian Stock originally used to describe eleventh- and twelfth-century movements 'based on a literate inner core, a set of written legislation, and a wider, unlettered membership united orally to the same norms' has certainly been lost (*Implications*, p. 238). But in 'textual communities' scholars have found a helpful way to describe the form of collective identity promoted by many medieval hagiographers, one grounded upon the written text though allowing its imagined members, literate to very varying degrees, to interact with that text in multiple ways.[13] Manuscript evidence might tell us a different story about who interacted with a given text (and how, when, where, etc.), but the textual communities envisaged by hagiographers vary little from one work to another (and even from Latin to the vernacular, and verse to prose). In the case of Jacobus's life of St George (as in countless other holy biographies), the saint, though in some respects a stranger, is presented as one of 'us'. The boundaries of our textual community are broadly drawn, but drawn they certainly are. By telling us which strangers are like us and which ones are anything but, the saint makes 'us'.

Saints' lives placed in their manuscript context can help expose the fiction of hagiography's united textual community. Taking as my corpus the surviving medieval French and Occitan lives featuring the George and the Dragon story (though focussing on a handful of these, mostly unpublished), I here consider the shifting boundaries between strangers and communities from one version of the story to another, and the grounds they give for welcoming some strangers and rejecting others. A look at the afterlife of one of the French versions of the legend will lead to a discussion of William Caxton's life of St George in relation to English national identity, before we return to Cazalet's triptych to ask whether it can ever be possible for our most famous dragon-slayer to patronize an ethically appropriate community.

Crusader St George and the Elimination of Alterity

For Kristeva (as for any self-respecting poststructuralist), subjectivity is unstable, incomplete, provisional, or, to use her own phrase, *in process* ('en procès'). The Freudian unconscious splits the Cartesian subject, alienating our selves from our-selves. Unfortunately (at least for some), Kristeva argues, human beings are wont to overcome this alienating strangeness within by projecting it onto their fellows: by casting (out) others as strangers, we (and our communities) create an illusion of stability, completion and permanence. In *Étrangers à nous-mêmes*, Kristeva seeks to remedy the totalitarian threat thus diagnosed by prescribing psychoanalysis. We must learn to live with our own strangeness (read: our unconscious) if we are to stand any chance of living with others. In sum, 'de le reconnaître en nous, nous nous épargnons de le détester en lui-même' ['By recognizing him within ourselves, we are spared detesting him in himself'].[14]

If Kristeva's foray into the political sounds familiar, it is because her figure of the stranger is to some extent indebted to that of the abject (discussed in Chapter 1). Though never explicitly equating stranger and abject, she provides ample oppor-tunity for doing so, as Noëlle McAfee has previously explored.[15] Where *Pouvoirs de l'horreur* strays from the personal to the political, the abject manifests itself in the guise of the stranger (p. 12). Echoes of the abject, meanwhile, are found in Kristeva's description of the role played by the stranger in the elaboration of collective identity, as described in *Étrangers*: 'l'étranger condense sur soi la fascination et l'abjection que suscite l'altérité' (p. 140) ['the foreigner concentrates upon himself the fascination and the repulsion that otherness gives rise to' (*Strangers*, p. 96)].

Not all of Kristeva's strangers, however, are provoked into provoking abjection. Some are welcomed into the fold: 'l'étranger est d'emblée situé comme bénéfique ou maléfique pour ce groupe social et pour son pouvoir, et, à ce titre, il est à assimiler ou à rejeter' (*Etrangers*, p. 140) ['the foreigner is at once identified as beneficial or harmful to that social group and its power and, on that account, he is to be assimilated or rejected' (*Strangers*, p. 96)]. Crucially, then, some strangers are considered objects within the realm of symbolic difference, while others are akin to the abject that threatens to collapse symbolic difference altogether. The latter are boundary-crossers, stubbornly refusing to stay in their proper place. And though they are radically other, there is also something uncannily familiar about them. For this reason, after Norma Claire Moruzzi, I shall refer to them here as 'familiar strangers'.[16]

For some medieval hagiographers, St George is first and foremost a literal *miles Christi*, who slew (and continues to slay) his pagan enemies assigned a role akin to the Kristevan familiar stranger. One such life, the unpublished French prose version here labelled number 13, survives in two fifteenth-century manuscripts, both legendaries that make heavy use of Jean de Vignay's rendering of the *Legenda aurea*. Version 13 of the George life stands out from the corpus of French and Occitan recensions as a whole for two reasons. Firstly, its structure is inverted, so that the *passio*, which is a rendering of Matzke's *Z*, actually precedes the dragon and Jerusalem miracles, which are given according to a unique rendering of the *Legenda aurea*. Secondly, the miracle tales are reworked in the light of the martyrdom sequence to cast all pagans, whether Romans of late Antiquity or late-eleventh-century Fatimids, as devil-worshipping idolaters who should, ideally, be annihilated at the earliest convenience.

Though the pagans of French prose version 13 are initially presented as victims of imperial tyranny and diabolical temptation (ff. 136v-137r), they soon receive less compassionate treatment. In the *Legenda aurea*, when George pretends to appease his persecutor by performing sacrifices, he craftily prays instead for Dacian's temples and idols to be destroyed. Lightning strikes, his wish is granted and the pagan populace is specifically spared (1, 446). But other Latin versions of the *passio* that share a common source with Jacobus's account, including Vincent de Beauvais's *Speculum historiale* and Jean de Mailly's *Summa*, are less forgiving: part of the crowd goes up in smoke.

Perhaps under the influence of this branch of Matzke's *Z* family, version 13 includes an even more complete fantasy of pagan annihilation. George kneels before Apollo and prays at some length for the destruction of devils and the conversion of Dacian's people (f. 138r). But God seems to misinterpret George's request. The divine fire that was supposed to facilitate evangelization envelops the entirety of the pagan population (apparently twice):

> Sitost comme saint George eut faicte sa priere, feu descendy du ciel qui embraza tout le peuple et ardist tous les faulx ymaiges et les evesques, et grant partie des mescreans. (f. 138r)

> [As soon as St George had pronounced his prayer, fire descended from the sky that inflamed all the people and burned all the false idols and bishops, and a large part of the infidels.]

This scene of abjectification is notable for its lack of converts: not only do all the pagans fall victim to the lightning strike, but not even the empress, absent from this version, is inspired to turn to the Christian God. George has given up proselytizing for good, and when lightning next strikes, this time avenging the saint's death, Dacian and the last few remaining pagans are burned to a crisp (f. 138v).

After George's martyrdom, the author of version **13** takes us backwards in time to the dragon miracle. The citizens of Silena here bear a striking resemblance to Dacian's pagan populace: identified as 'Sarrazins' (f. 138v) ['Saracens'], they too are depicted as temple-going idolaters (f. 140v). At the end of the miracle, moreover, the vernacular hagiographer cannot resist adding a scene of destruction to parallel the one he added to the martyrdom. And so the city's temples go up in smoke to make way for churches (ff. 140r-140v).

Fast-forwarding some 700 years to the Jerusalem miracle, we find a familiar epilogue to George's triumphant appearance before the Crusaders. Inspired by the saint,

> les Crestiens s'efforsoient tousjours, tant qu'ilz prindrent la ville par force et occirent les Sarrazins sans remedde. Et porterent les reliques saint George dedans la ville. Et destruirent les temples aux ydolles. Et en lieu de ce firent esglises des sains Nostre Seigneur, et la ville peuplerent de Crestiens. (ff. 140v-141r)

> [the Christians struggled on until they seized the city by force and killed the Saracens without restraint. And they carried St George's relics into the city. And they destroyed the temples dedicated to idols. And in their place they built churches devoted to the saints of our Lord, and they populated the city with Christians.]

Just as Dacian's temples and the temples of Silena had to be destroyed in the *passio* and the dragon miracle, Jerusalem's temples of idolatry had to disappear — and the more collateral damage to abject Saracens, the better — to make way for Christian colonization. Jacobus made little effort to link the diversely sourced sections of his entry for George, but the author of version **13** produces a coherent whole by homogenizing the pagan Other. The pagans' strangeness is familiar because we have already encountered it in the story (and as a literary *topos* elsewhere in our readings/ hearings). But, more importantly, these pagans make for familiar strangers because, in casting them as so radically other as to be abject, they are parodically (and paradoxically) more like us: the churches dedicated to saints can never completely displace the temples to the idols since the former inspired the latter.

Prose version **13** of the George life may feature heightened violence directed at pagans, but it does not explicitly incite violence beyond the diegesis. The same, however, cannot be said for French prose version **6** of the story. This text is known only in a paper volume (Brussels, KBR 10295-304) completed in Ath in 1429 by a certain Jehan Wagus and later found in the library of Charles I de Croÿ.[17] Alongside didactic and moralizing works including the *Fables* of Marie de France and Gossuin de Metz's *Image du monde*, this anthology preserves 41 saints' lives, many of which can be related to lives in a late-thirteenth-century volume (Paris, BnF, fr. 6447). There is no dragon in the George entry in BnF, fr. 6447, however, which is perhaps the reason why the compiler of KBR 10295–304 looked elsewhere for this particular biography.

In terms of the narrative, version 6 of the life of St George sticks closely to the *Legenda aurea* for both martyrdom and miracles. The saint here, however, behaves more like a *sacer luctator* than a *consiliator*. For one thing, in the opening dragon miracle he taps the full potential of the monster as a tool for terrorizing the pagan populace into submission. In the Latin source, George spikes the beast with his lance and instructs the princess to throw her girdle around its neck. And so the dragon is led to Silena 'velut mansuetissimus canis' (I, 442) ['like a well-trained dog']. But in version 6, the simile is rewritten: George and the princess are said to drag along a 'rabid hound' ('kien rabit', f. 65r). The vernacular author thus rejects the hagiographical *topos* according to which the civilizing saint tames the beast, instead leaving the dragon undomesticated. We should hardly be surprised, then, that Silena's citizens head for the hills and the strongholds of the city, terrified that George is about to feed them to the monster. Once George has summoned the fearful pagans back to the city, he duly delivers his ultimatum: sure, he will slay his rabid dog, as long as everyone believes in Christ.

Violence in version 6, moreover, is contagious, spreading from the diegesis to the imagined textual community. The author adds a prologue and an epilogue to his George biography, identifying the narrator as a soldier and dedicating the intervening text to his brothers-at-arms.[18] He begins by advising men-at-arms to carry the life with them at all times, before suggesting that other readers also have a vested interest in reading the text if they wish to triumph over their enemies:

> Chi aprés s'ensieut le vie monsigneur saint Jorge, le glorieus martir, comment il fu martirijés, lequel martire en remembrance cascuns hommes d'armes le doit porter en bataille et en tous lieus perilleus. Et quiconques le lira ou ora lire, ja icel jour nus maus li avenra, ne nus encombriés, mais qu'il ait boine foy et ferme creance ou Pere et ou Fil et ou benoit Saint Esperit et en monsigneur saint Jorge, qui li seront en ayuwe a tous les besoing qu'il aront. Et qui en devotion le portera, ja son anemi n'ara pooir ne victore sur lui. (f. 63v)

> [Hereafter follows the life of my lord St George, the glorious martyr, how he was martyred, whose martyrdom every man-at-arms, in remembrance, should carry into battle and in all dangerous places. And whoever reads it or hears it read, nothing bad or harmful will happen to him on that day, as long as he has good faith and firm belief in the Father, the Son and the blessed Holy Ghost, and in my lord St George, who will help him with everything he needs. And he who carries it with devotion, never will his enemy have power or victory over him.]

Soldier-readers are not just being urged to 'carry' the text with them in memory ('en remembrance'); they are to take a hard copy 'in memory' of the saint. The prayer that George pronounces before his decapitation in version 6 confirms that the narrator considers the physical text as a talisman that will guarantee soldiers victory over their enemies:

> Or vous prie jou pour tous chiaus qui mon non reclameront, en tiere, en mer et en baptaille, et en tous lieus perilleus, soit devant juge ou signeur terrijen,

que vous les delivrés de tous leur tourmens et de tous les perieus [...] Et a tous ciaus qui porteront ma vie en bataille, sire Diex, je vous requier que par vostre merite vous leur donnés victore encontre leur anemis. (ff. 67v-68r)

[I now ask, on behalf of all those who invoke my name, on land, at sea and in battle, and in all dangerous places, before a judge or a secular lord, that you deliver them from all their torments and all their perils [...] Moreover, Lord God, I request that, by your merit, you give all those who carry my life into battle victory over their enemies.]

It is unlikely, of course, that the 400 folios of KBR 10295–304 ever made it to the battlefield. On the contrary, the size of this codex suggests that Jehan Wagus was not the author of version 6 but borrowed it from elsewhere.

In the lengthy prayer that closes the epilogue to version 6, the narrator identifies himself and his readers more specifically as knights under George's chivalrous tutelage:

Voelliés prijer a lui qu'il voelle prijer a Dieu qu'il voelle ensaucier no prijeres [...] Sire sains Jorges, je vous prie que vous voelliés mi et mes amis warder de mal et d'encombrier si vorement que je met mon cors et mes biens en vostre dignez mains. Et, tres dous sires, je vous requierch que vous donnés mes anemis tel destourbier qu'il ne me puissent nuire ne grever en bataille nulle, quelle que ce soit, ne blecer mes armures. Et si vous prie que par vostre sainte merite et par vostre sainte chevalerie qui vit ou trone devant Dieu ou siecle des siecle, sire saint Jorges, vrais martirs, prijés a Dieu qu'il me voelle ensaucier mes prijeres et que Nostre Sires Jhesu Crist me voelle donner victore et jetter de l'an et dou jour a honneur. (ff. 68r-68v)

[May you ask him to ask God to hear our prayers [...] Lord St George, I ask that you protect me and my friends from evil and harm so sincerely that I place my body and everything I own in your worthy hands. And, fairest lord, I request that you cause so much trouble for my enemies that they cannot harm or injure me in any battle, whichever it is, nor damage my armour. And I ask that you, lord St George, a true martyr, who dwells in heaven ever-lasting before God, by your holy merit and your holy chivalry hear my prayers and may our Lord Jesus Christ give me victory and cast me into honour every year and every day (?).]

The narrator's prayer may be syntactically convoluted (Voeillés [...] qu'il voelle [...] qu'il voelle'), but it is nonetheless clear that the textual community imagined here is made up of fellow knights, and not just *milites Christi* in a figurative sense: these are knights who want to avoid injuries and scratched armour on the battlefield. Addressing us as 'you', but also subsuming us into a collective 'we', the narrator invites readers and listeners to participate in an imagined military community that turns to George and his fellow knights in Paradise to triumph over our enemies of flesh and blood.

Additions made to the Jerusalem miracle in version 6 forge intriguing links between fighting at the diegetic and extradiegetic levels. The vernacular hagiographer makes it clear from the outset that the aim of the Siege of Jerusalem in 1099 was to destroy all the Saracens within the city walls (f. 68r). He also adds a triumphant image of Christian colonization to Jacobus's account that sees the Crusaders as 'signeur de la chitet' (ibid.) ['lords of the city']. More importantly, however, the narrator links the tale of George's miraculous appearance at the end of the eleventh century to the present day. The Jerusalem miracle is introduced as an explanation for why knights continue to bear the distinctive arms of St George: it is, we are told, 'le raison pour quoy on a pris les armes monsigneur saint Jorge, qui estoient blancques a une rouge crois' (ibid.) ['the reason why the arms of my lord St George, which are white with a red cross, have been adopted']. Version 6 of George's biography, then, stages a re-enactment. If some soldier-readers carry George's biography to the battlefield to stand a better chance of destroying their enemies (just as George destroyed the Saracens), others dress up in his armour, too.

In French prose version 6 of George's biography, abject pagans owe their strange familiarity not simply to parody (as, say, in version 13). Nor can these familiar strangers be fully explained by René Girard's notion of mimetic violence, according to which opponents become increasingly similar as they exchange ever more aggressive blows (dissembling their similarity all the while).[19] Here we have the strange familiarity of re-enactment. As we ride into battle, equipped with George's biography and armour, our enemies are not familiar because we have already read or heard about them, but because the text, in part, has created them.

Conciliatory St George and Familiarizing Ourselves with Others

Having laid out her theoretical wares in the opening section of *Étrangers à nous-mêmes* (with nods aplenty to Camus), Kristeva proceeds to trace a genealogy of cosmopolitanism from Ancient Greece to the present. She considers the Stoics' complex notion of οἰκείωσις, or 'conciliation', by which the subject familiarizes himself with himself, but also with family, friends and, ultimately, all mankind. She connects the Old Testament Prophets' instructions to welcome strangers with the Israelites' status as a group of exiles. And in the writings of Sts Paul and Augustine she finds Christendom conceptualized as 'une communauté autre' (p. 113) ['a community that was other' (p. 77)], a society of strangers transcending all political structures, with Christ, the strangest of all, at its centre (p. 122). Though locating the origins of cosmopolitanism in stoical and biblical works, Kristeva nonetheless acknowledges that these precocious 'citizens of the world', however universalist in their outlook, only embraced 'ceux qui adoptent la *même* universalité' (p. 101) ['those who adopt the *same* universality' (p. 69)]. These cosmopolitan communities, in other words, still had entry requirements.

The metrical lives of St George in French and Occitan take a stance on alterity that is similarly conciliatory to that of Kristeva's early cosmopolites. Sources for both of these works have proved somewhat elusive. Though evidently independent of one another, both of these lives appear to bear the influence of the *Legenda aurea* as well as a Latin text like that preserved in Munich, BSB, Clm 14473 (or a lost source combining these) for the dragon miracle. And for George's martyrdom, both French and Occitan works belong to Matzke's *Y* tradition, but preserve (different) episodes apparently unique to Greek versions of the legend. The French text has come down to us in a single late-fourteenth-century manuscript, probably copied in the northern *oïl* zone and now in unknown (private) hands. The Occitan, meanwhile, survives in a fifteenth-century copy, no doubt made in Catalan-speaking country.[20]

If the author of the French metrical life did indeed follow the *Legenda aurea* for the dragon miracle, he departed from it by explicitly casting the dragon as a symbol of Silena's pagan religion. When George rides up to the maiden, she is suitably impressed by his heroic display, given the monster is scheduled to arrive at any moment (vv. 63–66). The saint modestly suggests that the maiden could be acting just as bravely as he, if only she were not a Saracen:

> Fille, vous estes sarrazine,
> Mais se vous voulez en Dieu croire
> Le serpent ne vous puet mal faire. (vv. 76–78)

[Girl, you are Saracen, but if you wish to believe in God the serpent cannot do you harm.]

Instead of converting alongside her father and his subjects in the city, the maiden embraces Christianity there and then with a triumphant cry of 'J'y croieray vraiment!' (v. 79) ['Truly I shall believe!']. By abandoning her pagan ways she has rendered herself immune to the dragon's attack.

That George's encounter with the dragon represents a battle between Christianity and paganism (as opposed to pagans *per se*) is further emphasized in the French life when the monster rears its ugly head. George has no need to reach for his famous lance here. Instead, as if literalizing the allegorical interpretation of the story we find in Jacobus de Voragine's sermons, he plays the role of the preacher, stopping the dragon in its tracks with the word of God:

> Saint George lui dist haultement,
> 'De par Dieu, le Roy tout puissant,
> Te conjur que n'aies povoir
> Que d'illec te puisses mouvoir!' (vv. 87–90)

[St George cried out to it loudly: 'By God, the almighty king, I command that you be powerless to move from this spot!']

Once the newly converted maiden has lassoed the dragon with her girdle, the monster that had hurtled towards them at breakneck speed is motionless for evermore: 'Onques le serpent ne bouga' (v. 96) ['The serpent never budged']. This is no over-determined tool — evil put to good use — for converting the pagan masses: the townsfolk erupt in joy when they spy the tamed monster rather than heading for the hills (v. 98). And no ultimatum is required for them to embrace Christianity: the maiden, having listened to George's sermon, preaches to her parents (more sympathetic sovereigns here than in the *Legenda aurea* because they do not refuse to abide by their own child-sacrifice legislation). Whereupon the whole city spontaneously turns to Christ with gleeful shouts of 'Nous croirons le Dieu de saint George!' (v. 110) ['We shall believe in St George's God!']. Conciliatory George has shown the Saracens how to defeat paganism *themselves*.

Generally speaking, the Occitan metrical life of St George follows the *Legenda aurea* more closely for the dragon episode, but like its French counterpart (and indeed French prose versions 2 and 7) it casts the conversion scene as voluntary. Having overpowered the monster with his trusty lance (he needs more than words here), George instructs the princess to lead the monster to Silena by her red hair (vv. 191–207). But the Occitan hagiographer excises the veiled threats of Jacobus's version, having the saint instead explain that the dragon is now utterly harmless:

> Adox le sans lur a cridat
> E facht senall de remanir,
> E ell ves elos a tenir,
> E correc fort aytant com poc,
> Tant que amb elos fom aloc.
> E diy al rrey e a sas gens,
> 'Baroys, aquest cruell cerpent,
> Per que fuges? Non a poder
> A voseutres plus de noser!' (vv. 208–16)

[And so the saint shouted and gestured to them to stay and headed towards them, and he ran as fast he could until he reached them. And he said to the king and to his people, 'Lords, why are you running away from this cruel serpent? It's powerless to hurt you now!']

George then explains that he has been sent by God to baptize Silena and destroy the city's dragon. Even though the conversions take place before the dragon is finally slain, the lack of Jacobus's ultimatum and the saint's reassurance that the 'cruell cerpent' is in fact powerless mean that, once again, there is no place for over-determinism of monstrosity in this life. George's domestication of the dragon shows his pagan onlookers how to purge themselves — voluntarily — of their own pagan dragons.

According to Jacobus's account of George's martyrdom in the *Legenda aurea*, the saint's torture-resistant body converts a small number of pagans (Dacian's chief sorcerer and his wife), but it is more often the site of his enemies' annihilation. In the French and Occitan metrical lives, which follow Matzke's Y for the *passio*, the sublime saint serves one purpose alone: conversion.

When George speaks out to comfort his fellow Christians in the French metrical life, he is dragged before Emperor Dacian to explain himself (vv. 156–63). In the Occitan, he finds himself face-to-face with Dacian of his own accord, but the ensuing exchange between saint and despot is comparable to the French: George advises the emperor to worship the Christian God, while Dacian commands his opponent to worship the pagan idols (vv. 288–328). In the French life, the emperor is so infuriated by George's sermonizing that he lunges at him with a knife. The blade, however, bounces back and falls to the floor (vv. 194–99). Dacian's futile attempt to inflict physical harm on George's body (to get him to be quiet) sets the tone for things to come: the saint's body is untouchable and will ensure that the imagined textual community is, too.

George is immediately sentenced to a first round of torture. In the French metrical life, George is crucified, his face crushed with a boulder and his body sliced into bits, before a razor-equipped wheel finally decapitates him (vv. 205–14). Dacian and his pagan henchmen celebrate the reduction of George to a few scraps of flesh until the Virgin Mary and her train of angels descend to resuscitate him (vv. 217–22). The scene is analogous in the Occitan version: George is sawn into pieces by eight expert sawyers, before Jesus arrives to put him back together again (vv. 335–62). The Occitan differs from the French, however, in that this first restoration of George's body triggers a first wave of conversions: 'Aqui gran conpanya de gent | Si convertiy demantenent' (vv. 371–72) ['Whereupon a large crowd of people converted right away'].

The saint performs his next trick in a poor widow's hovel that also serves as his prison. In the French version, George restores the woman's disabled son to full bodily unity, curing him of deafness, dumbness and blindness (vv. 262–66). At the same time, he restores to their senses over a thousand pagans, who are persuaded by what they have seen to embrace Christianity (v. 272). In the Occitan, meanwhile, George provides the widow's son with a partial miracle cure (vv. 418–23), but withholds treatment for his lameness until he has a more numerous pagan audience to dazzle into converting (vv. 502–2<).

Next, Dacian promises to convert to Christianity if George can make tree stumps (in the French) or twelve thrones (in the Occitan) bear fruit. In the French version, the saint is convinced of the emperor's recalcitrance — so wicked is his heart — but performs the miracle anyway at the request of his audience ('pour acomplir | A tout le peuple leur desir', vv. 306–07). The pattern has by now become a familiar one. The pagan spectators, amazed by the restoration of life and growth where previously there was but death and lack, immediately swell the ranks of George's cultic community:

> Tout le peuple les regarda,
> Chascun si s'en esmerveilla.
> Tous s'escrierent a haulte voix,
> 'Nous creons le Dieu que tu crois!' (vv. 320–23)

[The whole crowd looked at them and everyone was astounded. They all cried out loud, 'We believe in the God you believe in!']

The crowd is similarly impressed in the Occitan, crying out that 'May tan gran miracle no viy' (v. 466) ['They never saw such a great miracle'] and volunteering to become enthusiastic servants of Jesus Christ (vv. 467–68).

It is now George's turn to make a promise that he has no intention of keeping. As in the *Legenda aurea* account of his martyrdom, George offers to perform a sacrifice to Dacian's idols. But the verse lives (following Y, their chief source) differ from Jacobus's narrative in that George holds the pagan idols to account, commanding them to divulge their diabolical ways. The author of the French version had already branded the idols venerated at the emperor's festivals as devils ('Dÿables ont en leur querolles, | Car ilz creoient fausses ydoles', vv. 115–16 ['They have devils at their assemblies, for they believed in false idols']). But now, in both French and Occitan, the idols announce that they are responsible for tempting pagans away from the Christian God. One idol in the French text exclaims that he aims to 'mener les gens a contraire | Et destourner de leur preu faire' (vv. 366–67) ['lead folk astray and turn them away from doing good']. Likewise, Apolo the Idol in the Occitan claims that — much like Emperor Dacian, we may think — he forces his subjects to worship idols: 'Stas ydolas adorar | Lur fac, en lu[o]c de Dieu veray' (vv. 536–37) ['I make them worship these idols instead of the true God'].

In the corresponding passage in the *Legenda aurea*, George prays for the pagan idols to be obliterated by lightning and swallowed up by the ground, God answering his request by destroying not only the offending statues but the priests as well (I, 444–46). In the French metrical life, the idols' fate is more mundane, the saint simply throwing them into the street (vv. 368–69). The Occitan life, though lacking divine fire, is nonetheless closer to Jacobus's account:

> Vay dell pe en terra ferir
> E li terra si vay aubrir
> E asorbiy, vesent la gent,
> Las idolas demantenent.
> Mot de cels que an aysso vist
> Adoran Dieu Jhesu Crist. (vv. 543–48)

[He struck the ground with his foot and the earth opened up and swallowed up the idols at once, with everyone watching. Many of those who saw this (now) worship God Jesus Christ.]

When the ground swallows up the idols in the Occitan, it is noteworthy that no pagans disappear with them, but plenty turn to Christianity.

With his idols in the street or somewhere beneath the Earth's crust, Dacian subjects George to a second round of torture. In the French metrical life, George is dismembered and thrown into a cauldron of boiling water (vv. 376–83). Having died for a second time, an angel pops down from heaven to restore him to bodily wholeness (vv. 384–87). The Occitan life also features a vat of water, but this time the angel protects George's body from the outset and he is left unscathed (vv. 549–66). But whether we are dealing with the sublime body that bounces back into shape or the sublime body that never loses its shape, the result is the same: innumerable converts (French: vv. 390–93; Occitan: vv. 567–70).

George performs one final miracle before his definitive corporeal death. Dacian again promises to convert if the saint is able to resuscitate a group of Hell-dwelling pagans who have been dead for centuries. In the French life, it is plain to everyone that George has transformed ash ('pouldre', v. 444) into flesh and blood human beings ('en corps et en ames', v. 458). Similarly, in the Occitan life George takes dust and bone fragments ('pols' and 'oses dem[e]nis', vv. 649–50) and concocts 235 men and women (vv. 669–72). 'Grant est le Dieu des Crestïens!' cry the pagan crowd in the French text (v. 476 ['The Christians' God is great!']); they will never worship 'autre dieus may cel que Yorgi col', they announce in the Occitan (v. 716 ['a god other than the one George worships']). George's restoration of bodies restores the body of his Christian community to rude health.

In the Occitan metrical life, it is significant that Dacian has George gagged as he is being led to his place of execution:

Tantost sos mesagies sonet,
Als cals destrechamens mandet
Que yll ses bentansa fassan far
Un fren que Yorgi deya portar,
Per tall que non presic la gent. (vv. 733–37)

[(Dacian) immediately summoned his messengers, to whom he gave strict instructions to make a bridle, without delay, for George to wear, to stop him preaching to people.]

It is not surprising that Dacian commissions a harness for George to interrupt his preaching; it is, after all, his proselytizing activity that poses the greatest threat to the pagan emperor in both the French and the Occitan verse lives. In the *Legenda aurea* account of the *passio*, George abjectifies pagans as well as their idols, but here he is a true *consiliator*, destroying devils but making repeated attempts to counsel the infidel, his tyrannical tormentor included. He also counsels *us*. As he stretches out his neck, braced for beheading, George prays to protect his textual community from a variety of abstract (non-human) ills, including sin, sickness, diabolical snares and fire. But, unlike in other vernacular lives, protection from human foes is conspicuously absent here (French: vv. 507–14; Occitan, vv. 769–84). The members of the textual communities imagined in the metrical lives are all strangers, or, rather, they used to be, before George dispatched their dragon-faced strange*ness*. Our conciliatory saint advocates conciliation for all (or at least for 'ceux qui adoptent la *même* universalité').

Continuing her potted history of cosmopolitanism in *Étrangers à nous-mêmes*, Kristeva understands the Enlightenment as heralding a new form of community formation that transgresses both religious boundaries and, to a large degree, political ones. She dwells in particular on the 'neo-Stoicist' figures (and unlikely theoretical bedfellows) Montesquieu, who commendably privileges an *esprit général* over a nationalistic *Volksgeist* and Freud, who reveals the inner strangeness of the unconscious. Kristeva concludes by calling for a new type of community, now that religion is incapable of protecting strangers (even ones who adopt 'proper' universality) from rampant nationalism: we need 'une communauté paradoxale [...] faite d'étrangers qui s'acceptent dans la mesure où ils se reconnaissent étrangers eux-mêmes' (p. 290) ['a paradoxical community [...] made up of foreigners who are reconciled with themselves to the extent that they recognize themselves as foreigners' (p. 195)].

We might well query to what extent post-Enlightenment cosmopolitanism differs from its ancestors (Stoical οἰκείωσις, Pauline *ecclesia*, etc.). Kristeva's 'communauté paradoxale', made up of those conscious of their unconscious, of self-avowed strangers-to-themselves, is a community of strangers that — paradoxically, we are told — knows no strangers. But this is a paradox that can be solved easily enough if we recognize that both objects and abjects lurk behind Kristeva's *étranger* tag. A community of strangers-to-themselves does not abjectify its fellow men (that is, it does not produce *abject* strangers); it comprises subjects (and objects) reconciled with their inner strangeness, cognizant of their ever-provisional status (*en procès*).

The problem here is that Kristeva gives priority to the psyche over the *polis*. She asks us to see ourselves as strangers (thanks to psychoanalysis) and then, leaping headlong into the political, to see the other (strangers) as ourselves. The abject may be admirably abstracted in Kristeva's 'communauté paradoxale', as it was in the metrical lives of St George, but only at the expense of casting our human correlates as assimilable objects. Her cosmopolitanism is thus not as far removed from universalism as she claims: as Norma Claire Moruzzi notes, *Étrangers* constitutes something of a critical volte-face for Kristeva, as she seemingly spouts the 'soothing mottoes of humanism' that she lampoons elsewhere (p. 143). Is communication with the stranger enough, Derrida asks towards the start of *De l'hospitalité*, or should we let him speak in his own language, letting him stay strange?[21] Sign up for Kristeva's 'communauté paradoxale' and the only strangers we'd be familiarizing ourselves with would be ourselves.

We might learn a thing or two from French prose version 9 of the life of St George. This text is found exclusively in a late-fifteenth-century anthology of pious material, probably compiled in the north-east of the *oïl* zone for a laywoman by the name of Jehanne le Mouche. As Martina Di Febo observes in her edition of the *St Patrick's Purgatory* preserved in this volume, 'cette destination du manuscrit entraîne un changement au plan de la structure sémantique des textes' ['this audience for the manuscript leads to changes at the level of the semantic structure of texts'].[22] In the case of the George biography, this means a saint who strikes a more conciliatory tone towards pagans.

Jacobus's *Legenda aurea* is the primary source for both the dragon miracle and the *passio* in version 9. Though the George and the Dragon story is abbreviated overall, with direct speech cut or reported and the end of the miracle receiving particularly brief treatment, a cluster of additions were made to the saint's encounter with the princess and the monster. The vernacular rewriter adds a romantic overlay to the exchange between George and the maiden. According to the *Legenda aurea*, the saint came across the princess while she was waiting for the dragon and immediately asked her what the matter was (I, 422). In version 9, however, the saint is so struck by her pretty looks and noble attire (neither of which are mentioned by Jacobus at this point) that he jumps off his horse to greet her in the proper fashion: 'Quant saint Jorge vid sy belle demoiselle, sy bien paree et sy noblement, il descendit de dessus son cheval pour le saluer et pour lui demander de son estat et pourquoy elle plouroit' (f. 123v) ['When St George saw such a fair maiden, so finely and nobly adorned, he dismounted from his horse to greet her and ask how she was and why she was crying']. The princess, though remaining sceptical about George's ability to defeat the dragon, is likewise enchanted by his courtly demeanour:

> 'Certes,' dist elle, 'moult estes hardis chevalier de ce dire et entreprendre. Mais bien sçay que contre lui pooir n'arés. Mieux vault que vous en allez que sy noble chevalier que vous estes, et de sy noble atour, morut pour moy.' (f. 123v)

> ['Certainly,' she said, 'you are a very brave knight for saying so and for seeking to do this. But I'm very sure you'll be powerless against it. It would be better for you to leave than for such a noble knight as you are, and of such a noble demeanour, to die for me.']

George and the princess share such similar courtly values here that we might be forgiven for forgetting altogether that this damsel-in-distress is a pagan. As the dragon — particularly demonic in this variant of the tale — rushes towards the flirtatious pair, she has already made the first steps towards membership of George's textual community.

The author of the version 9 biography continues to cast the pagans in a more sympathetic light in the account of George's martyrdom. Beginning with Dacian's great idol-worshipping festival, absent from Jacobus, the version here seems to betray the influence of a non-*Legenda aurea* account of the short Latin *passio* (Matzke's *Z*). The pagan festivities provide the backdrop for George's denunciation of idolatry as devil-worship (which Jacobus does include). The next time Dacian throws an idolatrous party it is George who is supposed to be performing sacrifices. Jacobus had claimed that the entire city erupted in joy at the prospect of partying (I, 444–46), but in version 9 everyone is terrified of being invited: 'Adonc le peuple fust moult esbahy, et par especial les Crestiens' (f. 125v) ['And so the people were very afraid, and the Christians in particular']. Dacian's pagans are not abject creatures that could be destroyed by divine fire at any moment; behaving as pre-Christian proselytes, their baptism is cast as an inevitability.

George prays for Dacian's temples and idols to be destroyed 'affin que le peuple se peüst convertir' (f. 125v) ['so that the people might convert'], and his wish is realized (in accordance with the *Legenda aurea*), lightning taking out the idols and 'masters' of the pagan religion. But the second consignment of divine fire never arrives, leaving Dacian and his henchmen unpunished. Nor does George get the opportunity to annihilate the Saracens of Jerusalem, since the miracle tales habitually appended to the martyrdom story are also axed. In version 9 the saint deals with pagans by abjectifying a diabolical dragon and diabolical idols to convert the masses; George the *conciliator* welcomes pagans (minus the temple 'masters') into his textual community. But these strangers are not welcomed *in spite of* their strangeness, but because they turn out to be not so strange after all: the author has already given the saint a helping hand with assimilating the pagan other into the imagined textual community.

Translating George and the Dragon to England

William Caxton printed his *Golden Legende* at The Red Pale in Westminster between 1483 and 1484. This was by no means the first time George's dragon had been sighted in England. Manuscript volumes of Jacobus's Latin *Legenda aurea* were held by English religious houses and ecclesiastical libraries from the late thirteenth century. Copies of Jean de Vignay's fourteenth-century French rendering of the *Legenda aurea* (cf. prose version 4) circulated widely on the continent as 'pictures for aristocrats', and they also made their way across the Channel.[23] In English, the story of George and the Dragon was retold in the sermons of John Mirk's late-fourteenth-century *Festial* (heavily indebted to the *Legenda aurea*), in a late, Jacobus-inflected branch of the *South English Legendary*, in the *Legend of St George* composed by John Lydgate for the armourers of London *c.* 1430, and in the *Gilte Legende*, translated from Jean de Vignay's French by a 'synfulle wrecche' in 1438.[24] (Not to mention the countless oral, visual and dramatic retellings of the tale.) With Caxton's *Golden Legende*, however, a written text of St George and the Dragon was more widely available in England than ever before.

If the *Legenda aurea* had already been translated into English, why did Caxton feel the need to re-do a job already done by the 'synfulle wrecche'? Caxton justifies his enterprise by citing the discrepancies between French, Latin and English recensions of the text:

> Ageynst me here myght somme persones saye that thys legende hath be translated tofore; and trouthe it is. But for as moche I had by me a legende in Frensshe and another in Latyn, and the thyrd in Englysshe, whiche varyed in many and dyuers places, and also many hystoryes were comprysed in the two other bookes whiche were not in the Englysshe book, and therfore I haue wryton one oute of the sayd thre bookes, which I haue ordryd otherwyse than the sayd Englysshe legende is, whiche was so tofore made.[25] (f. i v)

Caxton seems to have worked chiefly from a printed edition of *c.* 1472–1475 that gave version *C* of Jean de Vignay's *Legende doree*. But he nonetheless performed careful collation with copies of the *Legenda aurea* and *Gilte Legende*, contributing material unique to each of the three traditions to produce a collection that was 'one of the largest ever compiled in any European language'.[26]

As the Middle Ages waned, countless communities claimed St George as their very own, yet he continued to be venerated across the length and breadth of Latin Christendom. Surveying George's late-fifteenth-century cult, David Morgan concludes that, despite increasing 'nationalization' by (amongst others) the English, even in England the saint remained 'readily expressive of the cosmopolitan ethos of the aristocratic world', evoking an 'internationalist vision of Christian harmony and united endeavour'.[27]

Caxton appears to recognize, in his *Golden Legende* entry for St George, that the saint's cult knows no borders. His version of the Jerusalem miracle, which celebrates George as the 'conduytour of the batayle', lets the Crusaders seize the city (f. 158v). But instead of the expected fantasy of Saracen annihilation, we find another miracle, also present in one manuscript of the *Gilte Legende* (London, BL, Add. 35298), that takes place at the Chapel of St George near Ramla. This, we are told, is the site of the saint's tomb, where Christian pilgrims (whether or not they pay the two ducats' entry fee) can expect to receive seven years' worth of indulgences. But it is also a pilgrimage destination for Saracens. Any Saracen who is of unsound mind and who places his head inside a hole in George's tomb 'shal anone be made parfytely hoool [sic] and haue his wytte ageyn' (ibid.). In the Ramla miracle, then, Caxton's George does not destroy Saracens, nor does he assimilate them; he lets them join his cultic community and interact with him in their own way (in their own tongue).

The St George of the *Golden Legende* may be cosmopolitan, but it is nonetheless clear where his allegiances lie. The intriguing story of St George's adoption by the English as their national patron is one that has often been told, but it still perhaps needs to be set in its European context to do justice to all its many twists and turns.[28] Suffice to say, for the present, that by the time Caxton came to set his type, the English had claimed George as theirs, just as the Catalans had, and the Georgians, and many others besides. In recognition of his peculiar patronage of the English, Caxton ends his George entry by trumpeting the saint as both benefactor of the Order of the Garter and 'patrone of thys roiame of Englond' (f. 158v). Though most of George's body is said to be entombed in Palestine, his head and his heart belong to Windsor's College of St George (ibid.). In the late Middle Ages, aristocrats across Europe had been engaged in a feverish hunt for George's relics, and his head in particular.[29] Now, Caxton tells us, the English have won.

What to make of this apparent contradiction between St George's late medieval cosmopolitanism and the special protection he would seem to accord the English? In *Étrangers à nous-mêmes*, Kristeva notes the incompatibility of cosmopolitanism and nationalism (which we might, for argument's sake, commute to 'nationism' when dealing with the pre-modern era). She recognizes, however, that the matter is more complex than it at first appears (p. 182). One of the ways she gestures towards this is by framing national identity in terms of translation. 'Le national,' she argues, 'se fonde donc sur une *traductibilité* élargie' (p. 262) ['national features are thus based upon a broadened *translatability*' (p 178)]. The nineteenth-century *Volksgeist*, in other words, was a rendering of a shared Classical and Biblical heritage, 'amplified' into national terms (and a national language). Derrida's characterization of the relationship between cosmopolitanism and nationalism is similar. In *L'Autre Cap* he suggests that

> Le nationalisme et le cosmopolitisme ont toujours fait bon ménage, si para- doxal que cela paraisse [...] Dans la logique de ce discours 'capitalistique' et cosmopolitique, le propre de telle nation ou de tel idiome, ce serait d'être un cap pour l'Europe; et le propre de l'Europe ce serait, analogiquement, de s'avancer comme un cap pour l'essence universelle de l'humanité.

> [Nationalism and cosmopolitanism have always gotten along well together, as paradoxical as this may seem [...] In the logic of this 'capitalistic' and cosmo- political discourse, what is proper to a particular nation or idiom would be to be a heading for Europe; and what is proper to Europe would be, analogically, to advance itself as a heading for the universal essence of humanity.][30]

A nation looks beyond its borders to the degree that it seeks to become a capital for (and to capitalize on) its analogues. In *Le Monolinguisme de l'autre* (and elsewhere), Derrida maintains that a text is neither fully translatable (if it can be grasped as a singular text that differs from another), nor fully untranslatable (if any meaning can be gleaned from its words).[31] The same applies to cultural identity in *L'Autre Cap*:

> Aucune identité culturelle ne se présente comme le corps opaque d'un idiome intraduisible mais toujours, au contraire, comme l'irremplaçable *inscription* de l'universel dans le singulier, le *témoignage unique* de l'essence humaine et du propre de l'homme. (pp. 71–72)

> [No cultural identity presents itself as the opaque body of an untranslatable idiom, but always, on the contrary, as the irreplaceable *inscription* of the uni-

versal in the singular, the *unique testimony* to the human essence and to what is proper to man. (*Other Heading*, p. 73)]

Cosmopolitanism and nationalism are opposed, but they are also in cahoots. No nation is so closed off as to be untranslatable, but insofar as each claims to be the authentic individualization of a universal — a translation that cannot be bettered — nor is it translatable. Every nation must have a flag, like any other, unlike any other. Every nation must have an anthem, recognizable to its neighbours whom it sings of crushing. And every nation must have relics of St George, with the best bits reserved for each (and every) one.

At the end of Caxton's *Golden Legende* entry for St George, we 'praye vnto hym that he be special protectour and defendour of thys royame' (f. 158v). We have read or heard a strange tale about a saint so universally revered that he can only be patron of the English. We have read/heard it in a strange tongue, a largely London-centric 'Chancery Standard' preserving some of Jean de Vignay's French forms that goes by the name of 'Englysshe'.[32] And, just as strange, we have been subsumed into a textual community imagined as cosmopolitan and yet — and *therefore* — English. There is more to William Caxton's 'Englishing' of George and the Dragon than at first appears.

Unravelling the Textual Community

Critics of Cazalet's Trinity Reredos and the St George's Day giants that it inspired generally seem to have been most irked by a lack of concern for historicity. Was the English patron saint not a born-and-bred Englishman? Or, if he were really Turkish, how could he have been black? And is he not supposed to have slain the dragon rather than setting him free?[33] Cazalet's visual retelling of the George and dragon story, like all retellings, lays bare the fictionality of the textual community imagined through the particular version we hold dear. As the heated response to Manchester's St George's Day parade testifies, a different version of the story not only challenges our 'proper' account; it challenges *us*.

Fighting over St George's biography has been going on since the fifth century (at least). In the later Middle Ages, French and Occitan versions of the George and the dragon tale may well have proved similarly contentious. They provide two models of engagement with strangers. On the one hand, George is sometimes portrayed as a *sacer luctator* who annihilates uncannily familiar strangers, whether the Saracens of the story or our flesh-and-blood enemies on the battlefield. On the other, George is represented as a *consiliator* who slays abstract strangeness to assimilate alterity. Even in the second case, however, the textual community promoted by the text fails to welcome the stranger in and on his own terms. I do not mean to suggest that all late medieval vernacular renderings of the George life fall into two categories. Only comparatively rarely can strangers be neatly divided into objects and abjects. But as Kristeva's *Étrangers à nous-mêmes* (read in conjunction with *Pouvoirs*) teaches us, it is precisely the alternate designation of the other as object and abject that is constitutive of subjectivity. Caxton's English St George, who sometimes performs miracles for the Saracens he still helps to destroy, is, if anything, even less tolerant of alterity than his counterparts in French.

Late-twentieth- and twenty-first-century theorists of various stripes have struggled to come up with an ethically appropriate concept of 'community', one that doesn't return to a mythical *Gemeinschaft* and raise the spectre of totalitarian menace. With their communities classified respectively as *désœuvrée, inavouable* and *sans communauté* ['inoperative', 'unavowable' and 'without community'], Jean-Luc Nancy, Maurice Blanchot and Jacques Derrida (amongst others) have drawn attention to the aporia of collectiveness without identity.[34] Without necessarily being more constructive, more positive are the formulations of community by Giorgio Agamben and in Nancy's later work. In *La Comunità che viene*, Agamben outlines his concept of *singolarità qualunque*, inassimilable singularity *such as it is*. Rather than looking backwards to a *Gemeinschaft* that never existed, Agamben looks forwards to a coming community of singularities that co-belong in their potentiality 'senza una rappresentabile condizione di appartenenza' ['without a representable condition of belonging'].[35] For Nancy, on the other hand, writing in *Être singulier pluriel*, we are always-already in community. To exist is to co-exist, since singular being is defined, inescapably, by its relations with others. If we are to speak of a 'we', it must be one whose constituent beings share nothing but an unsubstantial relationality.[36]

By comparing and contrasting various versions of a text (George and the Dragon will do nicely), we expose the fictionality of the *gemeinschaftlich* textual community, represented to 'us' as stable and secure. And in the transition from one version to another (one language to another, one manuscript to another, etc.), we may even be afforded glimpses, however partial, of communities that are not simply textual because they are formed in and through the text, but because they have the intricacy, mobility, relationality and incompleteness *of* a text. One of the aims of philological work is to work against, or to unravel, the fiction of the united textual community. First and foremost, this can be done by studying the relations between witnesses and placing them in their historical contexts, tracing the connections between a text and its Jehan Wagaces and Jehanne le Mouches. But perhaps, ultimately, philology seeks to show that, even as the texts with which we engage and the ways in which we engage with them are ever-changing, what relates all of us is some sort of engagement with those cultural artefacts that we broadly call 'texts'. To remedy the very human condition of abjectifying strangers Kristeva prescribes a dose of psychoanalysis. Maybe philology would prove just as effective a remedy (if not more).

Appendix

Medieval manuscripts preserving French and Occitan lives of St George with the dragon story are listed below, classified initially by language and medium (i.e. verse/prose) and thereafter by source and approximate date of composition.

Verse life in French

Dragon miracle: Jacobus de Voragine, *Legenda aurea* (?); martyrdom: *Y*.

> Fourteenth-century version in octosyllabic couplets (551 vv.). Whereabouts of manuscript currently unknown, but most recently held as Amsterdam, BPH 58 (saec. xv^{in}), ff. 187r-191r. Guilcher (ed.), *Deux versions*, pp. 95–109.

Verse life in Occitan

Dragon miracle: Jacobus de Voragine, *Legenda aurea* (?); martyrdom: *Y*.

> Fifteenth-century (?) version in octosyllabic couplets (806 vv.). Paris, BnF, fr. 14973 (saec. xv), ff. 27v-44v. Perhaps copied in Catalonia. Previously edited as Camille Chabaneau (ed.), 'Paraphrase des litanies en vers provençaux', *Revue des langues romanes*, 29 (1886), 209–55 (pp. 246–54), continued as 'Vie de saint George', *Revue des langues romanes*, 31 (1887), 139–55; but references here are to my own edition at <http://www.huwgrange.co.uk>.

Prose lives in French

[A] Jacobus de Voragine, *Legenda aurea*.

> 1. Paris, BnF, fr. 20330 (saec. xiii^{ex}), ff. 97v-100r; Le Puy-en-Velay, Bibl. du Grand Séminaire, unnumbered (saec. xiii^{ex}), ff. 90v-92r.
>
> 2. Version dedicated to Béatrice de Bourgogne. Paris, BnF, fr. 23114 (saec. xv^{ex}), ff. 119v-122r.
>
> 3. Modena, BEU, Estero 116 (saec. xiv^{in}), ff. 90r-92r; Tours, BM 1008 (saec. xiv^{in}), ff. 116v-118v.
>
> 4. Jean de Vignay's translation of the George biography survives in dozens of volumes, in three major redactions. For a list, see <http://www.arlima.net/no/15>. Hamer and Russell (eds), 'A Critical Edition'.
>
> 5. Florence, BML, Med. Pal. 141 (1399), ff. 128r-129v; Kraków, BJ, gall. f° 156 (c. 1440), ff. 125r-127v; Tournai, BV 127 (saec. xv^{med}), ff. 130r-132r.
>
> 6. Brussels, KBR 10295-10304 (1429), ff. 63v-68v.
>
> 7. Loose rendering, with George's martyrdom abbreviated. Paris, BnF, fr. 1534 (saec. xv^{ex}), ff. 39v-40v.
>
> 8. Semur-en-Auxois, BM 38 (saec. xv), ff. 188r-196v.
>
> 9. Slightly reworked (perhaps with another version of *Z*). Paris, BnF, naf 4464 (saec. xv^{ex}), ff. 122v-126r.
>
> 10. Lille, BM 452 (saec. xv^{ex}), ff. 465v-469r.
>
> 11. Cambridge, Fitzwilliam Museum, Charles Fairfax Murray 12 (saec. xv^{ex}), ff. 69v-71v.

[B] Martyrdom: *Y*; dragon miracle: Jacobus de Voragine, *Legenda aurea*;

12. Rouen, BM 1430 (saec. xv), ff. 38v-42r and 124r-125r. The dragon miracle appears separately towards the back of the manuscript.

[C] Martyrdom: *Z*; dragon miracle: Jacobus de Voragine, *Legenda aurea*;

13. A rendering of *Z*, though much of the wording seems to have been borrowed from the version of *Y* in Sainte-Geneviève 588. Tours, BM 1011 (saec. xv), ff. 155v-159v; Paris, BnF, fr. 15475 (saec. xv^(ex)), ff. 136v-141r.

[D] Martyrdom: *Z* and Jacobus de Voragine, *Legenda aurea*; dragon miracle: Jacobus de Voragine, *Legenda aurea*;

14. The martyrdom is an adaptation of French prose version 13 that also draws on the *Legenda aurea*. Cambrai, BM 811 (saec. xv^(med)), ff. 438r-441r; Cambrai, BM 812 (saec. xv^(med)), ff. 156r-159r. Note that BM 811 also gives the *Y* version of the martyrdom in full (ff. 432r-437v).

Prose life in Occitan

Jacobus de Voragine, *Legenda aurea*.

Paris, BnF, fr. 9759 (saec. xv), ff. 126v-129r; Paris, BnF, fr. 24945 (saec. xv), ff. 53r-55v; Paris, BnF, naf 6504 (saec. xv^(med)), ff. 46v-49r. Tausend (ed.), *Die Altokzitanische Version B*, pp. 120-26.

Notes to Chapter 2

1. Yakub Qureshi, 'Church Calls up "Black St George" to Fight Racism', *Manchester Evening News*, 20 December 2010 <http://menmedia.co.uk/manchestereveningnews/news/s/1400368_church_calls_up_black_st_george_to_fight_racism> (para. 9 of 21) [accessed 3 April 2016].
2. Ross Kaniuk, 'PC Crazes: St George Now Black', *Daily Star*, 21 December 2010 <http://dailystar.co.uk/posts/view/168380/PC-crazes-St-George-now-black> [accessed 3 April 2016]; Yakub Qureshi, 'Manchester Cathedral Event Depicting St George as Black Goes ahead Despite Hate Mail', *Manchester Evening News*, 7 May 2011 <http://menmedia.co.uk/manchestereveningnews/news/s/1420106_manchester-cathedral-event-depicing-st-george-as-black-goes-ahead-despite-hate-mail> [accessed 3 April 2016]; Jonathan Brown, 'Saint George, the Canon and a Flood of Right-Wing Hate', *The Independent*, 22 April 2011 <http://independent.co.uk/news/uk/home-news/saint-george-the-canon-and-a-flood-of-rightwing-hate-2271982.html> [accessed 3 April 2016].
3. References in parentheses are to Jacobus de Voragine, *Legenda aurea*, ed. Maggioni, I, 440-48.
4. The earliest extant manuscript is Greek and known as the 'Vienna Palimpsest'. John E. Matzke's division of the early Latin, Greek, Coptic, Arabic and Syriac lives of St George into 'apocryphal' and 'canonical' versions remains useful: 'Contributions to the History of the Legend of Saint George, with Special Reference to the Sources of the French, German and Anglo-Saxon Metrical Versions', in *Publications of the Modern Language Association of America*, 17 (1902), 464-535; and 18 (1903), 99-171.
5. See Christopher Walter, 'The Origins of the Cult of Saint George', *Revue des études byzantines*, 53 (1995), 295-326 (pp. 320-22).
6. Bartholomew's legendary (Vatican, BAV, Cod. Lat. 2300) is dated to c. 1245 and remains unedited.
7. The longer account is known as *Y* (Matzke, 'Contributions' [1902], pp. 492-535). Broadly speaking, Versions *Y* and *Z* correspond to BHL *passio* no. 3 (BHL 3386-96) and BHL *passiones* nos 1-2 (BHL 3363-85) and 1 respectively. By drawing on *Z*, Jacobus was following in the footsteps of fellow Dominican hagiographers Vincent de Beauvais and Jean de Mailly, although Jacobus does not abbreviate his source to the same extent.

8. Odilo Heiming (ed.), *Das ambrosianische Sakramentar von Biasca: Die Handschrift Mailand Ambrosiana A 24 bis inf.*, Liturgiewissenschaftliche Quellen und Forschungen, 51 (Münster: Aschendorff, 1969), pp. 116–17.

9. Georges Bataille, *Théorie de la religion* (Paris: Gallimard, 1974), p. 83.

10. See Samantha Riches, *St George: Hero, Martyr and Myth* (Stroud: Sutton, 2000), p. 1; Francesc Barriga i Pérez, *Sant Jordi i Catalunya: arrels de la identitat catalana* (Madrid: Edaf, 2007), p. 58; and Jonathan Good, *The Cult of Saint George in Medieval England* (Woodbridge: Boydell, 2009), pp. 113–14.

11. For a brief history of George's spectral appearances on medieval battlefields, see Riches, *St George*, pp. 12–15.

12. The three sermons are published in Jacobus de Voragine, *Sermones de sanctis per anni totius circulum* (Venice: Somaschi, 1573), pp. 189–93 (subsequent references to this edition). For the description of George's allegorical outfit, see p. 189; and on comparisons of knights' armour to monastic virtues, see Giles Constable, 'The Place of the Crusader in Medieval Society', *Viator*, 29 (1998), 377–403 (p. 382).

13. Closer to Stock's usage is Duncan Robertson's description of Barking Abbey as a 'textual community' in 'Writing in the Textual Community: Clemence of Barking's *Life of St Catherine*', *French Forum*, 21 (1996), 5–28. The term is employed in a less specific sense in Simon Gaunt, *Gender and Genre in Medieval French Literature*, Cambridge Studies in French, 53 (Cambridge: Cambridge University Press, 1995), pp. 212–13; and Campbell, *Medieval Saints' Lives*, pp. 123 and 133–34.

14. Julia Kristeva, *Étrangers à nous-mêmes* (Paris: Fayard, 1988), p. 9; and Julia Kristeva, *Strangers to Ourselves*, trans. Leon S. Roudiez (New York: Columbia University Press, 1991), p. 1.

15. Noëlle McAfee, 'Abject Strangers: Towards an Ethics of Respect', in *Ethics, Politics and Difference in Julia Kristeva's Writings*, ed. by Kelly Oliver (London: Routledge, 1993), pp. 116–34 (p. 123).

16. Norma Claire Moruzzi distinguishes run-of-the-mill 'foreigners' from abject 'familiar foreigners' in 'National Abjects: Julia Kristeva on the Process of Political Self-Identification', *Ethics*, ed. Oliver, pp. 135–49.

17. This information is gleaned from ff. 103r, 124r, 158r, 230v and 386r.

18. The prologue resembles the opening lines of the George lives in Lille, BM 453 (ff. 94v–99v); Paris, Bibl. de l'Arsenal 570; and Cambrai, BM 811 (ff. 432r–441r). The epilogue he adds is, as far as I am aware, unique.

19. René Girard, *Le Bouc émissaire* (Paris: Grasset, 1982), p. 23.

20. On the sources of the French, see Matzke, 'Contributions' [1903], pp. 115–19; Konrad M. Sandkühler (ed.), *Der Drachenkampf des hl. Georg in englischer Legende und Dichtung vom 14. bis 16. Jahrhundert* (Munich: Meindl, 1913), pp. 49–54; and Yvette Guilcher (ed.), *Deux versions de la Vie de saint Georges*, Classiques français du Moyen Âge, 138 (Paris: Champion, 2001), pp. 95–112. On those of the Occitan, see Maria Carla Marinoni, 'Il drago e la principessa: considerazioni su una Vita di S. Giorgio occitanica', *ACME*, 57 (2004), 161–82.

21. Jacques Derrida, *De l'hospitalité*, with Anne Dufourmantelle (Paris: Calmann-Lévy, 1997), p. 21.

22. *Les Versions en prose du 'Purgatoire de saint Patrice' en ancien français*, ed. by Martina Di Febo, Classiques français du Moyen Âge, 172 (Paris: Champion, 2013), p. 152.

23. Hilary Maddocks, 'Pictures for Aristocrats: The Manuscripts of the *Légende dorée*', in *Medieval Texts and Images: Studies of Manuscripts from the Middle Ages*, ed. by Margaret M. Manion and Bernard J. Muir (Reading: Harwood Academic, 1991), pp. 1–23. London, BL, Royal 19.B.XVII was produced in Paris in 1382, but owned by William FitzAlan, Earl of Arundel in the fifteenth century. Jean de Vignay's St George entry is edited in Richard Hamer and Vida Russell, 'A Critical Edition of Four Chapters from the *Légende dorée*', *Mediaeval Studies*, 51 (1989), 130–204.

24. See John Mirk, *Festial*, ed. by Susan Powell, Early English Text Society, 334–35, 2 vols (Oxford: Early English Text Society, 2009–2011), I, 117–20; M. Görlach (ed.), *An East Midland Revision of the South English Legendary: A Selection from MS C.U.L. Add. 3039*, Middle English Texts, 4 (Heidelberg: Winter, 1976), esp. pp. 33–35; John Lydgate, 'Legend of St George', in *Mummings and Entertainments*, ed. by Claire Sponsler (Kalamazoo: Medieval Institute Publications, 2010),

pp. 42–48; and *Gilte Legende*, ed. by Richard Hamer with the assistance of Vida Russell, Early English Text Society, 327–28 and 339, 3 vols (Oxford: Early English Text Society, 2006–2012), I, 268–75.

25. In the absence of a modern critical edition of the *Golden Legende*, folio numbers in parentheses refer to the copy in the Hunterian Library under the shelfmark Bg.1.1, [Wylyam Caxton], [*Golden Legende*] ([London]: [Caxton], [1487]).

26. M. Görlach, 'Middle English Legends, 1220–1530', in *Hagiographies: histoire internationale de la littérature hagiographique latine et vernaculaire en Occident des origines à 1550*, ed. by Guy Philippart (Turnhout: Brepols, 1994-), I (1994), 429–85 (p. 478).

27. David A. L. Morgan, 'The Cult of St George *c.* 1500: National and International Connotations', in *L'Angleterre et les pays bourguignons: relations et comparaisons XVe-XVIe siècles*, ed. by Jean-Marie Cauchies (Neuchâtel: Centre européen d'études bourguignonnes (XIVe-XVIe s.), 1995), pp. 151–62 (p. 162).

28. For one of the more recent accounts, see Good, *Cult of St George*.

29. See Kenneth M. Setton, 'Saint George's Head', *Speculum*, 48 (1973), 1–12; and Morgan, 'Cult of St George'.

30. Jacques Derrida, *L'Autre Cap, suivi de La Démocratie ajournée* (Paris: Minuit, 1991), p. 49; Jacques Derrida, *The Other Heading: Reflections on Today's Europe*, trans. by Pascale-Anne Brault and Michael B. Naas (Bloomington: Indiana University Press, 1992), p. 48.

31. Jacques Derrida, *Le Monolinguisme de l'autre, ou, La Prothèse d'origine* (Paris: Galilée, 1996), p. 103.

32. The classic study of Caxton's language is Helmut Wiencke, *Die Sprache Caxtons* (Leipzig: Tauchnitz, 1930). See also John H. Fisher, *The Emergence of Standard English* (Lexington: University Press of Kentucky, 1996), pp. 76, 128–29.

33. See the comments to the newspaper articles listed above.

34. See, most notably, Jean-Luc Nancy, *La Communauté désœuvrée* (Paris: Bourgois, 1986); Maurice Blanchot, *La Communauté inavouable* (Paris: Minuit, 1983); and Jacques Derrida, *Politiques de l'amitié, suivi de L'oreille de Heidegger* (Paris: Galilée, 1994), pp. 98–99.

35. Giorgio Agamben, *La Comunità che viene* (Turin: Einaudi, 1990), p. 59.

36. Jean-Luc Nancy, *Être singulier pluriel* (Paris: Galilée, 1996).

CHAPTER 3

❖

St Honorat of Hungary, Some Saracens, and their Queer Genealogies

Legend has it that the Provençal town of Draguignan takes its name from a dragon. Among the more recent accounts of Draguignan's monstrous etymon is a children's book by Max Ducos.[1] *Le Carnaval des dragons* is the charming tale of an international dragon-building competition that takes place (where else?) in Draguignan. Despite being too young to take part officially, local primary school pupils work hard to manufacture their own monster, and thanks to their colourful imaginations, an inspirational teacher and a hefty dose of teamwork, the Dracénois kids are able to see off the child-unfriendly dragons constructed by their adult rivals to steal the day. The children's creation is declared by the mayor to be 'le nouveau dragon de Draguignaaaan!' [sic] (p. 35) ['the new dragon of Draguignaaaan!'], is installed in the local museum for perpetuity, and becomes the town's new emblem (p. 37).

At first glance, Draguignan's 'nouveau dragon' would appear to have few traits in common with the dragon of the sixteenth-century *Discours de la vie, bonnes moeurs et saincteté de sainct Hermentere* by Jean de Nostredame (younger brother of the infamous prophet).[2] According to Jean, the Empus Valley was once plagued by a dragon that emerged from the humid earth and reduced the region to a barren wasteland with its fiery, pestilential breath (pp. 163–64). But one day a band of pilgrims whose path happens to take them close to the dragon's lair resolves to dispatch the monster. Led by the local hermit, St Hermentaire, and protected by the armour of the Lord, they succeed in their mission after much pious stone-throwing and beating with sticks (pp. 164–65). They all celebrate the dragon's demise with singing, embalming, the building of a chapel, and the naming of the spot 'Draguignan' (pp. 166–67).

Much easier to identify, however, is the affiliation between Nostredame's *Discours* and the Occitan *Life of St Honorat* composed by Raimon Feraut c. 1300.[3] Nostredame appropriated Raimon's account of the Draguignan legend more or less wholesale, although there are some striking differences. First and foremost, the protagonist in the Occitan text is not Hermentaire but Honorat (whom Nostredame relegates to playing an incidental part as Hermentaire's less successful brother). Secondly, Honorat needs no help from pilgrims to tame the beast in Raimon's version of the story: he is able to fetter it to the side of the Empus Valley all by himself (vv. 5087–88). Lastly, the *Life of St Honorat* lacks Nostredame's party atmosphere marking the taming of the monster. The saint's triumph is nonetheless commemorated when the nearby town is baptized Draguignan: 'E Draguignan a nom le castellz atressi, | Car en son terrador le mals dragons mori' (vv. 5094–95) ['Hence the town is called Draguignan, because the wicked dragon died on its land']. This is the earliest known account of the etymology of Draguignan.

Ducos's new dragon ostensibly inherits little (if anything) from the older ones given to us by Jean de Nostredame and Raimon Feraut. The twenty-first-century fairytale may have its fair share of terrifying monsters, but instead of rearing their ugly heads from an underground lair they are the product of robotics, pyrotechnics, and genetic engineering (cast as unfathomable fields that even the experts fail to master completely). And instead of Honorat or Hermentaire coming to the rescue with shackles or sticks and stones, Ducos's victor is a composite creature emblematic of the qualities that every good pupil should hone (creativity, fairness, co-operation, and so forth). *Le Carnaval des dragons* is a story for the *laïcité* generation, ideally kept in the dark about religion, yet sensitized to the man-made perils of science.

Though Ducos's beneficent dragon triumphs over the maleficent ones of present and past accounts of the Draguignan legend, perhaps its genealogy can nonetheless be traced back to the Middle Ages. perhaps it is not entirely 'new'. After all, Draguignan's monster has always been commemorated more than its saint has, even taking on a holy air at times. In Raimon Feraut's Occitan version, the beast's bones are said to have been displayed for many years, as if they were relics (vv. 5089–91). Nostredame picks up on the dragon's holiness, has the monster embalmed, and gives it a funeral (pp. 166–67). Neither, moreover, makes any link between St Hermentaire and the village of Saint-Hermentaire, but both point to the dragon as Draguignan's etymon. Perhaps it was only a matter of time before the saint actually turned into a dragon.

If Max Ducos was in any way troubled by older versions of the Draguignan legend, he certainly would not have been the first. In his *Annales ecclesiastici*, published between 1588 and 1607, the cardinal and ecclesiastical historian Cesare Baronio reports that his French colleague, Gilbert Génébrard, once unearthed a scandalous printed biography of St Honorat, replete with 'fables' ('fabulae') and 'insane ravings' ('dicenda deliria').[4] Baronio hardly minces his words: these tales, he says, 'cannot be read without nausea, except by one whose stomach is made of iron and entirely coated in the rust of ignorance' ('non sine nausea legi possunt, nisi ab eo, cuius sit stommachus ferreus, et ignorantiae undique obductus rubigine', ibid.).

A Latin biography of Honorat had been in circulation in Provence from the fifth century, telling the highly respectable tale of the saint's conversion to Christianity, his journey to the Orient with his brother, his banishment of snakes from the island of Lérins, his glittering careers as Abbot of Lérins and Archbishop of Arles, and, finally, his death at a venerable age.[5] The target of Baronio's condemnation, however, was no doubt the 1511 edition of the *vita* added to the saint's dossier in the second half of the thirteenth century. This later Latin text gives a rather more fanciful account of Honorat's life, re-casting the converted pagan from Gaul as a Saracen prince and claiming that he travelled not from Gaul to the Orient (as he did in the fifth-century biography), but from the Orient to Gaul. When he arrives in the

West, a fourth-century saint is suddenly plunged — anachronistically, some might say — into the world of Carolingian epic, rescuing Charlemagne from a Saracen prison, helping to expel Saracens and heretics from Provençal shores, and slaying the eponymous twin dragons Lirus and Rinus to found the island-monastery of Lérins. The bulk of the later Latin text narrates Honorat's miracles, with a sizeable final chapter dedicated to the so-called Passion of Porcarius and martyrdom of the five hundred monks of Lérins.[6]

It was this thirteenth-century Latin *vita* of St Honorat that Raimon Feraut drew on for his biography of the saint in Occitan verse. In his epilogue to the work Raimon helpfully states his name, current title (Prior of Roquesteron, vv. 9690–93) and previous employment (monk at Lérins, vv. 9694–95). He also provides us with the names of his patron (Gaucelm, Abbot of Lérins, vv. 9683–85) and a celebrity dedicatee (Maria of Hungary, vv. 9700–07), and gives the year in which he completed the text as 1300 (v. 9723). Translating the Latin prose into Occitan verse entailed considerable toil, he claims — and it would be difficult to disagree, given the sheer range of metres he employs — and so the least his critics can do is to respect the letter of his text (vv. 9697–99). Raimon himself made no vow of fidelity to his source, but close comparison to the Latin suggests that his substantive contributions were restricted to a prologue and epilogue, the odd additional chapter in the form of letters and laments, some colourful tracts of direct speech, a hot-off-the-press miracle story, and intratextual prayers that forge links between the various miracle stories.[7]

To judge by the number of manuscripts that have come down to us, the Occitan *Life of St Honorat* was a relative success in the later Middle Ages. It survives today in nine codices and a fragment, a decent total for an Old Occitan narrative work.[8] All of these are modest copies produced in Provence between the mid-fourteenth century and the end of the fifteenth. Several of the scribes left their names: one was a neighbour of Raimon's (Paris, BnF, fr. 13509), another a priest based near Hyères (Paris, BnF, fr. 24954). Provençal nobility were among the earliest owners, however, and lost copies are thought to have lined the shelves of the very highest echelons of Provençal society: in the later fifteenth century, the library of René of Anjou is likely to have contained several (Flachaire de Roustan, pp. 275–76).

Despite its fidelity to a Latin source and its late medieval success, the Occitan biography of St Honorat came in for particularly harsh criticism from some later readers. Baronio may have been talking about the thirteenth-century Latin *vita*, but Honoré Bouche, the author of a mid-seventeenth-century history of Provence, was not: he attributes a long list of anachronisms specifically to Raimon.[9] Two centuries on and Jean-Baptiste Disdier continues to hold Raimon responsible for the 'inventions fabuleuses' ['fabulous fabrications'] that were introduced (allegedly) by the vernacular author.[10] But both made the same mistake: they came to the Old Occitan text via the *Discours* and believed Nostredame to be a faithful translator and Raimon to be a teller of tall tales. Even such a grandee of nineteenth-century Romance philology as Gaston Paris could find Raimon guilty of introducing 'un incroyable anachronisme' ['unbelievable anachronism'] into the Honorat biography.[11]

Even scholars aware of Raimon's indebtedness to the late Latin *vita* of St Honorat have continued to criticize him on one account, however. For Augustin Carlone, writing in 1873, for instance, Raimon is found guilty of using his poetic licence to muddy all temporality and cast the saint as a Hungarian.[12] Carlone even goes as far as to suggest that the vernacular hagiographer convinced himself of his own lie: 'chez les hommes d'imagination, il se produit de ces phénomènes' (p. 58) ['such phenomena occur in men with active imaginations']. Paul Meyer, meanwhile, recognizes Raimon as a deft translator and master of verse-forms, but can only attribute Honorat's new-found Hungarian identity to his lack of geographical acumen.[13] Gustave Lambert, finally, struggles to decide whether Raimon made the saint a Hungarian 'par ignorance ou fiction poétique' ['out of ignorance or poetic fiction'].[14]

Old habits die hard in scholarship: the author of the Occitan *Life of St Honorat* faced one charge of anachronism after another from chronology-concerned students of positivism, some of whom (ironically enough) failed to establish the text's genealogy rigorously enough. The fact that Raimon Feraut's work has proved so disruptive to later readers' senses of chronology, however, only means that this study of the genealogies within and beyond the text has been a long time coming.

Queer Genealogies

'Genealogy' can be a confusing word in scholarly discourse, but it is hoped that something productive will emerge from the bringing together of two meanings here. On the one hand, genealogy is the study of the ancestry of a particular person or group. An obsession of the internet age it may be, but this 'ancestral' genealogy was also an obsession of the upper echelons of medieval European society from the eleventh century on. Out went a focus on horizontal kinship clans, replaced with an interest in vertical lineage. Highborn folk traced their bloodlines (or, more likely, had their bloodlines traced for them) drawing a continuous line towards their very origins, the further back the better. The development of this type of genealogy, it has been argued, was coterminous with a shift in how temporality was understood and with the development of a secular historiography. As Gabrielle Spiegel puts it, 'genealogy functioned to secularize time by grounding it in biology, transforming the connection between past and present into a real one, seminally imparted from generation to generation'.[15]

There is another use of the term 'genealogy' that is also pertinent here, even if it is somewhat at odds with the ancestral variety described above. Genealogy is the name given (retrospectively) to a mode of critical history developed first and foremost by Michel Foucault. Foucault's genealogical project can be considered 'une ontologie du présent, une ontologie de nous-mêmes' ['an ontology of the present, an ontology of ourselves'], or an enquiry into how the 'now' of the subject has been constituted contingently over time through knowledges and discourses.[16] In his reading of Nietzsche's *Zur Genealogie der Moral*, Foucault asserted that genealogy

> ne prétend pas remonter le temps pour rétablir une grande continuité par-delà la dispersion de l'oubli; sa tâche n'est pas de montrer que le passé est encore là, bien

vivant dans le présent, l'animant encore en secret, après avoir imposé à toutes les
traverses du parcours une forme dessinée dès le départ. Rien qui ressemblerait
à l'évolution d'une espèce, au destin d'un peuple. Suivre la filière complexe de
la provenance, c'est au contraire maintenir ce qui s'est passé dans la dispersion
qui lui est propre: c'est repérer les accidents, les infimes déviations — ou au
contraire les retournements complets –, les erreurs, les fautes d'appréciation, les
mauvais calculs qui ont donné naissance à ce qui existe et vaut pour nous; c'est
découvrir qu'à la racine de ce que nous connaissons et de ce que nous sommes
il n'y a point la vérité et l'être, mais l'extériorité de l'accident.

[does not pretend to go back in time to restore an unbroken continuity that
operates beyond the dispersion of forgotten things; its duty is not to demonstrate
that the past actively exists in the present, that it continues secretly to animate
the present, having imposed a predetermined form on all its vicissitudes.
Genealogy does not resemble the evolution of a species and does not map the
destiny of a people. On the contrary, to follow the complex course of descent
is to maintain passing events in their proper dispersion; it is to identify the
accidents, the minute deviations — or conversely, the complete reversals — the
errors, the false appraisals, and the faulty calculations that gave birth to those
things that continue to exist and have value for us; it is to discover that truth
or being does not lie at the root of what we know and what we are, but the
exteriority of accidents.][17]

If a Foucauldian genealogy traces a line back in time, it does so to show that that
line is a broken one. Unlike a medieval genealogical chart, which gives the illusion
of restoring 'une grande continuité', Foucault's genealogies problematize origins and
demonstrate a radical discontinuity in order to destabilize the identity categories of
the present. In other words, if ancestral genealogy draws on the past to naturalize
the present, Foucault's genealogies draw on the past to *denaturalize* the present.

Time to pour another confusing word into the mix: 'queer'. Odd, at odds with
a norm, at odds with a sexual norm, at odds with all social and sexual norms
(which, I suppose, more or less brings us back to 'odd'): queerness resists pithy
definitions, and therein lies part of its usefulness when it comes to revealing
and resisting identity constructions, especially those bound up with gender and
sexuality. Queer theorists, following in the footsteps of Foucault-inflected critics
such as Eve Sedgwick and Judith Butler, do not necessarily agree on the precise
nature of the normativity at stake. But they would agree that queerness exposes the
unnaturalness of normativity *per se*, revealing (much like the abject) how norms are
naturalized according to the logic of exclusion. But if the queer plays the role of
Butler's 'constitutive outside', unlike the abject it resists by carving out a space (and
time) that is liveable, or at least promises to be.[18]

I won't, then, specify exactly what I mean by 'queer' here, but I will be rather
more forthcoming about my usage of 'normativity'. Firstly, the norms that my
'queer' reveals and resists are norms in a Butlerian sense, i.e. performative citations
that have been (and are being) naturalized. And secondly, they embrace the
'logic of the missionary position', as Glenn Burger and Stephen Kruger put it in
their introduction to *Queering the Middle Ages*: man on top, woman on bottom,
reproductive imperative duly obeyed.[19] It is the constitutive outside of missionary

position logic (and, yes, that includes plenty of heterosexual shenanigans) that I shall here consider to be 'queer'.

Queer theory has taken a temporal turn of late. Or perhaps the concern with temporality was there all along: after all, queer theorists have long accused each other of doing history wrongly, of reifying categories we really should (as good Foucauldians) be collapsing, or of disrupting all continuity unthinkingly as we trace back that broken line from 'now'.[20] At any rate, if 'time is a medium for expressing social differences', as Peter Burke writes, in recent years it has certainly been found to express differences between normativity and queerness.[21]

Some have considered what might constitute 'chrononormativity', or 'the interlocking temporal schemes necessary for genealogies of descent', and more and more thinkers are outing queer temporalities, too: whereas chrononormativity has been variously characterized as origin-oriented, teleological, linear and future-oriented, queer time is said to resist origins, straight lines, final causes and finality.[22] For Burger and Kruger, queer theory 'suggests that the stabilization of a sequential "pre" and "post", cause and effect, might be thought otherwise. Sexual norms themselves demand not only a reified sexual positionality but also a stabilized temporality' (p. xii). The queer, in other words, is 'preposterous'.

Medievalists, likewise, and especially those interested in all things queer, have a particular investment in temporality. Karma Lochrie, amongst others, has warned against 'othering' the Middle Ages to throw modern genders and sexualities into artificially stark relief, as Foucault himself is alleged to have done in the *Histoire de la Sexualité*.[23] Where medievalists have read saints' lives through a queer lens, however, it is fair to say that temporality has not been at the top of their agendas.[24] The major exception is Carolyn Dinshaw, who, in *How Soon is Now?*, dwells on the queer time-travellers who feature in the hagiographical legend of the Seven Sleepers of Ephesus.[25] Dinshaw stresses that temporality was experienced diversely and multiply in the Middle Ages: medieval chrononormativity cannot be reduced, say, to Benedict Anderson's 'Messianic time' or to Jacques Le Goff's 'Merchants' time'.[26] It could be disrupted, moreover, by what she terms 'asynchrony', or 'different time frames or temporal systems colliding in a single moment of *now*' (p. 5). 'Saints' lives can be extreme spectacles of asynchrony', she writes (p. 59), and it is time to test that statement by exploring the anachronistic saints and monsters of the *Life of St Honorat*.

At the same time, however, I wish to consider what we might call hagiography's 'queer genealogies'. I should stress that I am not using this term in quite the same way as Laura Doan, who adopts it to refer to attempts to historicize sexuality using Foucault's genealogical method.[27] 'Queer genealogy' here refers to a Foucauldian genealogy *of* ancestral genealogy, an attempt to trace back a family line from the 'now' only to find that the straight line expected is contingent upon lines that are bent in all directions, are impossibly long, or connect points that are disturbingly multiple. With their stories of virgin births, miraculous longevity and incest, queer genealogies leave us fumbling in the dark, no longer sure which direction is up and which is down, turning (the page) in all directions in a vain bid to retrace the straight lines of repro- and chrononormativity. Queer and ancestral genealogies, the former both constitutive and (potentially) disruptive of the latter, make for odd bedfellows, I will argue, in the *Life of St Honorat*.

A Timeless Saint

Two young boys, the pride and joy of their well-to-do parents (the King and Queen of Hungary), are kidnapped while visiting their uncle (the Roman emperor). They had been groomed by three filthily clad old men who, hiding in the bushes, now take their chance to seize the boys — the 'treasure' (v. 1176) they have 'so desired' (v. 1046) — and traffic them to Provence. Their mother is quickly driven to the grave; their father would have been, too, had bystanders not stopped him from taking his own life. And the Occitan *Life of St Honorat* tells us that all this is a good thing.

Good because Honorat and his brother Venant are kidnapped from their family, who are pagans, by Christians. Honorat has been destined since time immemorial to become a holy man: before his birth, both king and queen dreamt that their first-born would one day crush the pagan religion they hold so dear (vv. 165–81). His upbringing in Hungary, far too cushy and far too pagan, is hardly conducive to that goal. It is also too chrono- and repronormative. The king and queen of Hungary live purely to perpetuate their line, and *what* a prestigious line it is, we are constantly reminded (e.g. vv. 718–34, 1074, 2049–50). Marriage bells are already ringing for Honorat (vv. 773–84). But he can have nothing to do with his pagan kin.

It will be instructive here to retread some of the ground covered by Emma Campbell in her study of the substitution of human family with spiritual family in Old French saints' lives.[28] 'Saints' lives,' writes Campbell, 'do not simply disrupt a particular ideology of the human family: these texts also develop models of kinship that elaborate patterns of descent and affiliation of their own' (pp. 73–74). Like so many budding saints, Honorat and his brother do not give up on family structures *per se* — indeed, when Honorat finds himself all alone on a beach, seemingly abandoned by all, he laments this 'bestial' condition (v. 2040) — on the contrary, they adopt new families in an altogether more becoming (read: spiritual) sphere. Much of this lexicon of spiritual kinship will be entirely familiar to us. Embracing Christianity, Honorat and Venant become 'sons' of Christ (v. 901), guided by their spiritual 'father' (and erstwhile abductor), St Caprasi (v. 2034). When Honorat slays the twin dragons Leri and Rins to found the monastery of Lérins, he in turn will be a 'father' (v. 3206) to a community of 'brothers' (v. 2664). Honorat and Venant, we might note, remain brothers after leaving Hungary, but consanguineous brotherhood is now secondary to spiritual fraternity.

In contrast to biological family ties, the kinship bonds formed with Christ — and with others in Christ — shun the chrono- and repronormativity of ancestral genealogy (or they certainly seem to at first glance). Honorat, of course, takes his chastity vow entirely seriously. But more importantly his extreme asceticism, whether he lives as a hermit in his alpine retreat, as abbot of Lérins, or as archbishop of Arles, annihilates his body (vv. 1314–16, 2680, 3305). As a result, Honorat lives in a state akin to that of the criminals and martyrs scrutinized by Robert Mills in *Suspended Animation*. He inhabits one time zone in Provence, playing a role in temporal society where time flows freely (*nunc fluens*), but — asynchronously — he also inhabits another, already partaking as he does of the timelessness of heaven (*nunc stans*).[29] A medieval superman in life, he is able to travel across Provence and to Paradise and back literally in a flash (vv. 3224–44, 3834–36). In death, likewise, with heaven now his permanent residence, he is constantly reappearing in Provence in the guise of a decrepit monk sporting the beautiful (yet untimely) baby-face of an angel (vv. 6214, 6306–07, 6514, 6666–67, 7379, 7497–98, 8624–25, 8670–71).

Insofar as a particular ideology of the human family is disrupted not only by the relationship between the saint and the divine but by the relationship between the saint and his textual community (at least at the level of the diegesis), Raimon's *Life of St Honorat* also takes us beyond Campbell's initial line of argument. It is with the two books of miracles, divided into *ante* and *post mortem*, that the extent of Honorat's new-found spiritual family becomes apparent. The saint is happy to fulfil any family role (spiritually speaking, of course) that his cultic community requires. When a blind woman's son, for example, is captured by Saracen pirates, who should step in as a replacement but Honorat (vv. 4760–4885)? When a poor girl from the town of Uzès is resurrected by the saint after being raped and murdered by a loathsome banker, Raimon sings the praises of a holy man who acts as 'payres de donnas e d'enfantz' (v. 4707) ['father to women and children']. Elsewhere, it is Honorat's maternal streak that appears to shine through: he is said, for instance, to 'feed' all children as he 'fed' the bastard child of one of his followers (v. 5357). But it is the wretched Clariana who perhaps expresses Honorat's flexibility as a family man most simply: having been wrongly accused of adultery by her stepsons she claims to be friendless and without kin ('non ay mays amic ni parent', v. 6509 ['I have no other friend or relative']) and thus asks for Honorat to step in.

Raimon Feraut made a concerted effort to extend the family ties between Honorat and his beneficiaries at the diegetic level of the narrative to us, his potential beneficiaries beyond the diegesis.[30] He begins the two books of miracles by claiming that everyone in Provence — husbands and wives, children and parents — should consider themselves siblings of the Lerinian saints:

> Meraviyllas mi don per ver
> Con en Proenza pot aver
> Seynor ni donna, fiyll ni payre,
> Que de l'islla ron sian confrayre
> E parsonier en los bens fatz
> De tantos santz benauratz (vv. 4206–11)

[I would truly be amazed, then, if there were any lords or ladies, children or parents, in Provence who weren't siblings of the island and who didn't share in the good deeds of so many blessed saints.]

The additions made by Raimon to the Latin *miracula*, moreover, have the effect of warmly welcoming us, his audience, into the saint's family. Firstly, Raimon contributes an entire miracle story, one that is particularly close to his heart because it features the child of a woman for whom he acted as priest and confessor (vv. 8694–763). We listen to Raimon's words now as his parishioners once did, in the expectation that we too could one day end up in his anthology. Secondly, Raimon contributes brief explicits to the miracles, in which he instructs certain members of the audience to identify with particular protagonists. The identifications he fosters are occasionally along geographical lines (vv. 6034–39) or social lines (vv. 8162–63), but more often than not they are along gender lines (vv. 4312–15, 5465, 5941, 6450–51, 6725, 7812–13, 8316–17). A third and final type of addition that makes us feel part of the saint's family takes the form of the numerous intertextual prayers pronounced by the protagonists of the miracle stories. Honorat's beneficiaries pray to him, they tell us, because they have heard miracle stories in which he rescued those accused of similar crimes or facing similar punishments.[31] With these prayers, Raimon turns the diegetic audience into models for us, the extradiegetic audience, and as they guide us in our interpretation of the text, we find ourselves subsumed into their big Provençal family.

We grasp Honorat's queerness not so much in his relationship with the divine, but in the multiplicity of spiritual family roles he plays for members of his cultic community. The story of a noblewoman from Avignon who falls on hard times is instructive in this regard. When our down-and-out lady decides to pimp out her own daughter to the highest bidder, Honorat intervenes, and in an erotically charged variant of the *sponsa Christi* motif, prepares to make the young girl 's'amigua o sa serventa' (v. 5397) ['his lover or his servant']. Honorat then hands over enough money for the woman to pay off her debts and instructs both mother and daughter to follow him to an abbey (vv. 5402–14). The epilogue to the tale, addressed specifically to women, casts Honorat in a role that is a queer combination of sexual partner, mother and father:

> Donnas, sant Honoratz es vostre mercadiers:
> Noyre vostres enfantz e dona sons deniers,
> Vos guarda de grantz blasmes e vos dona maritz. (vv. 5416–18)

[Ladies, St Honorat is your supplier: he feeds your children and distributes his wealth; he protects you from disgrace and gives you husbands.]

Having bought the girl for his pleasure, the saint is said both to suckle children (like a mother) and arrange marriages (like a father).

Honorat's familial ties to his cultic community may be queer, but the cultic community itself is inculcated time and time again in missionary position logic. Carolyn Dinshaw, in her work on Chaucer, has spoken of medieval works that 'construct queer effects in order finally to contain these disturbances of hetero-logic'.[32] Emma Campbell, similarly, notes that hagiography's queerness functions in a highly conservative fashion, reserving transgressive desires for the superior spiritual sphere in a bid to prohibit them all the more forcefully in the temporal (pp. 116–17). The miracles of the *Life of St Honorat* are, for the most part, tales of dysfunctional families rendered functional again by the saint. Sterile couples are given sons — never daughters — in order to secure the family line (vv. 4218–53, 4578–4641, 5572–5643, 6040–6345, 6808–6909, 6910–7003). Sons murdered by wicked stepmothers or jealous aunts are resuscitated to restore proper lineage (vv. 4219–63, 4264–4315, 6040–6345). A daughter who is raped is hastily married off so no one is any the wiser (vv. 4642–4707). Unhappy couples who succumb to adultery or violence are given the counselling they need miraculously to find happiness together (vv. 4396–4447, 4448–71, 5422–5519, 5786–5863, 6726–6807, 7356–7427). And debtors have their debts written off so that they can pass something on to the next generation (vv. 4316–33, 8066–8139). Little wonder, then, that Raimon introduced the miracle tales imagining a textual community made up of husbands and wives, children and parents. The *Life of St Honorat* prescribes ancestral genealogy in the temporal sphere, but it takes queer relations with a saint to straighten that genealogy out.

The majority of Honorat's miracle tales conclude with everyone playing happy families, with 'happiness' here defined as a man and wife who a) are alive, b) are unlikely to kill each other in the near future, and c) have at least one son to continue the bloodline. There are beneficiaries of Honorat's thaumaturgical exploits, however, who are trickier to marry off: motherless children, widowers and ex-lepers are typically excused from marital duties, instead following a monastic calling (e.g. vv. 4218–63, 4578–4641, 5864–5937, 6040–6345, 7746–93, 8320–61). Rarely, a miracle story will end with a perfectly marriageable man or woman entering a religious house. The adulterous Elena, for instance, may have been burned at the stake by her husband, but when Honorat rescues her from the flames, she does not head home with a (forced) smile on her face like her fellow punished adulterers in the *Life of St Honorat*; she gets herself to a nunnery instead (vv. 5938–6039). It is at times like these, when members of the saint's cultic community embrace a cloistered family over their consanguineous one, that we are afforded glimpses of vernacular hagiography's queer potential. Does Elena's rejection of repro- and chrononormativity simply serve to reinforce the boundary between temporal normativity and spiritual queerness? Or has she followed a vocation to live the asynchronous life of a saint, in (queer) imitation of Honorat? Is she, in other words, a warning or a model for us?

Honorat's Hungarian *jesta*

Within the enlarged textual community imagined by Raimon, there is one family that receives special treatment: the Hungarian royal family. The author of the thirteenth-century Latin *vita* had cast Honorat as the son of the erstwhile Christian King of Cumania and the Saracen princess from Iberia who led him astray (p. 40). Though Raimon does refer to Honorat's father as 'prinpce de Cumania' ['prince of Cumania'] early on (v. 138), he had already affiliated him to Hungary by calling him 'Andrioc d'Ongria' ['Andrioc of Hungary'] (v. 137). Hungary garners no mention in his Latin source, but Raimon will go on to make dozens of allusions to Honorat's Hungarian ancestry in the Occitan, compared to only one further mention of 'Cumania' (v. 157).[33] How could a saint of the fourth century, even one who hangs out with Charlemagne, be a Hungarian prince when the history of the Kingdom of Hungary supposedly starts with Stephen I in the eleventh century? For some modern readers of the *Life of St Honorat*, as we have seen, this was one anachronism too far.

Paul Meyer believed Raimon to have made an innocent mistake here: surely the land known as Cumania at the turn of the fourteenth century was near enough to Hungary for a vernacular author to get muddled ('Vie latine', p. 496)? The Turkic tribesmen known collectively as the Cumans had arrived in Hungary in vast numbers in the 1230s, forced westwards by the advancing Mongols. Welcomed by the royals, but loathed by everyone else, the Cumans had unwittingly plunged Hungary into internecine chaos by the time Raimon was writing.[34] It would have been a confusing political picture for anyone, let alone a troubadour-monk writing a thousand miles away.

As Augustin Carlone first noted, however, Raimon had a clear motive for conferring Hungarian nationality upon Honorat (pp. 48–49).[35] By rendering Cumania as Hungary and Cumans as Hungarians, the Occitan hagiographer was able to extend the saint's family tree to include his patron, Maria of Hungary. As Chrétien dedicated the *Charrette* to Marie de Champagne, so Raimon addresses his biography of Honorat to Maria of Hungary:

> Car a la pros reyna
> Que ves Dieu es enclina,
> A ma donna Maria,
> Filla de rey d'Ongria,
> E que porta corona
> De Cecilia la bona
> En volra far present. (vv. 56–62)

[For I wish to present (this life) to the worthy queen who is devoted to God, to my lady Maria, daughter of the king of Hungary, who wears the crown of Fair Sicily.]

Maria, Queen of Sicily by virtue of being married to Charles II of Anjou, belonged to a *beata stirps* if ever there was one: her aunt was St Margaret, fast-tracked to canonization on her death in 1271, and her great-aunt the ever-ascetic St Elizabeth (not to mention their illustrious ancestor St Ladislaus).[36] Here, however, Raimon connects Maria to St Honorat. And he does so not by dwelling on their shared Cuman heritage — Maria's mother, Elizabeth, was the daughter of a pagan tribal leader — but by presenting both as the children of Hungarian kings.

Raimon reiterates his opening dedication to Maria in the epilogue, with some minor differences. Maria now adds the crown of Jerusalem to that of Sicily (vv. 9704–05).[37] And here Raimon invokes her support to protect his text, citing several reasons for his request:

> Car es de l'auta manentia,
> Filha del noble rey d'Ongria,
> Et ama sancta gleyza tant,

> Parenta de nostre cors sant,
> Dell lignaje de Costanti,
> Don le verays cors santz yssi. (vv. 9708–13)

[For she is of great nobility, daughter of the noble king of Hungary, and she loves Holy Church so much, a relation of this saint of ours, of Constantine's lineage, from which the true saint was descended.]

As the daughter of the King of Hungary, Maria should not only rally to Raimon's cause because she is of noble birth; she should do so because she is directly related to the saint, both able to trace their ancestry back to Emperor Constantine.[38] Maria and Hungary, then, are not just analogously related as the children of Hungarian kings; they are related by blood.

With an untimely saint in the family, however, genealogical ties are unlikely to be straightforward. Back in the prologue, Raimon had asked Maria not to protect his work but to safeguard the Lérins monastery. He asks that she look after

> Cesta sancta mayson
> Que fey sant Honoratz
> Que d'Ongria fom natz
> Del sieu reyal lignage
> E que·l sant heretage
> Deu tostemps mantener
> A trastot son poder! (vv. 67–73)

[this house of religion founded by St Honorat, who was born of Hungary, of her royal lineage, and that she always support this holy heirloom, to the best of her ability!]

Why should Maria defend the interests of Lérins? Because she is related to its founder, Raimon tells us. But already we find hints that this *beata stirps* may not obey the chrononormativity of ancestral genealogy. Honorat is born into Maria's lineage — he is 'del *sieu* reyal lignage' — centuries before Maria herself was born. Honorat, meanwhile, forever casts a watchful eye over Lérins, a holy heirloom ('sant heretage') that is simultaneously his 'inheritance' from Maria and his 'legacy' to her.

Carlone was no doubt right to suspect that Raimon made his saintly protagonist a Hungarian for his patron's sake, but he stops short of a full explanation. More recently, Jean-Paul Boyer has suggested that Honorat was given Hungarian nationality to add the prestige of the Árpádian dynasty to the already prestigious Franco-Angevin house ('De force', p. 35). He goes on to argue that, by making Honorat an Árpádian (and even a proto-Angevin), Raimon was attempting to legitimize the Angevin presence in Provence: 'le récit indiquait [...] qu'avec les Angevins la Provence retrouvait ses protecteurs et ses maîtres légitimes' (p. 46) ['the story showed [...] that, with the Angevins, Provence had rediscovered its lawful protectors and masters'].

The Occitan hagiographer's sleight of hand also needs to be understood in the context of Hungary, however. While Raimon was composing his text, at the close of the thirteenth century, Maria was desperately trying to lay claim to the

Kingdom of Hungary on behalf of the Angevins. Her brother, Ladislaus IV, was heirless when he was killed by the Cumans he so adored in 1290, and Maria had since been attempting to install her son, Charles Martel, on the Hungarian throne. Despite papal support, it was only in 1310 that one of Maria's descendants, Martel's son Carobert, was finally accepted as King of Hungary.[39] If the Occitan life of St Honorat legitimized Angevin rule in Provence, then it also attempted to do the same for Hungary.

Thus, in the Occitan *Life of St Honorat*, a saint who forsook his royal parents for a more spiritual family is ostensibly celebrated in the prologue and epilogue for the royal blood he rejected so emphatically. This apparent contradiction can be resolved if we consider Honorat's Hungarian nationality in relation to the dysfunctional families of the miracle stories. The saint in the vernacular biography defies all repro- and chrononormativity, in life as in death, and is thus able to safeguard the normativity of the wider textual community. The Hungarian royal family is no exception. Maria's royal line may seem broken at first glance: we, the audience, are left wondering who succeeded Honorat's father as king of Hungary, just as we might have wondered who on earth would accede to the Hungarian throne at the turn of the fourteenth century. But our saint, who occupied multiple (queer) positions on the family tree as Maria's descendant and ancestor, promises to straighten out the very lineage he subverts.

In the epilogue to the *Life of St Honorat*, having traced his patron's ancestry back (and forwards) to Honorat and Constantine, Raimon presents his work to Maria with the following words: 'E d'aquella jesta valent | De la vida li fatz prezent' (vv. 9714–15) ['I present to her the life of this worthy *jesta*']. Occitan *jesta* (like its French cognate *geste*) is notoriously difficult to translate, and this is particularly the case in the *Life of St Honorat*.[40] 'Jesta' as Raimon employs the word often refers to the religion of the Saracens (Ricketts and Hershon, p. 156n), sometimes to Honorat's epic deeds and, most often of all, to the text itself (and to the Latin source in particular). Here in the epilogue, however, a genealogical sense cannot be excluded. Raimon not only presents an account of Honorat's life to Maria; having turned Latin history into Occitan family history, he presents a Hungarian princess with the first instalment of her *jesta*. If that *jesta* is 'valent' it is only because Honorat rejected it as valueless; if it has been rendered 'prezent' it is only because the saint disrupted its chronology. In other words, that *jesta* is only straight because it is queer.

Untimely Saracens and their Diabolical *jesta*

Having seen Honorat restore the sight of a Majorcan prince, a Saracen doctor heads to Lérins with a dozen of his students to learn about the saint's miraculous medicine. When Honorat reveals that the prince was actually cured thanks to the intervention of the Christian God, the doctor remains sceptical until he witnesses the following scene (vv. 4946–5037). Peering in at the chapel window, he watches Honorat celebrate the Pentecost mass. As the monks sing the Golden Sequence, he sees the choir stalls engulfed by flames, two singers rush out of the church and the choirboys burst into laughter. Without any explanation of these curious goings-on, the service resumes. Honorat administers Communion and the Saracen doctor sees the wafer transformed into the Christ Child.

With mass over, the choirmaster admonishes the children for laughing uncontrollably during the Halleluiah. They are not to blame, they answer: they laughed because they saw two Saracens, the ones who habitually 'tease' the cellarer and the sacristan, lead the two monks out of the church by the hand before showering them with kisses and rolling around with them on the floor. The choirmaster informs Honorat, who challenges the cellarer and sacristan directly. Asked why they left mid-service, they explain that they had found the heat insufferable. Honorat tells the monks that they have committed a crime more heinous than the one committed by the Babylonians against Susanna (cf. Daniel 13–14), decrees that they have been conquered by the devil, and expels them from the island forever. The Saracen doctor, meanwhile, converts as his ever-sceptical students make their way home to Majorca.

With its Saracens and queers (and its queer Saracens to boot), this scene is certainly an intriguing one. In terms of its representation of Saracens, however, it owes a great deal to medieval literary commonplaces. The appearance of Saracens here and elsewhere in the *Life of St Honorat*, which — lest we forget — is the biography of a fourth-century saint, has raised eyebrows among some modern readers. Even the author of the thirteenth-century Latin *vita* avoided the word at this point, referring to the companions of the cellarer and sacristan as 'Ethiopians' (p. 82). But Raimon's use of 'Saracen' here is no different from that of countless other medieval authors: 'Saracen', for him, is a catch-all term subsuming Muslims, pre-Christian Romans, and plenty of other religious and racial adversaries (Ethiopians included) into a single category. That Raimon's Saracens should disgrace Europe's chaste shores with their transgressive sexuality is hardly unusual for a work of medieval literature; that they should be in cahoots with the devil, moreover, is entirely humdrum.[41] No, what is most intriguing about this scene is the flagrant equation of racial/religious and sexual 'others'. Raimon effectively establishes an exchange rate: Lérins will swap one (convertible) Saracen for two queers.

If the two books of miracles in the Occitan *Life of St Honorat* teach us anything, it is that it is a good idea to watch out for marauding Saracens, who (like Christians in the woods) are always ready to assault our male heirs. No need to fret overly about our daughters, who — it would seem — are unlikely to interest these Saracen types. But we would do well to lock up our first-born sons, unless we want them to be abducted by Saracen pirates like the blind woman's son (vv. 4760–91), the sons of Enric de Sant Marcell (vv. 6452–6625), or the handsome Castellan (vv. 6808–6909). A less blatant threat to the chrono- and repronormativity of the imagined textual community's ancestral genealogy here, however, is posed by the Saracens' own family structure, which, as I shall argue in the remainder of this chapter, takes the form of horizontal kinship as opposed to vertical lineage.

The author of the thirteenth-century Latin *vita* of Honorat used a wide range of ethnonyms and demonyms to refer to the countless enemies of the Christian faith encountered by the saint. Raimon to a large extent rationalizes the nomenclature: the Agarenes (named after Hagar), the Ishmaelites (after Ishmael), the Ethiopians, the Berbers, and the unidentificable 'Gauni', all make way for *Sarrazins* in the Occitan.[42] As Krettek notes (p. 201), however, Raimon makes more extensive use of the term *Turc* than his Latin predecessor did, locating Turks not only in the Middle East, but also in Majorca (v. 4791) and Morocco (v. 8088), and situating the related (or even synonymous) 'Turcoples' in Murcia (v. 1421). Throughout the *vida*, but particularly in the course of the final book (the Porcarius Passion), *Turc* is employed as a synonym for the nonetheless much more commonly occurring *Sarrazi*.

If the Occitan author conflates multiple enemies of the faith using the terms *Sarrazi* and (to a lesser extent) *Turc*, his slippery deployment of the lexicon of heresy welcomes Manicheans of late Antiquity and late medieval Cathars into the family. Since his earliest biography, Honorat had been celebrated for combating the Manichean heresy that was particularly rife in Arles at the turn of the fifth century ('Sermo de vita S. Honorati', p. 69). In the thirteenth-century Latin *vita*, the saint is as adept at dispatching heretics from Provençal shores as he is Saracens, two groups that are generally discernible in the later work. For sure, the Latin author introduces the 'Mahometan' faith as a 'false heresy' ('perfida heresis', p. 40), predicting that this 'burgeoning heresy' ('heresis pululata', p. 43) would one day be extirpated by St Honorat. But after these initial allusions to the 'law of the Saracens' *qua* heretical sect, we find no further conflation of Saracens and heretics.[43]

Raimon Feraut, on the other hand, continues to refer to the Saracens' *heretge* time and time again.[44] He also hints at the parodic nature of the Saracen sect by alluding to that *matière de France* staple, the unholy Trinity: whether in joy or in rage, Raimon's Saracens turn to the gods Mahom (aka Bafumet), Apoly and Tervagant, the Occitan equivalents of the *Roland* trio (Mahum, Apolin and Tervagan).[45] The extent of the vernacular author's confusion of Saracens and heretics, which should not be underestimated, might be illustrated by a closer look at two of the most iconic episodes of the *Life of St Honorat*.

In the thirteenth-century Latin *vita*, the story of the foundation of Lérins begins with Honorat, weeping for his recently deceased brother, being spotted by three pirates anchored in the Rade d'Agay. The inimical trio are clearly identified as followers of Mani (p. 60). Having identified the saint as a companion of the local bishop, the one famed for destroying their 'sect', they believe that they have no choice but to kill him if they want to preserve what little remains of it (ibid.). The three Manicheans — and there is no doubt in the Latin that they are indeed Manicheans — proceed to leave Honorat on the island of Lérins as fodder for the dragons Leri and Rins.

In Raimon Feraut's rendering of the dragon episode, however, it is not at all clear that we are dealing with Manicheans. True, the boat lying offshore is said to be full of 'homes de fellonia, | Plens de gran malvestat e de folla heregia' (vv. 2066–67) ['men of treachery, full of great evil and mad heresy'], but such a description could equally apply to the Saracens in the vernacular text, who are routinely cast as heretics. Besides, the pirates fear that Honorat will extirpate their 'ley' (v. 2073) and their 'jesta' (v. 2083), terms reserved exclusively for Saracens and not Manicheans elsewhere in the Occitan *vida*. Having neglected to identify the pirates as followers of Mani, Raimon proceeds to forge a link between the twin dragons and Saracens: in the Latin, the reptiles were said to have slithered to Lérins after leaving their home in the surrounding woods (p. 60), but Raimon tells us that they hail from a specifically Saracen space, Las Mauras (v. 2098), to feed on the Saracen corpses discarded by Charlemagne. As members of Raimon's audience, we would be forgiven, I think, for assuming that Honorat's aggressors support Mahomet rather than Mani, or at least for concluding that they are closely related.

Another conflation of Manicheans and Saracens performed by Raimon takes place at the palace of La Trueylla, built by Emperor Constantine and adorned with a pagan idol. One day, Honorat arrives in Arles from Lérins to find an African giant in La Trueylla, brandishing a sword and spewing forth snakes throughout the city. The Latin had termed the giant an Ethiopian (p. 67), which Raimon renders as 'un Sarazin, | Gran e fer Arabin' (vv. 2816–17) ['a Saracen, a fearsome and imposing Arab']. The reason for the giant's appearance is stated quite bluntly in the Latin: it represents the Manichean heresy that has taken root in Arles following the death of the local bishop (p. 67). Raimon, too, mentions 'heregia' at this point, but — as we have seen — this could easily refer to Saracens in the vernacular biography. The 'heretics' in the Occitan, moreover, do not wish to elect a rival bishop, but are simply said to object to the Christian one (vv. 2842–49). In fact, there is nothing to suggest that the Arlesians have turned to heresy until the end of the miracle performed by Honorat in response to the giant (vv. 2972–77). And when Raimon does mention Manicheans he connects them to recent Occitanian history rather than relegating them to the ancient past: the heretics that Honorat exiled from Arles headed for Toulouse, where their descendants live to this day: 'Ancara n'i a, qui fort lo lur sufria, | De peccat e d'error, si fuecs non o delia' (vv. 3520–21) ['There are still some there (in Toulouse), which strongly supported them, in sin and error, unless fire has destroyed them']. Raimon, then, tells the tale of an ancient giant who enters a pre-Christian place of worship (where, incidentally, parodic 'masses' are held prior to the advent of the Christian original), to become a Saracen who (it eventually emerges) embodies some still extant Manicheans. The thirteenth-century Latin hagiographer began the process of relating Honorat's enemies from disparate time zones, but in the Occitan *Life of St Honorat* those enemies are not only related; they come crashing together asynchronously in the figure of the monster.

With his slippery terminology and his even slipperier monsters, Raimon relates the motley crew of pre-Christians, heretics and Mahometans that he found in his Latin source, subsuming them into one big heretical Saracen *jesta*. Though, corporeally speaking, Saracens come in many shapes and sizes in the Occitan *vida*, they have one physiognomic trait in common: the mark of the devil.[46] Saracens not only worship devils in the *Life of St Honorat* (vv. 1492–94); they are more or less devils themselves, we are told ('li jent d'Antecrist', v. 1762 ['Antichrist's people']). We may not be sure whether the giant of La Trueylla is a Roman, a Saracen or a Cathar, but its identity is to some extent stabilized by its initial presentation in manuscripts as the 'diable de la Trueylla' (rubric preceding v. 2766) ['devil of La Trueylla'].

We must wait, however, until the final book of the *Life of St Honorat*, the Passion of Porcarius, for the clearest account of the Saracens' diabolical kinship. When the long-awaited Saracens arrive on Lérins, Abbot Porcarius greets them with the following words:

> Ben fatz las hobras del Diable
> De cuy est fill e conestable:
> Ben recemblas a Lucifer,
> Las caras negras e·ll vis fer,
> Los heuls vermels, bocas espessas,
> Las golas grans et esdemessas
> A dire tota malvestat,
> Ben semblas de son parentat,
> Don aures pena tostemps mays
> En lo sieu doloyros palays. (vv. 9326–35)

[Truly you do the work of the Devil, whose sons and stewards you are: you look like Lucifer, with your black faces and fierce expressions, red eyes, big mouths, big throats quick to say all sorts of wickedness; you certainly seem to be of his kinship, from whom you'll have everlasting torment in his palace of pain.]

As well as offering familiar jibes of the type 'fill del Diable', the Occitan Porcarius compares the physiognomy of Saracens to that of devils. They are so similar, he concludes, that Saracens must be related to Lucifer. And before long there will be a hellish family reunion: the Saracens will be duly tormented by their kin for evermore ('tostemps mays').

It is worth emphasizing that Raimon's representation of Saracens in the *Life of St Honorat* — as sexual transgressors, as heretics, and as sons of the devil — is by no means extraordinary for a medieval author. More noteworthy is the cumulative effect, namely the conflation of enemies of the Christian faith from different time-periods into a single Saracen *jesta*. Like the saint, Saracens are creatures of asynchrony, dwelling in temporal time but already part-time residents of the infernal realm to which they are destined. If Honorat defied ancestral genealogy by popping up on the family tree whenever required to ensure perpetuation of the line, Saracen kinship structure is disruptive here because it has, as it were, been squashed until it is horizontal. For all their horizontality, however, Saracens do not (cannot) reside in our 'now'. In the *Life of St Honorat* Raimon stages one 'definitive' defeat of the Saracens by the saint after another, only for them to return time and time again. Saracens inhabit a time between past and future, and their apparition — 'furtive et intempestive' ['furtive and untimely'], like that of Derrida's *spectre* — always already haunts the 'now' that they make present.[47]

Positivist Panic

The *Life of St Honorat* is not recommended reading for positivists. Modern readers have already compiled enough lists of the anachronisms Raimon Feraut copied from his thirteenth-century Latin source or of those he himself 'committed'. For sure, in the etymological sense of 'against time', the *Life of St Honorat* is replete with anachronisms in the form of the saint and his Saracen opposition. Insofar as they dwell asynchronously in both our temporal sphere and the eternal *nunc stans*, saints and monsters are disruptive of chrononormativity. And with their kinship structures that put pay to patrilinearity (and not simply because they are sexual transgressors) they are disruptive of repronormativity, too. While we should be mindful of the conservative conception of medieval hagiography's queer genealogies (i.e. to prescribe ancestral genealogy all the more rigorously in the imagined textual community), they also provide a space (and a time) for queer potential. After all, there will always be someone who reads the rulebook as a revolutionary manifesto.

Hagiography's saints and monsters are not only constitutive of ancestral genealogy, however; they are also constitutive of a historiographical practice that is indebted to ancestral genealogy. In response to charges of anachronism brought against Raimon, we might respond that it is not so much the hagiographer who bolsters/ undermines history-writing — it is not he, in other words, who is committing 'anachronisms' in the sense of 'historiographical errors' — but the asynchronous saints and Saracens he represents. When bloodthirsty pirates are on their way, the monks of Lérins hide the treasure — the boys and the books — including the very text we are reading, the *Life of St Honorat* (vv. 9120–29). To protect ourselves from non-chrono- and non-repronormative marauders, it is not enough to lock up our sons and invoke a saint; we have to lock up our history, too.

In the Occitan *Life of St Honorat*, when the young saint is first accosted by the odd-looking St Caprasi *et al.* in the Hungarian forest, he is convinced that he is being attacked by devils (vv. 301–02). Medieval hagiography is punctuated by such moments of undecidability, when we wonder whether we are dealing with a saint or a monster, the sublime or the abject, the constitutive or the deconstructive queer. With so much in common, perhaps narrative chronology plays a key role in our ability to resolve whether these residents of multiple time zones bolster or undermine our 'now': to be told which came first in this game of chicken and egg is to decide between saint and monster, sublime and abject, constitutive and deconstructive queer. Good hagiography makes us fear that narrative chronology has been collapsed — has the monster really won? has control of the narrative really been lost? — only to re-impose the ever-expected triumph of good over evil all the more dramatically. We should stop reading hagiography as bad historiography; otherwise we risk reading anachronisms anachronistically.

For positivists, Max Ducos's *Carnaval des dragons* is perfect. We say goodbye to the timeless saint and the untimely Saracens of the earlier versions of Draguignan's legend, replaced with monsters of man's own making. Now *this* is a story that parents can read to their children, who will in turn be able to read it to their children (and so forth). That is, as long as they can forget that Draguignan's new dragon was once a saint.

Notes to Chapter 3

1. Max Ducos, *Le Carnaval des dragons* (Paris: Sarbacane, 2010).
2. References in parentheses are to Jean de Nostredame, 'Vie de saint Hermentaire', ed. by Camille Chabaneau, *Revue des langues romanes*, 29 (1886), 157–74.
3. References in parentheses will be to Raimon Feraut, *Vida de sant Honorat*, ed. by Peter T. Ricketts, with the assistance of Cyril P. Hershon, Association internationale d'études occitanes, 4 (Turnhout: Brepols, 2007). For Honorat's encounter with the Draguignan dragon, see vv. 5058–97. On the relationship between Nostredame's *Discours* and Feraut's *Vida*, see my 'Fraudsters or Patriots? The Authors of the Lives of St Honorat', *Romania*, 133 (2015), 201–18.
4. Cesare Baronio, *Annales ecclesiastici*, 12 vols (Venice: Hieronymus Scotus, 1600–1612), VI (1601), 26.
5. For an edition of the Latin *vita* of St Honorat by Hilary (BHL 3975), see Hilary of Arles, 'Sermo de Vita S. Honorati', ed. by Samuel Cavallin, in *Vitae sanctorum Honorati et Hilarii, episcoporum Arelatensium*, Skrifter utgivna av Vetenskapssocieteten i Lund, 40 (Lund: Gleerup, 1952), pp. 47–78.
6. An edition of the thirteenth-century Latin *vita* (BHL 3976) is available as Bernhard Munke (ed.), *Die 'Vita sancti Honorati' nach drei Handschriften*, Beihefte zur Zeitschrift für romanische Philologie, 32 (Halle an der Saale: Niemeyer, 1911).
7. For the most thorough comparison of the Occitan to the Latin, see Wilhelm Schäfer, 'Das Verhältnis von Raimon Ferauts Gedicht *La Vida de sant Honorat* zu der *Vita Sancti Honorati*', in Munke, *Vita*, pp. 134–62.
8. On the manuscript tradition of the *Life of St Honorat*, see Renée Flachaire de Roustan, 'Les manuscrits du poème de Raimon Féraut sur la vie de saint Honorat de Lérins', *Le Moyen Âge*, 35 (1924–1925), 255–84.
9. Honoré Bouche, *Chorographie ou description de Provence, et l'histoire chronologique du mesme pays*, 2 vols (Aix: David, 1664), I, 748.
10. Jean-Baptiste Disdier, *Recherches historiques sur saint Leonce, évêque de Fréjus et patron du diocèse* (Draguignan: Gimbert, 1864), p. 71.
11. Gaston Paris, *Histoire poétique de Charlemagne* (Paris: Franck, 1865), p. 88.
12. Augustin Carlone, 'Études historiques sur l'ancien comté de Nice, III: Le troubadour Raymond Feraud, son temps, sa vie et ses œuvres', *Annales de la Société des lettres, sciences et arts des Alpes-Maritimes*, 2 (1873), 5–68.
13. Paul Meyer, 'La Vie latine de saint Honorat et Raimon Féraut', *Romania*, 8 (1879), 481–508 (p. 496).
14. Gustave Lambert, *Histoire de Toulon*, 4 vols (Toulon: Le Var, 1886–1892), I, 52.
15. Gabrielle M. Spiegel, 'Genealogy: Form and Function in Medieval Historical Narrative', *History and Theory*, 22 (1983), 43–53 (p. 50). On the development and role of genealogies in medieval society, see also R. Howard Bloch, *Etymologies and Genealogies: A Literary Anthropology of the French Middle Ages* (Chicago: University of Chicago Press, 1983).
16. Michel Foucault, 'Qu'est-ce que les Lumières?', in *Dits et écrits, 1954–1988*, ed. by Daniel Defert and François Ewald, with the assistance of Jacques Lagrange, 4 vols (Paris: Gallimard, 1994), IV, 679–88 (p. 687).
17. Michel Foucault, 'Nietzsche, la généalogie, l'histoire', in Suzanne Bachelard et al., *Hommage à Jean Hyppolite* (Paris: Presses universitaires de France, 1971), pp. 145–72 (p. 152); Michel Foucault, 'Nietzsche, Genealogy, History', in *Language, Counter-Memory, Practice: Selected Essays and Interviews*, ed. and trans. by Donald F. Bouchard, trans. by Simon Sherry (Ithaca, NY: Cornell University Press, 1977), pp. 139–64 (p. 146).
18. Judith Butler, *Bodies that Matter: On the Discursive Limits of 'Sex'* (New York: Routledge, 1993), p. 3.

19. Glenn Burger and Stephen F. Kruger, 'Introduction', in *Queering the Middle Ages*, ed. by Burger & Kruger, Medieval Cultures, 27 (Minneapolis: University of Minnesota Press, 2001), pp. xi–xxiii (p. xi).

20. Consider, for instance, the rebuke to scholars who behave like 'tourists in the archives' in David Halperin, *How to Do the History of Homosexuality* (Chicago: University of Chicago Press, 2002), p. 60; or Scott Herring's emphasis on the impossibility of recuperative history in *Queering the Underworld: Slumming, Literature, and the Undoing of Lesbian and Gay History* (Chicago: University of Chicago Press, 2007). But on queer theory's presentism and the need to find some way of accessing 'rich and varied histories', see Eve Sedgwick, cited in Steven Maynard, '"Respect Your Elders, Know Your Past": History and the Queer Theorists', *Radical History Review*, 75 (1999), 56–78.

21. Peter Burke, 'Reflections on the Cultural History of Time', *Viator*, 35 (2004), 617–26 (p. 625).

22. For this definition of 'chrononormativity', see Elizabeth Freeman, *Time Binds: Queer Temporalities, Queer Histories* (Durham, NC: Duke University Press, 2010), p. xxii. Consider also the notions of 'reproductive futurism' in Lee Edelman, *No Future: Queer Theory and the Death Drive* (Durham, NC: Duke University Press, 2004); and 'repro-time' in Judith Halberstam, *In a Queer Time and Place: Transgender Bodies, Subcultural Lives* (New York: New York University Press, 2005).

23. Karma Lochrie, 'Desiring Foucault', *Journal of Medieval and Early Modern Studies*, 27 (1997), 3–16.

24. See, most notably, the reading of the *Life of St Euphrosine* in Simon Gaunt, 'Straight Minds/"Queer" Wishes in Old French Hagiography: *La Vie de sainte Euphrosine*', in *Premodern Sexualities*, ed. by Louise Fradenburg and Carla Freccero, with the assistance of Kathy Lavezzo (New York: Routledge, 1996), pp. 155–73; Robert Mills's study of male martyrdom in '"Whatever You Do is a Delight to Me!" Masculinity, Masochism, and Queer Play in Representations of Male Martyrdom', *Exemplaria*, 13 (2001), 1–37; and chapters 4 and 6 of Campbell, *Medieval Saints' Lives*.

25. Carolyn Dinshaw, *How Soon is Now? Medieval Texts, Amateur Readers, and the Queerness of Time* (Durham, NC: Duke University Press, 2012), pp. 41–72.

26. See Benedict Anderson, *Imagined Communities: Reflections on the Origin and Spread of Nationalism* (London: Verso, 1983), p. 24; and Jacques Le Goff, 'Au Moyen Âge: temps de l'Église et temps du marchand', in *Pour un autre Moyen Âge: temps, travail et culture en Occident* (Paris: Gallimard, 1977), pp. 46–65.

27. Laura Doan, *Disturbing Practices: History, Sexuality, and Women's Experience of Modern War* (Chicago: University of Chicago Press, 2013).

28. See, in particular, Chapters 3 and 4 of *Medieval Saints' Lives*.

29. On the contrast between the temporal 'now' and God's eternal 'now', see, for example, Augustine's *Confessions*: 'Sed praecedis omnia praeterita celsitudine semper praesentis aeternitatis et superas omnia futura, quia illa futura sunt, et cum venerint, praeterita erunt. Tu autem idem ipse es. [...] Hodiernus tuus aeternitas' (ed. by James J. O'Donnell, 3 vols (Oxford: Clarendon Press, 1992), I, XI:13/16) [But you precede all things past in the highness of your ever-present eternity, and you exceed all things future, because they are yet to come, and when they will have come, they will be past. But you are yourself, ever the same [...] Your today is eternity.]

30. On interpellation of the textual community in Old French hagiography, with particular emphasis on epilogues, see Campbell, *Medieval Saints' Lives*, pp. 131–35.

31. Lady Gualborc, for instance, having been wrongly condemned for adultery, appeals to Honorat because she knows he rescued a girl in a similar position once before (cf. the Orgon miracle). See vv. 4396–4447, 5821, and, for similar cases, vv. 4218–63, 4642–4707, 5938–6039, 6140–42, 6503–04, 6663. It doesn't seem to matter whether those who pray or those who are mentioned in the prayers are guilty or not. The tale of Diode provides an example of a miracle story in which the punishment is the intratextual glue: having been falsely accused of raping his stepmother, Diode is dragged to the beach by horses before being thrown into the sea, sensibly mentioning the miracle of the boy who was drowned in the Rhone by his wicked aunt when he invokes Honorat's aid (vv. 4264–4315, 6133). On a similar note, see vv. 4396–4447, 6040–6315, 6506–07, 6726–6807.

32. Carolyn Dinshaw, 'Chaucer's Queer Touches / A Queer Touches Chaucer', *Exemplaria*, 7 (1995), 75–92 (p. 79).

33. See Adolf Krettek, 'Die Ortsnamen der *Vida de sant Honorat* von Raimon Feraut, und ihrer lateinischen Quelle', in Munke (ed.), *Vita*, pp. 163–204 (pp. 184–85).

34. On the Cumans in Hungary and their relations with the ruling Árpádians, see Pál Engel, *The Realm of St. Stephen: A History of Medieval Hungary, 895–1526*, trans. by Tamás Pálosfalvi, ed. by Andrew Ayton (London: Tauris, 2001), pp. 90–100 and 107–10.

35. Jean-Paul Boyer also picks up on this, in 'De force ou de gré: la Provence et les rois de Sicile (milieu xiiie siècle-milieu xive siècle)', in *Les Princes angevins du XIIIe au XVe siècle: un destin européen*, ed. by Noël-Yves Tonnerre and Elisabeth Verry (Rennes: Presses universitaires de Rennes, 2003), pp. 23–59 (p. 35).

36. For a study of the Árpádian saints, see André Vauchez, '*Beata stirps*: sainteté et lignage en Occident aux xiiie et xive siècles', in *Famille et parenté dans l'Occident médiéval: actes du Colloque de Paris (6–8 juin 1974)*, ed. by Georges Duby and Jacques Le Goff (Rome: École française de Rome, 1977), pp. 397–406.

37. Charles I had bought what remained of the Kingdom of Jerusalem in 1277.

38. Constantine is named as Honorat's grandfather in BHL 3976 (p. 41) and the Occitan life (vv. 204–05).

39. On Maria's involvement in the tumult following Ladislaus's death, see Émile G. Léonard, *Les Angevins de Naples* (Paris: Presses universitaires de France, 1954), pp. 180–82 and 197–99.

40. See, for example, R. Howard Bloch, *Etymologies*, pp. 98–99.

41. On the transgressive sexuality of Saracens as represented in medieval theological writings, see Philippe Sénac, *L'Image de l'autre: l'Occident médiéval face à l'islam* (Paris: Flammarion, 1983), p. 56. Medieval Saracens are read as 'implicitly sodomitic' in Gregory S. Hutcheson, 'The Sodomitic Moor: Queerness in the Narrative of *Reconquista*', in *Queering the Middle Ages*, ed. Burger and Kruger, pp. 99–122 (p. 102). On the links between Saracens and the devil, see, for example, Armelle Leclercq, *Portraits croisés: l'image des Francs et des Musulmans dans les textes sur la Première Croisade*, Nouvelle bibliothèque du Moyen Âge, 96 (Paris: Champion, 2010), pp. 251–89.

42. Raimon omits references to the Agarene fiction and Ishmael's progeny. He renders Latin 'Ethiopes' (pp. 67, 82) and 'Gaunorum' (p. 53) as Saracens (vv. 1341, 2816, 5006).

43. On the representation of Islam as a heresy in the Middle Ages, see R. W. Southern, *Western Views of Islam in the Middle Ages* (Cambridge, MA: Harvard University Press, 1962), esp. pp. 38–39; and John V. Tolan, *Saracens: Islam in the Medieval European Imagination* (New York: Columbia University Press, 2002), pp. 155–69.

44. See, for example, vv. 583–85, 909–10, 952, 1793, 1812–13.

45. On the parodic Trinity in the Occitan *vida*, see Keith Busby, 'Hagiography at the Confluence of Epic, Lyric, and Romance: Raimon Feraut's *La Vida de sant Honorat*', *Zeitschrift für romanische Philologie*, 113 (1997), 51–64 (p. 56). Mahom/Bafumet and Tervagant are paired several times in the Occitan text (vv. 134, 188, 1141), with Apoly invoked by Andrioc alongside the Saracen deities Astarot, Jupiter and their messenger Mauhom (vv. 587–89).

46. On Saracens' corporeal difference (their 'Oriental' bodies), see Suzanne Conklin Akbari, *Idols in the East: European Representations of Islam and the Orient, 1100–1450* (Ithaca, NY: Cornell University Press, 2009), esp. p. 12. For criticism of the notion of the Saracen's 'Oriental' body, see Kathy Cawsey, 'Disorienting Orientalism: Finding Saracens in Strange Places in Late Medieval English Manuscripts', *Exemplaria*, 21 (2009), 380–97. On links between Saracens and the devil, see note 41 above.

47. Jacques Derrida, *Spectres de Marx: l'état de la dette, le travail du deuil et la nouvelle Internationale* (Paris: Galilée, 1993), p. 17.

❖

CHAPTER 4

St Enimia of France and the Wonders of the Tarn Gorges

Levez-vous parisiens engourdis, grands paresseux! Êtes-vous donc ici pour dormir? C'est indigne d'un touriste que de ne pas assister au spectacle magique du lever du soleil dans les gorges du Tarn.[1]

[Arise, you numb Parisians, you famous layabouts! Are you here, then, to sleep? It's shameful for a tourist not to witness the magical spectacle of the sunrise in the Tarn Gorges.]

Burle, le Couvent des Dames de Saint-Vincent-de-Paul, la Croix de St-Jean, le rocher de Chante, les 14 stations du Chemin de la Croix, distancées sur un sentier de renard, qui monte presque à pic, nous rendent un salut fraternel, car, en gens bien élevés, nous leur disons bonjour. Enfin nous arrivons à l'Ermitage suants, essoufflés, rompus. Entrons, la sonnette nous appelle [...]
La voilà cette vierge dans sa châsse, représentée en cire, étendue sur sa couche! sa main droite se lève pour bénir; à son côté repose la crosse abbatiale; ses membres sont revêtus de la robe monastique, couleur moirée [...] Pour les rives du Tarn, si catholiques, c'est un trésor à nul autre pareil. (Costecalde, p. 145)

[Burla, the Convent of Saint-Vincent-de-Paul, the Saint-Jean Cross, the rock of Chante, the 14 stations on the Way of the Cross (at intervals along a fox's track that rises almost vertically), they all greet us amicably, for, as well-mannered folk, we say 'good day' to them. We arrive at last at the Hermitage, perspiring, breathless, exhausted. Let us go in; the bell summons us [...]
And there is the virgin saint in her shrine, depicted in wax, lying on her bed! She raises her right hand in benediction; beside her lies the abbot's crozier; her limbs are covered by a monastic robe of shimmering hue [...] For the very Catholic banks of the Tarn, it is an incomparable treasure.]

Writing his *Voyage au pays des merveilles* in the final decade of the nineteenth century and under the enigmatic pseudonym 'Monsieur X.', Léon Costecalde imagines the reactions of a group of Parisians travelling to a little-known land full of untold wonder. The Frenchmen are ill-adapted to this wilderness realm, physically broken by the vertiginous slopes and struggling to climb tracks made by wild animals. There is no-one and nothing to say a friendly 'bonjour' to, only the ruined shells of dilapidated buildings. The sole sign of life, in fact, comes from a body that has been dead for over a thousand years but seems to raise its hand in a gesture of benediction. Contrary to what we might expect, however, this treasure is not found in a distant Orient but in the Tarn Gorges, a land of wonder that lies a little over 350 miles from Paris.

Though Costecalde himself hailed from the Tarn Gorges, here he adopts the perspective of visitors from northern France. He seeks to entice visitors who have already explored the four corners of Europe to his native land (p. 5) by depicting that land as an uninhabitable realm inhabited by an unusually animate cadaver and an infernal *drach* that 'pourrait bien sauter sur vous et vous croquer à belles dents' (p. 220) ['could easily pounce on you and gobble you up']. His tactics were hardly new. It is the medieval manipulation of the holy body that Costecalde's French travellers found so fascinating (that of St Enimia), and of its equally fascinating wilderness home, that is the subject of this chapter.

Entre-deux-morts

What do the martyrs, madmen, warriors and wizards of medieval French literature have in common? All have been read in recent years as inhabiting the uninhabitable space known as the *zone entre-deux-morts*, as theorized by Lacan in his *Séminaire* of 1959–1960.[2] Though contradictions aplenty lie in the Lacanian *zone*, since some of these appear to be of our own making, we would do well to return to Lacan's paradigmatic *zone*-dweller, Sophocles's Antigone.

Antigone is the daughter of Oedipus and Jocasta (not to mention granddaughter to the latter). In contravention of the law pronounced by her uncle Creon, she buries her brother's body, left on the battlefield for the vultures to peck at. Her punishment is to be exiled from the city and buried alive in a cave. Before Creon has had a chance to realize the error of his ways, Antigone has hanged herself within her living tomb. In *L'Éthique de la psychanalyse*, Lacan distinguishes two types of death here, real (biological) death and its symbolization. If the biological death of Antigone's brother, denied funeral rites, initially goes without symbolic recognition, Antigone conversely suffers symbolic death before she dies corporeally. As Lacan notes, her symbolic death occurs even before she enters the cave:

> [Antigone] franchit l'entrée de la zone entre la vie et la mort, où prend forme au-dehors ce qu'elle a déjà dit qu'elle était. Il y a longtemps en effet qu'elle nous a dit qu'elle était déjà dans le royaume des morts, mais cette fois-ci la chose est consacrée dans le fait. Son supplice va consister à être enfermée, suspendue, dans la zone entre la vie et la mort. Sans être encore morte, elle est déjà rayée du monde des vivants. (*Seminaire 7*, p. 326)

> [She crosses the entrance to the zone between life and death, that is to say, when what she has already affirmed herself to be takes on an outward form. She has been telling us for a long time that she is in the kingdom of the dead, but at this point the idea is consecrated. Her punishment will consist in her being shut up or suspended in the zone between life and death. Although she is not yet dead, she is eliminated from the world of the living. (*Seminar 7*, p. 280)]

When a living body leaves the representable world it undergoes symbolic death, the erasure of its identity in the eyes of society, its 'death to the world'. When a living body enters the realm of the unrepresentable, it undergoes real (biological) death.

In *Antigone*, these deaths do not always coincide, opening up another space, a *zone entre-deux-morts*.

Nor do they coincide in the works of the Marquis de Sade, which Lacan reads in *L'Éthique* alongside Sophocles. Sadeian victims can seemingly endure endless torment and yet, not unlike Antigone, they are 'toujours parées, non seulement de toutes les beautés, mais de la gràce même' (pp. 303–04) ['always adorned not only with all kinds of beauty, but also with grace' (p. 261)]. It is as though, even beyond corporeal death, their bodies live on because death fails to register at a symbolic level. Like Antigone, they inhabit an uninhabitable *zone entre-deux-morts*. As the impious Pope Pius suggests in Sade's novel *Juliette*, published anonymously at the turn of the nineteenth century, one death is not enough: 'le meurtre n'ôte que la première vie à l'individu que nous frappons; il faudrait pouvoir lui arracher la seconde' ['murder only takes the first life of the individual we strike down; one should be able to deprive him of the second'].[3] This 'second death' both is and is not the death that brings to an end being in the *zone*. In Sade, the *zone*-dwelling victim sustains the fantasy of an absolute death heralding the eradication of all natural laws: this 'second death' promises to be 'le point où s'annihile le cycle même des transformations naturelles' (*Séminaire 7*, p. 291) ['the point at which the very cycles of the transformations of nature are annihilated' (*Seminar 7*, p. 248)], but in the end, at least according to Lacan's reading, it will only restart the cycle.

This brief outline of the Lacanian *entre-deux-morts* already raises several questions. If the uninhabitable *zone* is home to figures as varied as Antigone and the Sadeian victim, creatures sublime and abject (and no doubt a bit of both), how do we distinguish them? Does it matter which death comes first (i.e. real or symbolic)? Whether they act or are acted upon? Whether they defy or defend the Law? Can they ever be properly distinguished? And what happens when a psychic *zone* beyond representation is (impossibly) represented as physical space, Antigone's symbolic death, for example, figured by her living tomb? What happens, in other words, when Lacanian topologics are mapped onto topography?

These are the questions I shall explore here in relation to the medieval lives of St Enimia. The story of this Merovingian princess, leper and hermit who makes her home in the dragon-infested Tarn Gorges has come down to us in three fourteenth-century manuscripts. The earliest version (BHL 2549–51), a *vita*, an *inventio* and *miracula* in Latin now thought to have been composed in the mid-eleventh century, survives in Paris, BnF, lat. 913, and (minus the miracles) in a codex in private hands.[4] As the final passage of the *vita* proper reveals (pp. 275–77), the text was intended to be read on Enimia's feast day. Two later Latin versions of the legend, also panegyrics, are shorn of the earlier text's rhetorical niceties and heavily abbreviated in comparison to BHL 2549–51. The first (BHL 2552), for instance, omits the account of the saint's *inventio* centuries later, while the second (BHL 2553) makes no mention of the dragon episode at the centre of the longer Latin narrative. Both abbreviated lives survive in BnF, lat. 913.[5]

Better known in scholarship is the Occitan biography of St Enimia in octosyllabic verse composed by Bertran de Marselha in the early thirteenth century at the request of the Priory of Sainte-Énimie (vv. 1–20).[6] This survives in a single early-fourteenth-century copy (Paris, Bibl. de l'Arsenal 6355). A loose rendering of the longer Latin life (but perhaps betraying the influence of the later *panegyrici*), the vernacular version was written with both a monastic and a lay audience in mind (e.g. v. 1631). And while the Occitan text certainly appeals to the local population (vv. 1629–48), it is also thought to have acted as something of a guidebook to the holy sites of Sainte-Énimie for pilgrims visiting from afar.[7]

It is my contention here that Bertran de Marselha, writing at a time of increasing French influence on the Gévaudan as a result of the Albigensian Crusade, effects a remarkable transformation in his Occitan rendering of Enimia's biography in terms of the portrayal of the saint's homeland, France, and that of her place of exile, the wilderness of the Gévaudan.[8] In all four medieval versions of her biography, the saint inhabits a series of uninhabitable spaces akin to the Lacanian *zone entre-deux-morts*. The representation of these zones varies from one life to the next, but this is particularly the case for the wilderness of the Tarn Gorges. When we compare the Occitan verse life of St Enimia to its Latin sources, it emerges that the Gévaudan is no longer represented as a zone forever uninhabitable save for a handful of sublime and abject creatures trapped in-between deaths, but as a full-fledged community grounded upon antipathy towards France.

From Riches to Rags

All four extant lives of St Enimia initially present the saint as a beautiful French princess.[9] It is an identity that the young saint soon learns to reject as she rebels against the worldliness of court life. The courtly body, E. Jane Burns argues, can be understood 'as a set of clothes that make, mark, delimit, and define the body presumed to lie beneath'.[10] Enimia's four medieval biographers all use clothing to chart her trajectory from court darling to court pariah. In each case, the saint replaces her gorgeous garments with the plainest of rags, but the social skin she sheds — the courtly identity she relinquishes — will vary from one version of her story to the next.

The author of the eleventh-century Latin life (BHL 2549–51) gives Enimia's royal ancestry pride of place at the beginning of the narrative. The opening words not only give credit to Enimia for being a virgin but for her 'illustrissimam prosapiam' (p. 252) ['very distinguished ancestry']. He goes on to establish that Enimia is the great-granddaughter of Clovis, the first Frankish king to convert to Christianity, the daughter of another King Clovis, and the sister of a future King Dagobert (p. 253). But this princess is an unruly royal. Her philanthropic endeavours, though apparently sanctioned by the king and queen, make her a rose among thorns: she prefers the company of the poor, to whom she gives all her belongings, to that of courtiers, and she likes nothing better than to touch the sores and ulcers of the sick (ibid.). When Enimia swaps jewellery for rags her transformation is complete: the princess has become a pauper (p. 254).

In the vernacular version, it is not courtliness *per se* that poses a problem for Enimia, but the French court in particular. Bertran's Enimia bears a close resemblance to the archetypal lady of troubadour song. The Occitan hagiographer addresses her, just as the troubadours do their ladies, as the androgynous 'midons' (vv. 19 and 1732) ['my lady']. He dwells on her bodily beauty, claiming that 'natura non poc far | Negun temps de beltat sa par' (vv. 53–54) ['Nature was never able to produce anyone to rival her beauty']. And he tells us that she possesses all courtly virtues in abundance but is immune to the anti-courtly characteristic par excellence, *orgolh*, or 'pride' (v. 60).

Pride belongs to the aristocracy in general in the Occitan life (vv. 67–76). It is also, however, a peculiarly French trait, recalling the treatment of the northern invaders by the anonymous author of the *Canso de la Crozada*. Bertran introduces France as a barbarous realm, the last bastion of the pagan world to convert to the true faith. Where the Latin author had simply suggested that Germania had adopted Christianity thanks to the proselytizing zeal of the apostles' successors (pp. 252–53), Bertran makes special mention of the particular recalcitrance of the French:

> Mas cant foro las encontradas
> Vas Dieu totas per pauc tornadas,
> Tot deriers lo regne de Fransa
> Pres pels discipols baptizansa,
> Car totz temps fo ferma e dura
> En aco que cre, per natura. (vv. 29–34)

[But when more or less all the countries had turned to God, last of all the kingdom of France was baptized by the apostles, for it was always unyielding and inflexible in matters of faith, by its very nature.]

The author of BHL 2552 had considered the French to be God's new chosen people (p. 109). But here Bertran redirects the *translatio studii et imperii* topos. When Enimia refuses to wear 'polpra ni sendat' in the Occitan (v. 120) ['crimson cloth or silk'], it is the backward French court she is rejecting rather than the troubadours' *cortezia*.

The later panegyric (BHL 2553) also foregrounds Enimia's bodily beauty. The saint is said to behave like an old maid in the flower of youth — an image also found in the long Latin life and the earlier panegyric — but here it is precisely her non-nubile behaviour that keeps her body in bloom: 'pudor oculos, veritas linguam, modestia vultum, largitas manum, motum gravitas, animum pietas condiebat' (p. 132) ['shame preserved her eyes, truth her tongue, modesty her face, generosity her hand, dignity her gestures, piety her soul']. Whereas rumours circulate about Enimia's charitable acts in BHL 2549–51 and BHL 2552, here it is news of her 'pulchritudinis gratia' (p. 133) ['charm of beauty'] that travels across the Frankish realm. As in the Occitan, then, when Enimia shuns sartorial finery in favour of humble rags (p. 132), her new outfit offsets her dazzling bodily beauty.

The link between body and clothing is more complex, however, in the first panegyric (BHL 2552). Here, Enimia is said to be ever-mindful of the words of Revelation 14.4 predicting the appearance of 144,000 (male) virgins on Mount Zion heralded by the sounding of the seventh angelic trumpet:

Angelicum illud auribus eius insonuit: 'Hii sunt qui cum mulieribus commisceri fugiente, virgines permanserunt; virgines enim sunt et sequuntur Agnum quo-qumque ierit'. (p. 110)

[The angelic (trumpet) resounded in her ears: 'These are they which were not defiled with women, for they are virgins; these are they which follow the Lamb whithersoever he goeth'.]

This lesson, that God's true followers are those who flee the corrupting influence of women, is one which Enimia must also learn, according to the author of BHL 2552. And it is one that she should be able to grasp despite being a woman, we are told (given that Eve was created from Adam's side and that women can sometimes understand Scripture, if only through male, sacerdotal mediation, pp. 110–11). Enimia takes off her jewels and puts on rags 'ut inde Deum sibi placabilem redderet, unde hominibus displiceret' (p. 111) ['to please God and displease men']. But it is never entirely clear in BHL 2552 whether she is making herself repulsive to men to prevent her own body from being polluted, or to prevent her own body from polluting those of the male virgins slated to appear on Judgment Day. Does Enimia's donning of rags signal the rejection of her gender? Or has she been kitted out with attire more becoming of her gender? The Enimia of BHL 2552 is in possession of what Burns would call a 'sartorial body', made of fabric and flesh so interwoven that it is impossible to distinguish outer from inner (*Courtly Love Undressed*, p. 12).

Leprosy: Sin or Salvation?

During Enimia's youth, a pauper's rags are seemingly sufficient to protect her body from courtly corruption. When she reaches marriageable age, however, the threat posed by her numerous suitors cannot be averted by cloth alone. With the devil summoning hot-blooded males from across the Frankish empire, Enimia needs a thicker antisocial skin. She prays for God to preserve her body and soul intact. And as she asks for her body to be kept white, God turns her skin black with leprous pustules.[11]

The author of the long Latin life draws a parallel between Enimia's rags and her wilfully acquired leprosy. Both humble cloth and the disease that mortifies her flesh protect her from court life, allowing her to become a true disciple of Christ: 'Beata Enimia, abjectis regalibus pompis, corporis mortificatione ac diuturna maceratione effecta est discipula Christi' (p. 256) ['Having abandoned royal ostentation, St Enimia became a disciple of Christ through the mortification and daily maceration of her body']. But those black pustules make her stand out from the crowd more than her rags ever did. Lepers were often considered to be 'dead to the world' in the European Middle Ages, and Enimia is no exception.[12] In BHL 2549–51, the royal family mourn Enimia 'quasi mortuam' (p. 256) ['as if she were dead']. As a leper, Enimia inhabits an uninhabitable symbolic space akin to the Lacanian *zone entre-deux-morts*.

In the Occitan version of Enimia's biography, it is once again not so much courtliness in general as its French manifestation that calls for leprosy. Bertran de

Marselha presents the diabolic institution of marriage, for instance, as a particularly French threat. Whereas noblemen come from the whole of 'Germania' in BHL 2549–51 (p. 254), they hail from closer to home in the vernacular text ('Fo per molher trop demandada | Per los baros de l'encontrada', vv. 123–24 ['She was often asked by the noblemen of the country to be their wife']). If the king and queen ask their daughter about her views on marriage in the Latin (pp. 254–55), they are generous enough to allow her to select any baron of her choosing in the Occitan, with the proviso that he be a Frenchman ('Qal voletz per marit aver | De Fransa dels onratz baros?', vv. 144–45 ['Which one of the honourable noblemen of France would you like to be your husband?']). And once Enimia has contracted leprosy it is not only the royal household that is devastated by the cancellation of the princess's wedding (cf. the long Latin life, p. 256), but the entire realm of France:

> E qui poiria remembrar
> Lo dol c'om comenset a far
> Per tot lo regisme de Fransa? (vv. 221–23)

[Who could recall the grief that was felt throughout the kingdom of France?]

In this case, Enimia's putrified skin signals her symbolic departure not only from the aristocratic marriage circuit but also from France.

In the long Latin life and the Occitan rendering, what marks Enimia as different from run-of-the-mill lepers — and what guarantees that her disease is a mark of divine favour — is that she has specifically asked to be infected. Her symbolic death, in other words, is of her own volition. Leprosy was, of course, a profoundly ambiguous disease in the Middle Ages, 'the sickness both of the damned sinner and of one given special grace by God', as Brody puts it (pp. 100–01). It was, moreover, one that lustful and menstruating women in particular apparently needed to fear.[13] The author of BHL 2552 seems to have been uneasy about God infecting Enimia with leprosy. On the one hand, he makes it clear that the disease is a preventive measure to avoid licentiousness (whether Enimia's or that of her male suitors) (p. 113). On the other, there is a lingering suspicion — confirmed later on — that Enimia cannot have asked for leprosy in all innocence but must have done something to deserve her affliction. The black pustules that cover the saint's body are said to be wounds curing wounds ('vulnera vulneribus sanans', p. 114). And with the words of Hebrews 12.6 ('For whom the Lord loveth he chasteneth'), Enimia is told to accept her condition as just desserts, dispensed by a father who lovingly corrects his child (p. 114).

Into the Wild

Enimia's medieval biographers express the sartorial and leprous barriers that separate saint from society in spatial terms. Even before she sets foot elsewhere, her rags and her disease make her a heaven-bent pilgrim wandering away from worldliness. In the long Latin life (BHL 2549–51), by removing her elegant dresses and donning the rags of a pauper, 'angusti callis tramitem gressu sancte conversationis surgente conscendit' (p. 254) ['she ascended the narrow path of this world, climbing upwards through her saintly conduct']. Similarly, with the threat of nuptials hanging over her, Enimia prays to be allowed to wander heavenwards 'felici calcaneo' (p. 255) ['with a happy foot']. It is hardly surprising, then, that spatial separation should become the primary marker of Enimia's saintly alterity. But if Enimia takes up the pilgrim's staff in all four of her biographies, she does not, I would argue, leave the same France and reach the same Gévaudan each time.

After several years living the symbolic death of leprosy at the Frankish court, Enimia is informed by an angel that she can be cured of her disease by bathing in the Burla spring beside the River Tarn in the Gévaudan. Off Enimia trots, with a retinue befitting a princess. The journey southwards is an arduous one for two reasons. Firstly, the Gévaudan is depicted as a 'far-away land', a 'borderland' realm some distance away from France.[14] And secondly, it is a rocky wilderness made up of seemingly impassable mountains and gorges. Bertran de Marselha in particular goes to great lengths to convey the sterility of the landscape, prompting Gérard Gouiran to wonder whether 'l'occitan est capable de fournir assez de synonymes pour rendre compte de la terrible minéralité de ce paysage' ['Occitan is capable of providing enough synonyms to describe the terrible stoniness of this landscape'].[15] Though not quite 'vierge de toute inscription humaine' ['untouched by human hands'] (as Cristina Álvares suggests), this inhospitable realm lacks life except for a band of hostile creatures entirely foreign to the royal court.[16]

The native inhabitants of the Gévaudan garner little mention in the two abbreviated panegyrics, but they are given colourful portraits in both the long Latin life and Bertran's Occitan rendering of it. The first native encountered by Enimia is a brazen woman who marches right up to the royal party to ask what the princess thinks she is doing 'in their country' ('nostras [...] per partes', p. 257; 'per sesta nostra encontrada', v. 293). But when the Gévaudanaise spots Enimia's affliction she is only too happy to help. The princess may have made a bad impression, but before long she is convinced that the local girl must be an angel sent by God to guide her to Burla (p. 258 in BHL 2549–51; vv. 316–17 in the Occitan).

Unfortunately, however, the native woman misdirects the French visitors and a genuine angel must be sent to get Enimia back on track. The next locals whom Enimia encounters are a group of shepherds, as strange as the Gévaudanaise (if not stranger). In BHL 2549–51, the shepherd accosted by the saint demands money in return for directions to the spring at Burla (p. 259). Bertran might be said to mellow the depiction of these inhospitable natives since he adds a comic description of the shepherds running for their lives when they spot the northern knights approaching (vv. 429–32). But Enimia's interlocutor is just as keen to make a fast buck out of the foreign visitor (vv. 451–52 and 461–62). Bemused by Bertran's portrayal of the shepherds, Gouiran wonders why an Occitan author would describe his fellow Occitanophones as 'salvatges' ['wild'] ('Regard sur l'autochtone', p. 116). The answer perhaps lies in 'sly civility', the act of the indigenous population duping the colonial power by 'performing' stereotypes held by the colonists. In the Occitan life of St Enimia, the shepherds, coarse-spoken rustics who flee in (mock) terror, are able to make even greater material profit from their mightier northern neighbours.[17]

The shepherd agrees to lead Enimia to Burla, for a fee. The miraculous spring itself is located in the darkest and deepest part of the Gévaudan. As before, the Occitan hagiographer makes a particular effort to communicate the harshness of the environment. Burla lies at the bottom of a deep valley (vv. 469–70), so overshadowed by cliffs that the sun's rays barely reach it (v. 380). The description of the French travellers' first glimpse of the valley is typical:

> Esdevengron per aventura
> En una val prionda e fera,
> On Burla el fluvi de Tarn era,
> E domeyns que emiey la val
> Descendion d'aqui aval,
> Per us desrancs, per us belencs,
> Per unas rochas, per us bencs,
> Car adoncas non hi avia
> Per la val estrada ni via,
> Auziro, si coma Dieu plac,
> Pastors layns per miey lo blac. (vv. 396–406)

[They happened, by chance, upon a deep and wild valley, where Burla on the Tarn river was, and as they descended the slopes into the middle of the valley, over scree, between boulders, across rocks, around crags, for there was no path or road through the valley at that time, they heard, as God wished, some shepherds in the woods.]

Hidden in the humblest of places, the water of Burla is cool and clean. When Enimia dips her body into the pool three times and invokes the Trinity her pustuled skin becomes as pure as it once was: as white as snow and milk for the author of BHL 2549–51 (p. 260) and as white as a dove's feathers for the Occitan author (vv. 502–04).

Enimia's leprosy returns, however, as soon as she tries to ascend the slopes of the valley (or stray more than half a league from the spring in the Occitan text, v. 679). The author of the first panegyric (BHL 2552) makes the link between malady and topography explicit: 'Virgo in *valle* residens ad sanitatem *erigitur, excelsa conscendens*, infirmitate *deprimitur*' (p. 120, my italics) [The virgin, staying in the *valley*, is *raised* to health, but *ascending* the *heights* she is *lowered* by her affliction]. Having found her spring, Enimia has exchanged the 'depths' of illness for the 'depths' of the Tarn Gorges. In other words, Burla is the topographical equivalent of leprosy.

The long Latin life (BHL 2549–51) establishes that the Gévaudan lies in opposition to the worldliness *of* Enimia's native land (rather than in opposition to her native land *per se*). Each time the saint is miraculously cured by the spring-water she longs to return home. Her body cleansed for the first time, she cannot wait to tell her parents the good news (pp. 260–61), but God frustrates her desire for repatriation ('repatriandi denegat iter', p. 261 ['God again refuses to let her go home']). After bathing for a second time she is still keen to head home, but God keeps her in the Gévaudan 'nolentem' (p. 262) ['unwillingly']. When she finally understands that she is being granted a choice of leprosy or Burla and takes a third dip in the spring, she is said to have opted for the wilderness to avoid worldliness in general (p. 263). The Latin hagiographer make his position clear: if Enimia were to return home she would be akin to a dog returning to its own vomit or a spotlessly pink pig returning to the mire (p. 262; cf. II Peter 2.22). But it is the courtiers who are wallowing in muck rather than the French as a whole.

In the Occitan, however, spatial separation keeps both worldliness and France at bay. Rather than referring obliquely to Enimia's 'patria', Bertran de Marselha makes a habit of mentioning 'Fransa' by name. After bathing at Burla for the first time, Enimia is struck down by leprosy for heading towards 'Fransa' (v. 547). (It is a fair few lines before the vernacular author explains that it is the 'honors terrenals' of France that pose the problem, v. 559 ['worldly honours'].) After the second cure, Enimia heads homewards not because she is homesick (as in BHL 2549–51) but to placate the rest of her party and her kingdom: 'Per dar al regne alegransa | La verges volc lor voler far' (vv. 644–45) ['The virgin wanted to do their will to make the kingdom happy']. And when she prays for her leprosy to disappear for the final time, she simply asks to be kept away from 'her home' ('mon repayre', v. 722), making no mention whatsoever of temporal snares. France, then, is able to stand in metonymically for worldliness in the Occitan life.

What marks Enimia as different from the native inhabitants of the Gévaudan is that she finds herself in the wilderness of her own accord, having left worldliness up north. The stark relief throws her holiness into stark relief. There is nonetheless a suggestion in the first panegyric (BHL 2552) that the saint is not quite so at odds with her environment.

When Enimia bathes at Burla three of her biographers (the authors of BHL 2549–51, BHL 2552 and the Occitan) compare the saint to Naaman, the Syrian general of II Kings 5 who was cured of leprosy (or, more accurately, of Tzaraath) after bathing in the Jordan. Interpreted typologically, the passage tended to be understood by medieval commentators as prefiguring Christian baptism: Naaman's leprosy represents his misguided pagan ways; his dip in the Jordan ridding him of his disease as he embraces the God of Israel (Brody, pp. 122–23). When readers and listeners are asked to see Enimia as the new Naaman, the assumption is that, prior to her arrival at Burla, the saint is flawed in both soul and body.

Perhaps prompted by the Naaman reference, the author of BHL 2552 sees the asperity of the Gévaudan as reflective of Enimia's sinfulness. The scene in which the shepherd leads the leper to Burla is glossed as a priest leading a sinner to salvation:

> Quis hic pastorum auctoritatem et sacramentorum mysterium huic facto involutum non intelligat? Quid enim signat ductu pastoris leprosam ad fluenta sanitatis descendere, nisi animam immundorum lepra vitiorum infectam pastorali officio sacerdotum ad sacramenta salutis pertingere? Hoc utique indicio est neminem a criminibus posse sanari, nisi prius se confitendo exhibuerit suo pastori. (p. 117)

> [Who does not understand the authority of the shepherds here and the mystery of the sacraments hidden in this event? For what is signified by a shepherd leading a leper down to a restorative spring if not a priest with pastoral duties bringing a soul infected with the leprosy of filthy vices to the sacraments of salvation? This is certainly proof that no-one can be cleansed of their sins unless they first present themselves to their priest for confession.]

Found guilty without charge, Enimia is thus placed firmly under the thumb of the priesthood (foreshadowing her reliance on episcopal authority during the dragon episode). Likewise, the saint's trips back and forth between miraculous spring and the limits of the valley are said to signify recidivistic sinners punished by God for failing to learn from their repeated transgressions. Enimia may have needed several dips to be cured of her 'lepra criminum' (p. 120) ['leprosy of sins'], but the author of BHL 2552 hopes his audience will be quicker to learn that lesson.

Saint and/or Monster?

The Lacanian *zone entre-deux-morts*, which 'can contain either sublime beauty or fearsome monsters' (Žižek, *Sublime Object*, p. 135), finds an analogue in the Gévaudan wilderness of medieval biographies of St Enimia. No longer wishing to stray far from Burla, Enimia instructs her followers to spread throughout the valley and live as hermits before she sets up shop herself in the most inaccessible location of all, a cave high above her spring. Costecalde's account of the ascent to Enimia's hermitage is confirmed by the medieval descriptions. According to the author of BHL 2552, the grotto is so difficult to access that 'non nisi experto credendum est' (p. 122) ['it is not to be believed without experiencing it']. For Bertran de Marselha, meanwhile, the cave is so high that it surely touches the sky ('diratz que sus al cel tocha', v. 828 ['you'd say it touched the sky']). Even before any talk of asceticism in the Latin lives, exile in this wilderness is said to be akin to death, Enimia's own Gethsemane (BHL 2552, pp. 121–22), a place where she will suffer like Christ (BHL 2549–51, p. 265).

Merely inhabiting such an uninhabitable spot is enough in the Occitan life to grant Enimia sainthood. She leads a 'sancta vida' as a hermit (v. 865 ['holy life']) and founds a house of nuns that is 'digne e sant' (v. 1310 ['worthy and holy']), but she has no need to dabble in asceticism. As the rags and leprosy did previously, the bare rock shows off Enimia's spiritual and corporeal beauty. That beauty has already begun to remould the surrounding landscape: when she resuscitates a boy who has drowned an impression in the rock is left where she sat to perform the miracle (vv. 991–1002).

In the Latin biographies, however, the asperity of the landscape is transferred onto Enimia's body, asceticism taking her into yet another *zone entre-deux-morts*. According to the long Latin life, Enimia eats nothing but grass (with a little bread) and, even after establishing the abbey, she spends her days in constant prayer (pp. 267, 272–73). The harshness of this lifestyle is said to make her fully deserving of a martyr's crown (p. 273). The later panegyric (BHL 2553) remains relatively faithful to the long Latin life in terms of the saint's asceticism, but the author of BHL 2552 gives the budding saint an even more punishing regime. Enimia takes her grass-eating, vigils, fasts and exposure to the elements to such extremes that she descends into animality. As if eating grass and living in a 'den' ('latibulum', pp. 122 and 123) were not enough, while foraging for roots she is said to completely forget her humanity ('oblita se esse hominem', p. 122 ['she forgot she was a human being']).

Indeed, so forgetful is she of her body that she is prone to bouts of levitation. Having undergone symbolic death, she awaits real, corporeal death in a literal state of suspended animation (pp. 122–23). This long, drawn-out martyrdom, the author of BHL 2552 tells us, is easily as worthy as being burned at the stake or beheaded at the hands of a pagan persecutor (pp. 127–28).[18]

Enimia here, then, is analogous to Antigone as read by Lacan in *L'Éthique de la psychanalyse*: though 'un être inhumain' ['inhuman'], she does not belong to 'le registre de la monstruosité, car qu'est-ce que ça voudrait dire de notre part?' ['the level of the monstrous, for what would that mean from our point of view?'] (*Séminaire 7*, p. 306; *Seminar 7*, p. 263). What makes Antigone and Enimia sublime rather than monstrous is their apparent agency. Both seem to enter their respective *zones entre-deux-morts* of their own volition. And yet it would only be human for us to doubt the inhuman conviction of such martyrs. As soon as we question the absoluteness of their desire, however — as soon as we recognize the part we play — then, as Lacan intimates with his rhetorical question, we start creating monsters.

Lest we spend too long questioning Enimia's sublime status, we soon encounter a creature that is indisputably monstrous. When the saint attempts to erect a church near her hermitage, the devil appears every night in the guise of a terrifying dragon, razing the half-built edifice to the ground. Enimia's monstrous antagonist has traditionally been read as a symbol of a pre-Christian cult.[19] The cumbersome circumlocutions used by the author of the long Latin life to refer to the dragon — 'diabolical trickery', 'cunning plague', and so forth — give ample room for such an interpretation.[20] The author of BHL 2549–51, moreover, draws a direct comparison, albeit one that is difficult to decipher, between the dragon and the strange natives of the Gévaudan:

> Nam fraus diabolica immanis draconis, qui predicti fluminis discurrebat per alveum et ceu colonus littoris observabat cavernas, se fudit per artus et quicquid per septimanas ebdomadarum cimentarii implebant in opere, nocturnis horis pestis illa dolosa, facto impetu, ruebat ad ima. (p. 270)

> [For the diabolical trickery of a huge dragon, which roamed up and down the river and spied out the caves of the banks like a local, extended its limbs, and by night that wicked plague assailed however much of the church had been completed in the course of the week and reduced it to rubble.]

The diabolical force represented by the dragon moves up and down the valley, looking for dark holes in the banks of the river like a local. Whether it figures paganism or not, the monster would appear to be completely at home in the Tarn Gorges.

Enimia herself is not up to the task of ridding the valley of the dragon and must instead enlist the help of the local bishop, Hilary of Mende.[21] The saint, however, is the brains behind the operation, instructing Hilary to put on the allegorical armour of a *miles Christi* to slay the beast (p. 271). Hilary assaults the dragon armed with the sign of the Cross and the 'armour of salvation' ('arma salutaria', ibid.), but he also carries a crucifix, hastily assembled from two branches picked up along the way. When the monster is cornered it cunningly hews a hole in the rock to escape and

Hilary realizes that this is no flesh-and-blood serpent but an illusion created by the devil himself: 'Cernens miles Christ: diabolicum hoc fore nec in serpente hec esse velocitas, sed maligni spiritus potius videretur temptatio' (p. 272) ['The soldier of Christ sees this devil and it is clear to him that that is not the speed of a serpent but rather the temptation of an evil spirit']. He raises his cross and prays for the dragon to crash down defeated to the bottom of the valley. Rocks fall from the flanks of the mountains but they do not kill a living animal; they figure the defeat of an abstract entity. In BHL 2549–51 Hilary is a symbolic soldier fighting a symbolic dragon in a symbolic landscape.

The dragon sheds its abstraction to a large extent in the first panegyric (BHL 2552) and in the vernacular life. In BHL 2552, epithets such as 'antiquus hostis' (p. 125) ['ancient enemy'] and 'nequissimo impugnatore' (p. 127) ['most wicked assailant'] certainly establish the beast's allegiance to the devil, but elsewhere it simply goes by the name of 'draco' (p. 126) ['dragon']. Bishop Hilary's encounter with the monster is much condensed overall, but the author nonetheless adds a graphic description of its demise. The dragon crashes to the ground, spilling its guts and breaking its neck (p. 127). Hilary, then, seems to have dispatched a creature of flesh and blood.

'Colobra', 'serpens', 'drago' and 'dracs' are used interchangeably to refer to the dragon in the Occitan text, with 'adversiers', 'enemics' and 'malfat', which might be said to ally the beast more closely with the devil, used considerably less often.[22] Where the Latin author of BHL 2549–51 casts the dragon as a creature indigenous to the Tarn Gorges, Bertran de Marselha professes complete ignorance as to the monster's origins ('Venia una grans colobra, | No say d'on', vv. 1038–39 ['A great serpent came, I don't know where from']), as does Enimia herself at the level of the diegesis (v. 1078). And where the Latin author of BHL 2549–51 stresses from the outset that the dragon is a devilish apparition, his Occitan counterpart lends bodily actuality to the monster. As in the Latin, Bishop Hilary chases the dragon away from the construction site with a homemade cross, but the monster slithers away into a crack in the rock. The Occitan hagiographer expands the episode in which the clergyman prays for the dragon's expulsion:

> Cant fo la orazos finida,
> Lo dracs brama laïns e crida
> Et ab lo bram es fors anatz
> Per yeis lo loc on era intratz,
> Si que·l locs e la fendeduda
> Son encar en la roca dura.
> Aqui eus que·l dracs fo issitz
> Sairchz Ylis fo amanoïtz
> E a lo ferit ab la crotz,
> Si que·l sancs cazet fers e ros
> En una roca, on encar
> Per senhal lo pot hom trobar;
> So dizon li clerc e·l gens layga. (vv. 1163–75)

[When the prayer was over, the dragon shrieked and screeched inside (the rock), and with a cry emerged the same way it had gone in, so that the place and the crevice are still in the hard rock. As soon as the dragon had emerged the devoted Hilary was ready and he struck it with the cross, so that bright red blood poured onto the rock, where you can still find the mark to this day; so say clerics and layfolk.]

As in the long Latin version, Bishop Hilary acts as a *miles Christi*, wielding his cross 'like a military banner' ('a guiza de gonfayno', v. 1133). But this Frère Jean *avant la lettre* goes on to use his cross as if he were a literal soldier rather than an allegorical one. Whereas the dragon in BHL 2549–51 simply forges a path through the rock to escape Hilary's clutches, here the bishop prays for the monster to be expelled from its hiding-place, before whacking it with his cross, spilling so much blood that the stains are said by the narrator to be still visible. Before continuing in pursuit of the dragon, Hilary delights in the bloodshed (v. 1197) and promises to erect a church to mark the location of his heroic display (vv. 1179–83). Bertran de Marselha, then, leaves evidence of an encounter with a flesh-and-blood monster in the form of red stains and a chapel. Hilary may realize, as he does in the Latin texts, that this creature must have been sent by Satan himself (vv. 1213–14), but the Occitan hagiographer literalizes the monster and literalizes the landscape, complicating any association with a local pagan cult.

Revolution in the Tarn Gorges

How revolutionary is Antigone? According to Lacan's reading of Sophocles in *L'Éthique de la psychanalyse* she both incites and quells revolution. On the one hand, Antigone inhabits a symbolic space — the *zone entre-deux-morts* — that necessarily poses a threat to the Law because it lies beyond symbolization, supporting the fantasy of Sade's truly revolutionary 'second death'. On the other, her lament as she prepares to be entombed alive triggers a cathartic response in the chorus (and audience) that paves the way for a return to normality. Jane Gilbert's distinction between the 'two acts' of Antigone's drama, as Lacan reads it, is elucidating here:

> Her drama as Lacan tells it comprises two acts: the 'ethical' drive to death, followed by the 'moral' rehabilitation into, and consequent regeneration of, the established order. Lacan's assessment of the figure's capacity for enabling workable, durable resistance to that order is therefore lukewarm. Insofar as she has a social and political function, Antigone is normality's sacrifice to itself. (*Living Death*, p. 21)

Antigone, in other words, has revolted so (that) we don't have to.

In response to Lacan, however, some commentators have understood Antigone's revolutionary potential to be less limited. Slavoj Žižek, for example, reduces her drama to a single act. When Antigone says 'No!' to her uncle's law, she commits an act that is 'literally suicidal', exiling herself from her community, 'whereby she offers nothing new, no positive program — she just insists on her unconditional demand'.[23] Where Lacan argued that Antigone incarnates 'le pur et simple désir de mort' (*Séminaire 7*, p. 329) ['the pure and simple desire of death' (*Seminar 7*, p. 282)], Žižek suggests that, with no sign of moral rehabilitation, her refusal to give way on her desire shifts her 'from the modality of desire into the modality of pure drive'.[24]

Insofar as her 'feminine' *act* of negation may, in desperation, be repaired through subsequent 'masculine' *activity*, however, Antigone can be understood to pave the way for 'the great founding gesture of a new order' (*Enjoy Your Symptom*, p. 46).

In her reading, Judith Butler is critical of Lacan for elevating Antigone from specific cultural context to universal status: 'by separating the historical drama she lives through from the metaphysical truth she exemplifies for us, Lacan fails to ask how certain kinds of lives, precisely by virtue of the historical drama that is theirs, are relegated to the limits of the ineffaceable'.[25] Butler also distances herself from Žižek. Antigone does not merely say 'No!' to Creon; 'she also approximates the stubborn will of Creon and circumscribes a rival autonomy by her negation' (p. 68). At the cusp of representability, Butler's Antigone has undergone symbolic death but nonetheless makes provisions for her symbolic legacy. The revolutionary potential of Sophocles's heroine lies in transforming the unliveable space of her own particular historical drama into a circumscribed space that is liveable for others.

It is to some extent possible to reconcile Žižek's and Butler's stances on Antigone by recalling the logic of perversion. Positioning himself as the object of the drive (as opposed to desire), the perverse subject appears to find the naughtiest of ways of contravening the Law. In Lacanian terms, however, perversion is a *père version* — a turning towards the symbolic Father — an attempt to bring the Law into being. The pervert's rude defiance, in other words, is more conservative than at first meets the eye; his 'No!' is issued in the disavowed expectation of a more authoritative 'No!' in reply. But because drive and desire appear to be aligned in perversion, we cannot tell whether the pervert invokes the Law for himself or for the Other. Similarly, if Sophocles's Antigone has revolutionary potential, we cannot know for sure whether she is a posthumous poster-girl of the revolution — new legislation passed after the *passage à l'acte* (as in Žižek's reading) — or whether she fires the first shots in full cognizance of what she is starting — new legislation passed, as it were, *en passant* (as in Butler's reading). The insoluble question Antigone makes us ask is perhaps less 'What does she really want?' (Žižek, *Sublime Object*, p. 120) than 'Does she really want at all?'.

The author of the long Latin life of St Enimia (BHL 2549–51) restrains the saint's revolutionary potential in much the same way Lacan does Antigone's. Once the dragon has been defeated, Enimia continues to fight devils in the Tarn Gorges for the rest of her days: 'Post immensos quos contra hostem decertavit agones atque post innumeras temptationum victorias...', p. 273 ['After the unending battles she fought with the enemy and innumerable victories over temptation...']. For sure, the wilderness affords her glimpses of heaven (e.g. p. 266), but Burla only appears paradisiacal because it is so very far removed from the worldliness of court life. Both *ante* and *post mortem*, the landscape of the Gévaudan is represented as an unrepresentable *zone entre-deux-morts*, fit only for fights between sublime and abject creatures. Revolution might be taking place in the Tarn Gorges, but — safely confined by rock — nothing changes beyond their borders.

If the wilderness remains a barren space in BHL 2549–51, the later Latin *panegyrici* hint at its future transformation. In BHL 2552, Enimia instructs her followers to develop the surrounding terrain ('quae possint loca excolere [...] disponit', p. 121

['she told them which places to develop']), and on her deathbed she tells them to harvest the fruits of their labour ('pacis fructus colligere valeret monuit', p. 128 ['she instructed them to reap the fruits of harmony']). More significantly, the author of BHL 2553 makes it clear that God did not place Enimia in the Gévaudan arbitrarily or because it was the only place sufficiently removed from worldly society to be pure; Enimia was sent there, we are told, to make an inhospitable valley fruitful:

> Nec ideo, ut opinor, omnipotentis censura regrediendi obstitit, quin templum suum inviolatum ubique conservare vellet et posset, sed ut terram praecipitiis ac parva fructuositate pene inviam et inhabitabilem habitabilem faceret, nostratibus quoque in ea virginitatis exemplum formans et patrocinium donans. (p. 136)

> [In this way, God's censure, I suppose, did not block her return so that she would want and be able to conserve the temple of her body inviolable wherever she went, but so that she would render inhabitable a land of great peaks and little abundance, one that was uninhabitable and barely accessible, providing us with an example through her virginity and giving us protection.]

For the author of the second panegyric, Enimia has transformed the Tarn Gorges from an uninhabitable *zone entre-deux-morts* into a liveable and fully representable space. But it is not clear whether it was her (feminine) *act* or the (masculine) *activity* it inspired that triggered the revolution.

In Enimia's Occitan biography, the dragon is the last abject creature to be expelled from the Gévaudan (v. 1072). Perhaps encouraged by the fleeting references to future prosperity in the panegyrics, Bertran de Marselha converts the wilderness into an earthly paradise. During the closing stages of the narrative, he deviates entirely from BHL 2549–51 to address his audience directly:

> Baro, prohome, ar vejatz,
> Vos qu'en aquela val istatz,
> Home e femnas, laics e clergue,
> Si deuratz ben a cesta verge
> Portar honor digna e bona,
> Car ilh no volc que sa persona
> En fos en altre luec portada,
> Per so que la vals grans e lada,
> Que non portava negu fruch
> Adoncs, et aquo sabem tuch,
> Ni neguna ren don hom viva,
> Tan era sela vals esquiva,
> Pogues tostemps pel sieu istar
> Vinhas e blatz e fruchs portar.
> E tot aysso porta per ver
> Per ley, e poyratz ho vezer,
> Car aqui istan ganre gens
> Cuminalmem mays que dos cens,
> Et ha hi ben cent e vihnt fuecs;
> Ples e vestitz es bon lo luecs. (vv. 1629–48)

[Lords, gentlemen, now you see, you who stay in this valley, men and women, layfolk and clerics. You should honour this virgin well and properly, for she didn't want her body to be carried elsewhere in order that that great, wide valley, which didn't bear any fruit at that time or sustain the life of man, as we all know — so wild it was — might, through her presence, always bear vines, corn and fruit. And all that it truly bears thanks to her, and you can see it, for there are a great many folk here now, more than 200 in total, and there are 120 homes; it's a well-supplied and cultivated place.]

It is not simply Enimia's presence in the valley that transforms the landscape (as per BHL 2553); here, like Butler's Antigone, she *wills* revolution. Thanks to the saint, a wilderness unable to support human existence is now replete with vineyards, wheat-fields and orchards. Those creatures once elevated to the sublime or relegated to the abject can now emerge from their rocky hideaways to live as men and women, clerics and laypeople.

Given the hostility that Bertran de Marselha displays towards France elsewhere in his biography of Enimia, it is unsurprising that he should contrast this new community in the former desert with its northern neighbours. In BHL 2549–51, Enimia is desperately homesick when she realizes that she will have to spend the rest of her days in the Tarn Gorges. Not only does she miss her parents (and fear God's wrath for disrespecting them and thus breaking the fourth commandment, p. 264); she follows in the footsteps of the Desert Fathers and prays for the family and country she has deserted:

> Non illis deero, sed communem Dominum jugi prece pro illorum salute exor-abo, ut et in presenti regnum ipsorum pacatissima pace conservet integrum et in futuro ad commune sanctorum omnium felici transmigratione regnaturos faciat pervenire. (p. 266)

> [I will not abandon them but will ask the Lord with constant prayers to give them salvation so that he preserves their kingdom in peace and harmony in the present life and allows them to cross over to heaven and rule with all the saints in the future life.]

Casting the king and queen as rulers on earth as well as in heaven, the passage comes surprisingly close to conflating the kingdom of France with the kingdom of Heaven.

Bertran, in contrast, makes it clear that Enimia is relieved not to return to France. 'Anc pueys no la pres voluntat | Que s'en tornes en son regnat' (vv. 741–42 ['She never again wanted to return to her kingdom']), we are told in the Occitan. Given the opportunity, she wouldn't mind seeing her parents again (vv. 759–60). She will, moreover, continue to pray for her family, but France is conspicuously absent from her prayers:

> Aysso lur prec yeu caramen,
> Car tos temps lor profeitaray
> Ab los precs que per els faray. (vv. 800–02)

> [I ask this of them fondly, for I'll always advance their cause with prayers on their behalf.]

When Enimia invites her compatriots to stay, the Occitan text (like BHL 2552) lacks the large contingent of travellers who decline her offer and prefer to return to France. Bertran invents excuses for the handful of the saint's companions who do choose to return home: either they are keen to broadcast Enimia's story or else they have children whom they sorely miss (vv. 779–86).

News of Enimia's exemplary lifestyle and her thaumaturgical exploits eventually reaches the Frankish court. The saint's father, Clovis, and her brother, Dagobert, want to do everything in their power to enrich their kinswoman, sending messengers to buy up the land surrounding the abbey at Burla in Enimia's name. This explains the priory's considerable possessions, according to the authors of the long Latin life and the two *panegyrici* (BHL 2549–51, p. 273; BHL 2552, p. 127; BHL 2553, pp. 142–43). But Bertran de Marselha, writing at a time when French encroachment on the priory's lands was a very real concern, is manifestly unhappy with the foundation's unpaid debts to the French monarchy. Enimia and her nuns acquire the surrounding land from the royal family, but Bertran stresses that they owe the French nothing in return:

> E hereteron la maion
> De tot aquo qu'es deveiron:
> Vilas, terras, mas eissamen,
> Feu et alo entieyramen,
> Don encar ten tot per entier
> So que li fo dat em primier
> Senes tot cas e ses rancura,
> Aquitiadamen e pura. (vv. 1337–44)

[The abbey came into possession of all the surrounding area: farms, land, smallholdings too, entire fiefs and allods. And it still owns everything it was originally given in its entirety, without legal proceedings or appeals, fairly and squarely.]

The priory owns the land fair and square: there are to be no court cases and no attempts at retribution. There has been a revolution in the Tarn Gorges: this once lawless realm now makes its own rules, free from French interference.

Invention in/of the Tarn Gorges

The rediscovery, or *inventio*, of Enimia's body at Burla several centuries after her death constitutes a narrative distinct from the *vita* proper in the two manuscripts featuring the longer Latin life (and is consequently given a separate number — BHL 2550 — by the Bollandists). The story is entirely absent from the first *panegyricus* (BHL 2552) and only garners the briefest of mentions in the second (BHL 2553). But Bertran de Marselha allows the Occitan *vita* to flow seamlessly into the *inventio* and gives this final section of the narrative considerably more prominence by devoting a little over a quarter of the total number of his verses to the rediscovery of the saint's body. As we shall see, he also allows himself to make far greater departures from his chief Latin source in this section.

The author of the Latin *inventio* begins the story in praise of the French royal family. Enimia's father, King Clovis II, distinguished himself as a fine monarch and when he died he passed on a divinely sponsored kingdom to his son, Dagobert II:

> Cum rex Clodoveus, vir strenuus et in rerum administratione preclarus, post indultum sibi a Deo regnum migrasset de corpore, filiusque eius Dagobertus regni Francorum adeptus foret gubernacula... (p. 278)

> [When King Clovis, a vigorous man and distinguished in affairs of state, had departed in body from the kingdom granted to him by God, and his son Dagobert had inherited governorship of the kingdom of the Franks...]

The 'kingdom granted to him by God' clearly refers to the land of the Franks inherited by Dagobert. When he renders this passage into Occitan, Bertran seems to give it one of his anti-Frankish glosses:

> Cant Clodoveus, lo reis de Fransa,
> Fo issitz de la malanansa
> E del caytivier d'aquest aire,
> Lo filh renhet apres lo paire
> E governet tot lo regisme. (vv. 1479–83)

> [When Clovis, king of France, had left the evil and wickedness of this realm, son succeeded father and ruled the entire kingdom.]

'Aquest aire' may, of course, refer to the worldly *saeculum*, but — considering the Latin — might it not also refer to 'Fransa'? In the vernacular text, France is no longer a heaven-sent gift but a realm characterized by evil and wickedness.

For both the Latin and Occitan hagiographers, Dagobert is a renowned collector of relics.[26] But the author of BHL 2549–51 is not overly critical of the Frankish king. Dagobert wanted to adorn Saint-Denis with the holiest of relics out of love ('multo deflagrasset amore', p. 278 ['he was greatly consumed by love']) and his interest in Enimia's in particular is perfectly understandable given that noblemen across Latin Christendom are also after them (ibid.). Needless to say, Bertran omits anything that could be construed as an excuse for the King's behaviour. He stresses, moreover, the topographical distinctness of the Tarn Gorges. In the Latin version of the *inventio*, Enimia's abbey sometimes lies within the borders of Dagobert's realm and sometimes without. Enimia's *patria*, likewise, is seemingly both France and the Tarn Gorges.[27] But Bertran irons out this geographical fuzziness: France constitutes one province among many (v. 1490) and once Dagobert has pillaged other provinces near and far (v. 1491) he takes all the relics he finds back to France (vv. 1495–96). There is no question, in other words, of Burla lying within the borders of Dagobert's realm.

Dagobert's attempted theft of Enimia's body from Burla is not actually described in the Latin text. Enimia is praised for having the foresight to instruct her fellow nuns to place her body in an unmarked grave beneath that of her maid (who also happens to be called Enimia), thus ensuring that the king takes the wrong Enimia up to Saint-Denis (p. 279). But the event itself is absent from the text, the author simply asserting that things must have happened as she had planned: 'quod negozium ita foret peractum apud nos nulli dubium est' (ibid.) ['that things happened here in this way is beyond doubt'].

Bertran de Marselha expands on Dagobert's visit to Burla more than on any other episode of the Latin life, inventing roles for Enimia's fellow nuns and giving the saint's successor as abbess a particularly colourful part to play. The heated exchange between the French visitor and his southern hosts bolsters the geographical alterity of the Tarn Gorges. Dagobert begins by announcing, politely but presumptuously, that he wants to take Enimia's relics 'en mon païs, | Al ric mostier de Saint Danis' (vv. 1521–22) ['to my country, to the noble basilica of Saint-Denis']. The abbess is appalled: what would the nuns do 'in their moorlands' ('en cestas landas', v. 1526) if Enimia were taken to Dagobert's 'land' ('ta terra', v. 1528)? Dagobert promises to give the abbey vast wealth in exchange for his sister's corpse (vv. 1531–38). The abbess is just as aghast as before, her exasperation effectively conveyed by the repetitiousness of her words:

> Senher reis, per que·ns desconortas?
> Que farem nos si tu l'en portas?
> Si tu l'en portas, que farem?
> Certas, reis, certas nos morrem.
> Ilh es nostra dompna carnals
> E nostra dompna spiritals
> E·ns garda de tot encombrier
> Nos totas et aquest mostier,
> E per re non la ti daram,
> Qu'avans aucir nos laisaram. (vv. 1541–50)

[My royal lord, why are you causing us such grief? What will we do if you take her away? If you take her away, what will we do? Surely, king, surely we will die. She is our carnal lady and our spiritual lady, and she protects us from all harm, all of us and this abbey. We will not give her to you for anything in the world, for we'd rather let ourselves be killed.]

Enimia, by her physical presence as much as by her spiritual presence, protects the valley from harm and sustains life in this erstwhile wilderness. But without her relics the Tarn Gorges would become a *zone entre-deux-morts* once again, the nuns facing certain death.

Dagobert says he is resolved to seize Enimia's body, however much the nuns protest. He bursts into the chapel with his knights, the nuns running after them, tearing at their wimples ('E las sanctas monjas ab els | Tiran e derumpen lors vels', vv. 1579–80 ['And the faithful nuns with them pull and tear their wimples']). The nuns slyly tell the King that he will find Enimia's relics if he looks hard enough ('Quer lo tu, que be·l trobaras', v. 1586 ['Have a look yourself, you'll find her sure enough']). When they see their royal guest stealing the wrong body they put all their acting skills to the test and pretend to be distraught:

> Las mongas cant vezon aquo,
> Dins lor coratge lur sap bo,
> Cant vezon qu'el cuida aver
> Lo cors de sa soror per ver,
> Mas no fan ges semblan ni bruch,
> Per so que el no fos descuch,

Ans fan semblan que sion tristas:
'Lassas que mala fom anc vistas,
C'om ne porte nostre thesaur!
Que farem mays en cesta vaur?
Lassetas e que poyrem far,
C'om nos vulha aissi raubar?'
Tot aco dizon en ploran
Per so que·l reis s'an mielhs pessan
Que lo cors d'aquel monumen
Fos de sa soror veramen. (vv. 1663–78)

[When the nuns see this — when they see that he thinks he's actually found his sister's body — they are overjoyed in their hearts, but they make no sign or sound at all lest he find out the truth. They instead pretend to be sad: 'Alas, woe is us for ever being seen, that our treasure should be taken away! What will we do now in this valley? Poor us, what can we do now that people want to rob us like this?' All this they say while crying, so that the king believes more firmly that the body in that tomb is truly his sister's.]

Having branded Dagobert a thief, the nuns continue their charade, urging him to give generously to the abbey in compensation for the theft of their most prized possession: 'membre ti | D'aquest mostier religos | Que·l sias bos e caritos!' (vv. 1694–96) ['Remember this house of religion; may you be good and charitable towards it!'].

In the Latin version of the *inventio*, then, Enimia thwarts an attempt to take her relics from the wilderness — a suitable location for a body that signifies beyond death — to her *patria*. But in the Occitan text the saint's relics remain at the centre of a community living in a former wilderness that must be protected from the noisome influence of those up north. The joke is not only on a Frankish king of bygone years who was once 'enganatz e escarnitz' (v. 1704) ['tricked and mocked']; it is also on Frenchmen of the thirteenth century who remain gullible enough, according to Bertran, to believe that they own Enimia's body ('Don encar cudon ben aver | Sancta Enimia per ver', vv. 1713–14 ['And they still think they actually have St Enimia for real']).

Three centuries or so after the aborted *translatio*, a community of monks has replaced Enimia's nuns, and the knowledge that the saint still resides in the Tarn Gorges has been lost. Fortunately, however, a particularly pious monk called Johannes learns of the hidden relics in a dream. A little slow on the uptake perhaps (a trinity of visions is required before Johannes is convinced), the monk eventually reveals all to his monastic community and preparations are made for Enimia's tomb to be opened. The Latin *inventio* pays lip-service to ecclesiastical hierarchy here, the attendance of the Bishop of Mende and other clergymen contributing to the pomp and circumstance of the spectacle (p. 279). But Bertran de Marselha recognizes that Enimia's body acts as a pillar for a much broader community. In the vernacular text, Johan and his fellow brothers send for laypeople as well as monks and clerics; both laymen and clergymen are afforded a vision of paradise as the tomb is opened (vv. 1963–68); and both lay and clerical audiences are invited to pray to the saint alongside the narrator with the closing words of the *roman*:

> Aras pregem tuch, layc e clerge,
> Que Dyeus pel nom d'aquesta verge,
> De qui avem fach cest romans,
> Nos meta sus am los syeus sanhs. (vv. 1997–2000)

['Now let us all pray, layfolk and clerics, that God, in the name of this virgin whose *roman* we have made, place us in heaven with his saints.]

The story of Enimia's *inventio* here is not, then, a glimpse of heaven, reserved for a few sublime subjects eking out an impossible existence in the wilderness; it is a story for all to enjoy in their earthly paradise, inhabitable thanks to the ongoing presence of their saint.

Guides to the Wild

When the Parisians of Costecalde's *Voyage au pays des merveilles* finally reach St Enimia's hermitage, they find a dead body that is disconcertingly mobile. In the late nineteenth century the saint's corpse might have been alive and well in the Tarn Gorges, but her textual corpus had long since left. The only manuscript known (at the time) to preserve the medieval Latin biographies of St Enimia, once in the hands of Gévaudanais nobility, was in the collections of the Bibliothèque nationale.[28] (Festooned with *fleurs-de-lys*, this volume's new home is perhaps not wholly inappropriate.) The only copy of Bertran de Marselha's Occitan life of St Enimia, for its part, had already made it onto the shelves of the Bibliothèque de l'Arsenal. Enimia may have thwarted her brother's plans to head northwards with her relics, but her protection plan does not seem to have covered her texts.

In St Enimia's medieval biographies — Latin and vernacular — the saint endures a series of symbolic deaths prior to undergoing bodily death. In each version of the story her departure from temporal affairs is figured by clothing (a pauper's rags), disease (leprous pustules) and landscape (the wilderness). In each version she inhabits an uninhabitable space akin to the *zone entre-deux-morts* theorized by Lacan in *L'Éthique de la psychanalyse*. What distinguishes her from *zone*-dwelling monsters is her agency: what makes Enimia holy and her body sublime is that she has *chosen* to wear rags, acquire leprosy and live in the Tarn Gorges. But, as we have seen, not all of her biographers are fully convinced.

The greatest difference between Enimia's lives, however, concerns the representation of the Tarn Gorges as a wilderness. In the eleventh-century Latin life (BHL 2549–51), Enimia continues to subsist in the topographical equivalent of Lacan's topological *zone*. If she defies the Law, her unrepresentable revolution is safely contained. But in the early thirteenth-century Occitan text by Bertran de Marselha, Enimia — like Judith Butler's Antigone — moves boundaries. Plausibly under the influence of the two entirely neglected Latin *panegyrici* — the Occitan hagiographer rejected the early Latin author's mapping of topologics directly onto topography. The Tarn Gorges may once have been a zone only fit for sublime and abject bodies, but the presence of Enimia's beautiful body — never mortified and always as dazzling as a troubadour's lady — transforms the wilderness into a realm inhabitable by all. The new community that Enimia founds and fosters, moreover, is in stark opposition to the French, consistently portrayed by Bertran (writing during or in the aftermath of the Albigensian Crusade) as a proud, thieving, foolish, irreligious and barbarous people.

Today, Enimia's textual bodies are still in Paris (or, in the case of the more recently discovered copy of the Latin, in unknown hands), and there has been no sign of her relics since 1970 (when a modern-day Dagobert stole them from her grotto). According to Bertran de Marselha, the prospect of Enimia's body being removed from the Tarn Gorges provoked no end of consternation in the nunnery founded by the saint. But perhaps the sisters needn't have fretted. After all, it is the Occitan hagiographer's reading of the wilderness that endures (rather than those of the Latin hagiographers or Costecalde). Twenty-first-century guidebooks point out the landmarks associated with the saint's story — her hermitage, the rocky 'seat' sculpted to her holy posterior, the boulders that crushed the dragon — to the tourists who flock to Sainte-Énimie every summer. Enimia's body may have gone, but the Tarn Gorges have not reverted to a wilderness because the saint's presence is imprinted in the very landscape.

Notes to Chapter 4

1. Léon Costecalde, *Voyage au pays des merveilles, Cagnon du Tarn, vademecum du touriste* (Mende: Pauc, 1892), p. 133.
2. Scholars of medieval French (and Occitan) literature have drawn on the *zone entre-deux-morts* to discuss figures as varied as saints, madmen, *chanson de geste* warriors, and the knights and ladies of Arthurian romance. See, most notably, Kay, *Courtly Contradictions*; Sylvia Huot, *Madness in Medieval French Literature: Identities Found and Lost* (Oxford: Oxford University Press, 2003); Miranda Griffin, *The Object and the Cause in the Vulgate Cycle* (Oxford: Legenda, 2005); Simon Gaunt, *Love and Death in Medieval French and Occitan Courtly Literature: Martyrs to Love* (Oxford: Oxford University Press, 2006); Campbell, *Medieval Saints' Lives*; Luke Sunderland, *Old French Narrative Cycles: Heroism between Ethics and Morality*, Gallica, 15 (Cambridge: Brewer, 2010); and Jane Gilbert, *Living Death in Medieval French and English Literature*, Cambridge Studies in Medieval Literature, 84 (Cambridge, Cambridge University Press, 2011).
3. Marquis de Sade, 'Histoire de Juliette, ou les Prospérités du vice', in *Œuvres complètes*, ed. by Annie Le Brun and Jean-Jacques Pauvert, 15 vols (Paris: Pauvert, 1986–1991), VIII–IX (IX, 173).
4. For an edition of BHL 2549–51, see Clovis Brunel (ed.), 'Vita, inventio et miracula sanctae Enimiae', *Analecta Bollandiana*, 57 (1939), 237–98 (references to this edition). See Brunel's introduction for a description of the manuscript and provenance information. On the copy in private hands, see Clovis Brunel, 'Un nouveau manuscrit de la *Vita sanctae Enimiae*', *Analecta Bollandiana*, 75 (1957), 366–72. Brunel dates the life to the beginning of the twelfth century ('Vita', pp. 244–45), but the mid-eleventh century has been suggested as more probable given the content of the miracle tales. See Pierre Bonnassie, Pierre-André Sigal and Dominique Iogna-Prat, 'La Gallia du Sud, 930–1130', in *Hagiographies*, ed. Philippart, I, 288–344 (pp. 309–10).
5. For editions of the later *panegyrici*, see Pierre Pourcher (ed.), *Acta sanctae virginis Enimiae et Francorum Clotarii II filiae regis, ex Biblioteca nationali, lat. n° 913 edita* (Saint-Martin-de-Boubaux: the editor, 1883), pp. 109–28 [BHL 2552] and pp. 129–44 [BHL 2553].
6. Line numbers refer to Bertran de Marselha, *La Vie de sainte Énimie: poème provençal du XIIIe siècle*, ed. by Clovis Brunel, Classiques français du Moyen Âge, 17 (Paris: Champion, 1916). See the introduction to this edition for a description of Paris, Bibl. de l'Arsenal 6355 and a discussion of its history and provenance (pp. xii-xiv).
7. A thesis put forward in Albert Grimaud and Marius Balmelle, *Précis d'histoire du Gévaudan rattachée à l'histoire de France* (Mende: Planchon, 1925), pp. 157–58; and taken up in Geneviève

Brunel-Lobrichon, Anne-Françoise Leurquin-Labie, and Martine Thiry-Stassin, 'Langue française, ixe-xve siècle', in *Hagiographies*, ed. Philippart, II, 291–371 (p. 297).

8. The Priory of Sainte-Énimie prided itself on being independent from both secular and local ecclesiastical control and yet it was inevitably involved in the tussle between France, Toulouse and Aragon for control over the Viscounty of the Gévaudan during the Albigensian Crusade. With the Treaty of Paris of 1229, the French not only threatened the autonomy of the Viscounty; they also threatened the lands held by the Priory of Sainte-Énimie, demanding, for instance, that every man living on the prior's estate give 40 days' military service to the French king. See Ferdinand André, 'Histoire du monastère et prieuré de Sainte-Énimie, au diocèse de Mende', *Bulletin de la Société d'agriculture, industrie, sciences et arts du Département de la Lozère*, 18 (1867), 1–140; Charles Porée, *Études historiques sur le Gévaudan* (Paris: Picard, 1919), esp. pp. 410–15; and Jan K. Bulman, *The Court Book of Mende and the Secular Lordship of the Bishop: Recollecting the Past in Thirteenth-Century Gévaudan* (Toronto: University of Toronto Press, 2008).

9. 'Francia' in the Latin and 'Fransa' in the Occitan inevitably conflate the Merovingian kingdom of the Franks and the Capetian kingdom of the French.

10. E. Jane Burns, *Courtly Love Undressed: Reading through Clothes in Medieval French Culture* (Philadelphia: University of Pennsylvania Press, 2002), p. 12.

11. It is unclear where Enimia 'catches' her leprosy from, but possible contenders include the bride of St Licinius, who was struck with the disease on her wedding night, and St Néomaye, who is given webbed feet (a symbol of leprosy and also of menstruation) to avoid unwanted suitors. See Karena Gupton Akhavein, '*Reman say in aquesta terra*: The Function of *translatio* in the Occitan *vita* of Saint Enimie' (unpublished doctoral thesis, Columbia University, 2002), p. 4; and Cristina Álvares, 'Sainteté et sexualité: la *Vida de santa Enimia* de Bertrand de Marseille', *Diacrítica*, 7 (1992), 197–216 (p. 208).

12. On lepers' symbolic death, see Saul Nathaniel Brody, *The Disease of the Soul: Leprosy in Medieval Literature* (Ithaca, NY: Cornell University Press, 1974), p. 81; and Peter Lewis Allen, *The Wages of Sin: Sex and Disease, Past and Present* (Chicago: University of Chicago Press, 2000), pp. 35–37.

13. On leprosy as a punishment for lust, see Brody, pp. 52–53. On the links between leprosy and menstruation, see François-Olivier Touati, *Maladie et société au Moyen Âge: la lèpre, les lépreux et les leproseries dans la province ecclésiastique de Sens jusqu'au mlieu du XIVe siècle*, Bibliothèque du Moyen Âge, 11 (Brussels, De Boeck, 1998), pp. 109–13.

14. In BHL 2549–51, for example, Enimia introduces herself to the shepherds in the Gévaudan as a visitor from a 'longinqua patria' (p. 259) ['distant homeland']. The author of BHL 2553, similarly, says the party reached the 'Gabalitanos fines' after many days on the road (p. 135) ['Gévaudanais borders'] .

15. Gérard Gouiran, 'Le regard sur l'autochtone: sainte Énimie en Gévaudan', *Perspectives médiévales*, 22 (1996), 105–17 (p. 107). In the Occitan text, see vv. 380, 395, 401–04, 827–28, etc.

16. Cristina Álvares, 'Le corps féminin dans *La Vie de sainte Énimie* de Bertrand de Marseille', in *Le Rayonnement de la civilisation occitane à l'aube d'un nouveau millénaire: actes du 6e Congrès international de l'Association internationale d'études occitanes*, ed. by Georg Kremnitz et al. (Vienna: Praesens, 2001), pp. 301–09 (p. 303).

17. See Jeffrey Jerome Cohen, 'Hybrids, Monsters, Borderlands: The Bodies of Gerald of Wales', in *The Postcolonial Middle Ages*, ed. by Cohen (Basingstoke: Macmillan, 2000), pp. 85–104 (p. 87).

18. On 'le martyre « sans effusion de sang »', see Dominique Iogna-Prat, 'La femme dans la perspective pénitentielle des ermites du Bas-Maine (fin xie-début xiie siècles)', *Revue d'histoire de la spiritualité*, 53 (1977), 47–64 (p. 53).

19. See, for instance, Eugène Jory, *Histoire de sainte Énimie: vierge mérovingienne, fondatrice d'un monastère royal en Gévaudan au commencement du viie siècle* (Mende: Masseguin, 1873).

20. The following epithets refer to the dragon: 'plurimas [...] insidias demonum' (p. 270) ['manifold snares of the devil']; 'fraus diabolica immanis draconis' (ibid.) ['diabolical trickery of a huge dragon']; 'pestis illa dolosa' (ibid.) ['that cunning plague']; 'iniqui zabuli [...] insidias' (ibid.) ['snares of a wicked devil']; 'moles cuiusdam valida draconis' (ibid.) ['great might of a certain dragon']; and 'diabolica moles et immanis draco' (p. 272) ['diabolical might and a huge dragon'].

21. Enimia does dispatch the monster in popular versions of the legend recorded in the nineteenth century. See Henri Fromage, 'Sainte Énimie et le drac', *Bulletin de la Société de mythologie française*, 65 (1967), 1–18.

22. 'Colobra' (vv. 1038 and 1105 ['snake']); 'serpens' (vv. 1077, 1092, 1115, 1127, 1153, 1223, and 1255 ['serpent']); 'drago' (vv. 1134, 1144, 1147, 1156, 1233, 1245, 1254, and 1262 ['dragon']); 'dracs' (vv. 1140, 1164, 1169, 1183, 1193, and 1201 ['dragon']); 'adversiers' (vv. 1064 and 1124 ['adversary']); 'enemics' (v. 1200 ['enemy']); 'malfat' (v. 1108 ['devil']).

23. Slavoj Žižek, *Enjoy Your Symptom! Jacques Lacan in Hollywood and out* (London: Routledge, 1992), p. 46.

24. Slavoj Žižek, *Looking Awry: An Introduction to Jacques Lacan through Popular Culture* (Cambridge, MA: The MIT Press, 1991), p. 172n.

25. Judith Butler, *Antigone's Claim: Kinship between Life & Death* (New York: Columbia University Press, 2000), p. 50.

26. The relics of local saints Privat and Hilary were supposedly taken by Dagobert to Saint-Denis. As Brunel points out ('Vita', pp. 241–42), Enimia may have been associated with Dagobert to render her cult as prestigious as those centred on Mende.

27. Dagobert, for example, plunders relics from his own kingdom ('de diversis regni sui partibus', p. 278 ['from various regions of his kingdom']) and yet France is clearly understood as separate from the Gévaudan when news of Enimia's holiness travels 'per finitima regna' (ibid.) ['through adjoining kingdoms']. When Dagobert wishes to take his sister's body back to France ('ad patriam', ibid. ['to the homeland']), it remains unclear whether this is the king's homeland or that of both siblings. But when the Latin author says that the saint's body cannot leave Burla even after death he says that she may never be 'exiled' to France: 'a suis exulem nunquam sineret excubiis' (ibid.) ['she may never be exiled from her watchtower'], implying that Enimia is now perfectly at home down south.

28. On the Randon family, whose arms also appear in Paris, BnF, lat. 913, see Isabelle Darnas and Fernand Peloux, 'Évêché et monastères dans le Gévaudan du haut Moyen Âge', *Annales du Midi*, 122 (2010), 341–59 (p. 354).

CONCLUSION

❖

The Example of St Syrus and the Basilisk

Once upon a time, an over-sized, dragon-like creature known as the Basilisk plagued a city. The monster boasted a cockerel's crest and impenetrable skin, but its most powerful weapon was undoubtedly its deadly gaze. When confronted with those awful eyes, the inhabitants of the city were utterly helpless. Fortunately, however, a real hero soon arrived to save the day.

The above plot summarizes several Marvel Comics storylines of recent decades: basilisks have appeared on the pages of comic books in various guises since the 1970s, terrorizing New York until their eventual defeat by the likes of Spider-Man, the Thing and Morbius the Living Vampire.[1] It also sums up the Latin *vita* of St Syrus, composed in 1292 by Jacobus de Voragine (compiler of the *Legenda aurea*), in which Syrus rescues the city of Genoa, Jacobus's home turf, from the terrifying monster.[2] There is no direct genealogical link here — the basilisk has a long and illustrious pedigree stretching back to Pliny the Elder's *Naturalis historia* — but the least we can say is that the story of the crested creature's futile quest to destroy civilization is an enduring one.

Jacobus's Basilisk, which not only launches fire from its eyes but shoots plague from its mouth (as medieval dragons were wont to do), lives in a well beside Syrus's church. The saint takes pity on his public and announces three days of prayer and fasting, at the end of which he lowers a bucket into the dragon's hole and orders the monster to climb inside. Hauling the basilisk up to the surface, he commands it to launch itself into the sea, and never again are the Genoese pestered.

The Latin life of St Syrus is unusual among medieval saints' lives because it comes with a ready-made hermeneutic framework. The saint's encounter with the monster is given the following gloss:

> Sic igitur in beato Syro completum esse videtur verbum propheticum quod dicit, 'Super aspidem et basiliscum ambulabis', et verbum evangelicum quod dicit, 'Ecce dedi vobis potestatem calcandi super serpentes et scorpiones, et super omnem virtutem inimici' [...] Serpens iste serpentis antiqui gerit ymaginem, et similitudinem representat. Ipse enim super omnes filios superbie tumore cristatus multos visu sue astutie decepit, et flatu malitie venenose corumpit. Sicut igitur sanctus Syrus populum suum eripuit a serpente visibili, sic credamus quod suis meritis a serpente eripiat infernali. (p. 371)

> [It is thus clear that the word of the Prophets was completed in St Syrus, which says 'Thou shalt tread upon the lion[3] and adder' [Psalm 91.13], and the word of the Gospel which says 'Behold, I give unto you power to tread on serpents and

scorpions, and over all the power of the enemy' [Luke 10.19] [...] That serpent bears the appearance of the ancient serpent, and manifests its likeness. For, [king] over all the children of pride [Job 41.34], crested with the protuberance [of pride], he deceives many with the cunning of his gaze, and corrupts with the wickedness of his venomous breath. And so, just as St Syrus saved his people from a visible serpent, so let us believe that by his merits, he may save [us] from the infernal serpent.]

As Alain Boureau has noted, the Basilisk here slithers between the four levels of allegory of medieval exegesis.[4] There is, of course, the literal level, the story of a 'visible serpent' common to the medieval biography and Marvel Comics. But Jacobus also advances a more ambitious hermeneutical programme than we might expect to govern, say, our reception of a comic book. The tale of St Syrus had been told long before he donned his mitre, since the saint fulfils, typologically, the word of both Old and New Testaments. The story also plays out in the present, tropologically: the basilisk represents the diabolical snares we face, snares from which, with Syrus's help, we should strive to protect ourselves. And finally, looking forward anagogically to Judgment Day, the basilisk foreshadows the 'ancient serpent' of the Book of Revelation, who will be cast into the lake of fire. According to Jacobus, St Syrus makes for a perfect 'example of sanctity' ('sanctitas exemplum', p. 366), but he is not explicitly a model for us to follow. We find no incitement to imitation here. On the contrary, our response should be to pray for the saint's intercession (pp. 376–77); to pray, that is, for a further retelling of the story.

The saints and monsters of medieval French and Occitan hagiography are, for the most part, slipperier customers than St Syrus and the Basilisk. Even if they do not subscribe to Jacobus's four-way hermeneutics, however, vernacular hagiographers nonetheless encourage audiences to look beyond the literal level of the story. Prologues and epilogues, and prayers pronounced by the saint, or by the narrator on our behalf, present the intervening narrative as evidence that the story can and, moreover, *should* repeat itself in the present and future: with the saint's intercession, we may be able to steer clear of all forms of allegorical monsters ('ancient serpent' included). Upon reading or listening to a holy biography in the vernacular, we are instructed to say a prayer, or perhaps light a candle or set off on pilgrimage, in honour of our saint and to the glory of God. Never are we exhorted to model ourselves directly on the holy protagonist him- or herself. As Patrick Geary writes, 'These are not lives to be emulated but rather to be admired. They glorify God; they do not provide models for mortals'.[5]

And yet, vernacular hagiographers persistently refer to saints as 'examples'. The author of one French life of St Margaret, prose version 1, seeks to disseminate her story so that Christians far and wide may find a 'bon essample' (Sainte-Geneviève 587, f. 21r ['good example']). Likewise, in the Occitan life of St Enimia, Bertran de Marselha calls upon us all to follow the saint's example:

> Ans devon penre tuch essemps
> Excemple e tener tostemps
> En aquesta sancta pieusela,
> De cui vos recomtam novela. (vv. 77–80)

[Rather we must all together and at all times take and hold this holy maiden, whose story we are telling you, as an example.]

There is a need here, however, to make a distinction between these various examples of exemplarity. In Jacobus's Latin life of St Syrus, saint and monster typologically and anagogically embody a text and, tropologically, body one forth. Their exemplarity implies a particular configuration of body and text, according to which lives lived and told are indistinguishable, and aesthetically impossible bodies are invoked to testify to the truth of an ethical framework. The sublime and abject bodies of medieval hagiography signal that the examples set by holy and monstrous protagonists are worth copying or countering. But their worth is dependent on their being out of the reach of mere mortals like you or me.

There is nonetheless some scope for following or fleeing the examples of saints and monsters at the tropological level. Having read or listened to French prose version 1 of the life of St Margaret or the Occitan life of St Enimia, we are not supposed to set off in search of a pagan tyrant to martyr us, or a wilderness to mortify us. It is saints' devotional practices, and not their complete form of life, that we are asked to imitate. In Enimia's case, it is specifically her almsgiving that we are instructed to mimic, lest we prove overly proud. In Margaret's, at least in version 1, how we imitate her devotion is left to our own interpretation. And after reading hagiographical texts without detailed prescription, we might even find ourselves on the battlefield charging Saracens, dressed as St George, in imitation of his particular brand of militaristic devotion (cf. French prose version 6).

The body-text of medieval saints' lives is represented as immutable: the ethical framework bodied forth seems to be as resistant to change as the body of a rubbery martyr or a wraith-like ascetic. Indeed, in a world of shifting identities, a saint's life might offer its audiences a moment of stasis, a locus of identity formation that promises to hold everything together (if only for a moment), a contact relic that guarantees protection by the saint from the monster in reality as well as the one in the story.

Exemplarity at the tropological level, however, inevitably disrupts the stable body-text upon which we rely. As Catherine Sanok has written in relation to hagiography and gender, an invitation to imitate an ancient saint's devotional practices in our present inevitably prompts us to reflect upon cultural contingency:

> The expectation that vernacular legends could or should serve as devotional models is, paradoxically, what made them vehicles for thinking about cultural change and ethical variability, as hagiographers and their audiences sought to distinguish the imitable from the inimitable, the transhistorical from the contingent.[6]

To compare multiple versions of lives of saints, as I have done in this book, in a bid to unknot hagiography's sublime and abject configurations of body and text is, in a way, to misinterpret these texts. To show how vernacular hagiographers write the maternal body in and out of vernacular lives of St Margaret; how they shift the boundaries between communities and strangers in lives of St George; how Raimon Feraut rewrote St Honorat's family tree to give him Hungarian royal blood in the Occitan verse version of his life; and how Bertran de Marselha transformed a southern wilderness into a zone of liveability; in sum, to show how saints and monsters — their bodies and their lives — mutate in response to shifting religious, genealogical, gender and proto-national identities, is a flagrant act of misinterpretation. And yet such misinterpretation is sanctioned by these texts that, paradoxically, challenge the transhistoricity they simultaneously promote. Comparing and contrasting hagiographical tales, whether to cast doubt upon the old or authenticate the new, has a long scholarly pedigree indeed.

Hagiographical narratives (and sometimes even hagiographical protagonists) make occasional, albeit ephemeral, appearances in twentieth- and twenty-first-century comic books. After all, they remain great stories. But the example of St Syrus and the basilisk reminds us that medieval saints' lives come with layers of meaning that are supposed to play out in our own lives. With their sublime and abject bodies, these are lives that want to live.

Notes to the Conclusion

1. See, for example, the appearances by basilisks in *Marvel Team-Up* 16 (December 1973); *Morbius the Living Vampire* 4 (December 1992); and *New X-Men* 135 (December 2002); and subsequent issues.
2. The life is sometimes considered a supplementary chapter to the *Legenda aurea*. It is published in Jacobus de Voragine, 'Leggenda e inni di S. Siro, vescovo di Genova', ed. by Vincenzo Promis, *Atti della Società ligure di storia patria*, 10 (1874), 355–83 (references in parentheses to this edition).
3. The Hebrew *sháchal* (used poetically to refer to a lion) is rendered *aspís* ('asp') in the Septuagint, hence the discrepancy in the translation here.
4. Alain Boureau, 'La geste épiscopale de Jacopo da Varagine, de la Légende de saint Syrus à la Chronique de Gênes', in *Jacopo da Varagine: atti del I convegno di studi (Varazze, 13–14 aprile 1985)*, ed. by Giovanni Farris and Benedetto Tino Delfino (Cogoleto: SMA, 1987), pp. 79–100.
5. Patrick J. Geary, *Living with the Dead in the Middle Ages* (Ithaca, NY: Cornell University Press, 1994), p. 22.
6. Catherine Sanok, *Her Life Historical: Exemplarity and Female Saints' Lives in Late Medieval England* (Philadelphia: Pennsylvania University Press, 2007), pp. xiv-xv.

BIBLIOGRAPHY

❖

Primary

AUGUSTINE OF HIPPO, *Confessions*, ed. by James J. O'Donnell, 3 vols (Oxford: Clarendon Press, 1992)

BERGER, ROGER, and ANNETTE BRASSEUR, eds, *Les Séquences de sainte Eulalie* (Geneva: Droz, 2004)

BERTRAN DE MARSELHA, *La Vie de sainte Énimie: poème provençal du XIIIe siècle*, ed. by Clovis Brunel, Classiques français du Moyen Âge, 17 (Paris: Champion, 1916)

BRUNEL, CLOVIS, ed., 'Une nouvelle Vie de sainte Marguerite en vers provençaux', *Annales du Midi*, 38 (1926), 385–401

—— 'Vita, inventio et miracula sanctae Enimiae', *Analecta Bollandiana*, 57 (1939), 237–98

Calendarium Romanum, ex decreto sacrosancti œcumenici Concilii Vaticani II instauratum (Vatican: Typis polyglottis Vaticanis, 1969)

CHABANEAU, CAMILLE, ed., 'Paraphrase des litanies en vers provençaux', *Revue des langues romanes*, 29 (1886), 209–55

—— 'Vie de saint George', *Revue des langues romanes*, 31 (1887), 139–55

CHICHMAREV, VLADIMIR, ed., 'Vie provençale de sainte Marguerite', *Revue des langues romanes*, 46 (1903), 545–90

COSTECALDE, LÉON, *Voyage au pays des merveilles, Cagnon du Tarn, vademecum du touriste* (Mende: Pauc, 1892)

DI FEBO, MARTINA, ed., *Les Versions en prose du 'Purgatoire de saint Patrice' en ancien français*, Classiques français du Moyen Âge, 172 (Paris: Champion, 2013)

DUCOS, MAX, *Le Carnaval des dragons* (Paris: Sarbacane, 2010)

GÖRLACH, M., ed., *An East Midland Revision of the South English Legendary: A Selection from MS C.U.L. Add. 3039*, Middle English Texts, 4 (Heidelberg: Winter, 1976)

GUILCHER, YVETTE, ed., *Deux versions de la Vie de saint Georges*, Classiques français du Moyen Âge, 138 (Paris: Champion, 2001)

HAMER, RICHARD, ed., *Gilte Legende*, with the assistance of Vida Russell, Early English Text Society, 327–28 and 339, 3 vols (Oxford: Early English Text Society, 2006–2012)

HAMER, RICHARD, and VIDA RUSSELL, eds, 'A Critical Edition of Four Chapters from the *Légende dorée*', *Mediaeval Studies*, 51 (1989), 130–204

HEIMING, ODILO, ed., *Das ambrosianische Sakramentar von Biasca: Die Handschrift Mailand Ambrosiana A 24 bis inf.*, Liturgiewissenschaftliche Quellen und Forschungen, 51 (Münster: Aschendorff, 1969)

HILARY OF ARLES, 'Sermo de Vita S. Honorati', ed. by Samuel Cavallin, in *Vitae sanctorum Honorati et Hilarii, episcoporum Arelatensium*, Skrifter utgivna av Vetenskapssocieteten i Lund, 40 (Lund: Gleerup, 1952), pp. 47–78

JACOBUS DE VORAGINE, *Legenda aurea: con le miniature dal codice Ambrosiano C 240 inf.*, ed. by Giovanni Paolo Maggioni, trans. by Francesco Stella and others, Edizione nazionale dei testi mediolatini, 20, 2 vols (Florence: Galluzzo, 2007)

—— 'Leggenda e inni di S. Siro, vescovo di Genova', ed. by Vincenzo Promis, *Atti della Società ligure di storia patria*, 10 (1874), 355–83

—— *Sermones de sanctis per anni totius circulum* (Venice: Somaschi, 1573)

JEAN DE NOSTREDAME, 'Vie de saint Hermentaire', ed. by Camille Chabaneau, *Revue des langues romanes*, 29 (1886), 157–74

JEANROY, ALFRED, ed., 'Vie provençale de sainte Marguerite d'après les manuscrits de Toulouse et de Madrid', *Annales du Midi*, 11 (1899), 5–55

JOHN LYDGATE, 'Legend of St George', in *Mummings and Entertainments*, ed. by Claire Sponsler (Kalamazoo: Medieval Institute Publications, 2010), pp. 42–48

JOHN MIRK, *Festial*, ed. by Susan Powell, Early English Text Society, 334–35, 2 vols (Oxford: Early English Text Society, 2009–2011)

JOLY, A., ed., 'La Vie de sainte Marguerite: poème inédit de Wace', *Mémoires de la Société des antiquaires de Normandie*, 30 (1880), 173–270

KNIAZZEH, CHARLOTTE S. MANEIKIS, and E. J. NEUGAARD, eds, *Vides de sants rossellonesos*, Publicacions de la Fundació Salvador Vives Casajuana, 48, 3 vols (Barcelona: Dalmau, 1977)

MUNKE, BERNHARD, ed., *Die 'Vita sancti Honorati' nach drei Handschriften*, Beihefte zur Zeitschrift für romanische Philologie, 32 (Halle an der Saale: Niemeyer, 1911)

NICHOLAS BOZON, *Three Saints' Lives*, ed. by M. Amelia Klenke (St. Bonaventure: Franciscan Institute, 1947)

ORYWALL, INGELORE, ed., *Die alt- und mittelfranzösischen Prosafassungen der Margaretelegende* ([Bonn]: n. pub., 1968)

POURCHER, PIERRE, ed., *Acta sanctae virginis Enimiae et Francorum Clotarii II filiae regis, ex Bibliotheca nationali, lat. n° 913 edita* (Saint-Martin-de-Boubaux: the editor, 1883)

RAIMON FERAUT, *La Vida de sant Honorat*, ed. by Peter T. Ricketts, with the assistance of Cyril P. Hershon, Association internationale d'études occitanes, 4 (Turnhout: Brepols, 2007)

REICHL, KARL, ed., 'An Anglo-Norman Legend of Saint Margaret (ms. BM Add. 38664)', *Romania*, 96 (1975), 53–66

SADE, MARQUIS DE, 'Histoire de Juliette, ou les Prospérités du vice', in *Œuvres complètes*, ed. by Annie Le Brun and Jean-Jacques Pauvert, 15 vols (Paris: Pauvert, 1986–1991), VIII–IX (1987)

SANDKÜHLER, KONRAD M., ed., *Der Drachenkampf des hl. Georg in englischer Legende und Dichtung vom 14. bis 16. Jahrhundert* (Munich: Meindl, 1913)

SOLEIL, FÉLIX, ed., *La Vierge Marguerite substituée à la Lucine antique: analyse d'un poème inédit du XVe siècle* (Paris: Labitte, 1885)

SPENCER, FREDERIC, ed., 'The Legend of St. Margaret', *Modern Language Notes*, 5 (1890), 71–75 and 107–11

SYMEON THE METAPHRAST, 'Martyrium sanctae et egregiae et curationum virtute praeditae martyris Marinae', trans. by Laurentius Surius, in *De probatis sanctorum historiis*, 7 vols (Cologne: Calenium & Quenelios, 1576–1586), IV (1579), 274–84

TAMMI, GUIDO, ed., *Due versioni della leggenda di S. Margherita d'Antiochia in versi francesi del medioevo* (Piacenza: Scuola Artigiana del Libro, 1958)

TAUSEND, MONIKA, ed., *Die altokzitanische Version B der 'Legenda aurea': ms. Paris, Bibl. nat., n. acq. fr. 6504*, Beihefte zur Zeitschrift für romanische Philologie, 262 (Tübingen: Niemeyer, 1995)

WACE, *La Vie de sainte Marguerite*, ed. by Elizabeth A. Francis, Classiques français du Moyen Âge, 71 (Paris: Champion, 1932)

——*La Vie de sainte Marguerite*, ed. by Hans-Erich Keller, Beihefte zur Zeitschrift für romanische Philologie, 229 (Tübingen: Niemeyer, 1990)

ZINGERLE, WOLFRAM, ed., 'Zur Margarethen-Legende', *Romanische Forschungen*, 6 (1891), 414–16

Secondary

AGAMBEN, GIORGIO, *La Comunità che viene* (Turin: Einaudi, 1990)

AKBARI, SUZANNE CONKLIN, *Idols in the East: European Representations of Islam and the Orient, 1100–1450* (Ithaca, NY: Cornell University Press, 2009)

ALBERT, JEAN-PIERRE, 'Légende de sainte Marguerite: un mythe maïeutique?', *Razo*, 8 (1988), 19–31

ALLEN, PETER LEWIS, *The Wages of Sin: Sex and Disease, Past and Present* (Chicago: University of Chicago Press, 2000)

ÁLVARES, CRISTINA, 'Le corps féminin dans *La Vie de sainte Énimie* de Bertrand de Marseille', in *Le Rayonnement de la civilisation occitane à l'aube d'un nouveau millénaire: actes du 6ᵉ Congrès international de l'Association internationale d'études occitanes*, ed. by Georg Kremnitz and others (Vienna: Praesens, 2001), pp. 301–09

——'Sainteté et sexualité: la *Vida de santa Enimia* de Bertrand de Marseille', *Diacrítica*, 7 (1992), 197–216

ANDERSON, BENEDICT, *Imagined Communities: Reflections on the Origin and Spread of Nationalism* (London: Verso, 1983)

ANDRÉ, FERDINAND, 'Histoire du monastère et prieuré de Sainte-Énimie, au diocèse de Mende', *Bulletin de la Société d'agriculture, industrie, sciences et arts du Département de la Lozère*, 18 (1867), 1–140

ASHLEY, KATHLEEN, and PAMELA SHEINGORN, 'The Translations of Foy: Bodies, Texts, and Places', in *The Medieval Translator / Traduire au Moyen Âge*, 5, ed. by Roger Ellis and René Tixier (Turnhout: Brepols, 1996), pp. 29–49

ASHTON, GAIL, *The Generation of Identity in Late Medieval Hagiography: Speaking the Saint*, Routledge Research in Medieval Studies, 1 (London: Routledge, 2000)

BARONIO, CESARE, *Annales ecclesiastici*, 12 vols (Venice: Hieronymus Scotus, 1600–1612)

BARRIGA I PÉREZ, FRANCESC, *Sant Jordi i Catalunya: arrels de la identitat catalana* (Madrid: Edaf, 2007)

BATAILLE, GEORGES, *Théorie de la religion* (Paris: Gallimard, 1974)

BERRESSEM, HANJO, 'On the Matter of Abjection', in *The Abject of Desire: The Aestheticization of the Unaesthetic in Contemporary Literature and Culture*, ed. by Konstanze Kutzbach and Monika Mueller, Gender in Modern Culture, 9 (Amsterdam: Rodopi, 2007), pp. 19–48

BERTONI, GIULIO, 'Sulla Vita provenzale di S. Margherita', *Revue des langues romanes*, 49 (1906), 299–301

BLANCHOT, MAURICE, *La Communauté inavouable* (Paris: Minuit, 1983)

BLOCH, R. HOWARD, *Etymologies and Genealogies: A Literary Anthropology of the French Middle Ages* (Chicago: University of Chicago Press, 1983)

BONNASSIE, PIERRE, PIERRE-ANDRÉ SIGAL, and DOMINIQUE IOGNA-PRAT, 'La Gallia du Sud, 930–1130', in *Hagiographies: histoire internationale de la littérature hagiographique latine et vernaculaire en Occident des origines à 1550*, ed. by Guy Philippart (Turnhout: Brepols, 1994-), I, 288–344

BORLAND, JENNIFER, 'Violence on Vellum: St Margaret's Transgressive Body and its Audience', in *Representing Medieval Genders and Sexualities in Europe: Construction, Transformation, and Subversion, 600–1530*, ed. by Elizabeth L'Estrange and Alison More (Farnham: Ashgate, 2011), pp. 67–87

BOUCHE, HONORÉ, *Chorographie ou description de Provence, et l'histoire chronologique du mesme pays*, 2 vols (Aix: David, 1664)

BOUREAU, ALAIN, 'La geste épiscopale de Jacopo da Varagine, de la Légende de saint Syrus à la Chronique de Gênes', in *Jacopo da Varagine: atti del I convegno di studi (Varazze, 13–14 aprile 1985)*, ed. by Giovanni Farris and Benedetto Tino Delfino (Cogoleto: SMA, 1987), pp. 79–100

BOYER, JEAN-PAUL, 'De force ou de gré: la Provence et ses rois de Sicile (milieu XIIIe siècle-milieu XIVe siècle)', in *Les Princes angevins du XIIIe au XVe siècle: un destin européen*, ed. by Noël-Yves Tonnerre and Elisabeth Verry (Rennes: Presses universitaires de Rennes, 2003), pp. 23–59

BRODY, SAUL NATHANIEL, *The Disease of the Soul: Leprosy in Medieval Literature* (Ithaca, NY: Cornell University Press, 1974)

BROWN, JONATHAN, 'Saint George, The Canon and a Flood of Right-Wing Hate', *The Independent*, 22 April 2011 <http://independent.co.uk/news/uk/home-news/saint-george-the-canon-and-a-flood-of-rightwing-hate-2271982.html> [accessed 3 April 2016]

BRUNEL, CLOVIS, 'Un nouveau manuscrit de la *Vita sanctae Enimiae*', *Analecta Bollandiana*, 75 (1957), 366–72

BRUNEL-LOBRICHON, GENEVIÈVE, ANNE-FRANÇOISE LEURQUIN-LABIE, and MARTINE THIRY-STASSIN, 'Langue française, IXe-XVe siècle', in *Hagiographies* (see Bonnassie, above), II, 291–371

BULMAN, JAN K., *The Court Book of Mende and the Secular Lordship of the Bishop: Recollecting the Past in Thirteenth-Century Gévaudan* (Toronto: University of Toronto Press, 2008)

BURGER, GLENN, and STEPHEN F. KRUGER, 'Introduction', in *Queering the Middle Ages*, ed. by Burger & Kruger, Medieval Cultures, 27 (Minneapolis: University of Minnesota Press, 2001), pp. xi-xxiii

BURKE, PETER, 'Reflections on the Cultural History of Time', *Viator*, 35 (2004), 617–26

BURNS, E. JANE, *Courtly Love Undressed: Reading through Clothes in Medieval French Culture* (Philadelphia: University of Pennsylvania Press, 2002)

BUSBY, KEITH, 'Hagiography at the Confluence of Epic, Lyric, and Romance: Raimon Feraut's *La Vida de sant Honorat*', *Zeitschrift für romanische Philologie*, 113 (1997), 51–64

BUTLER, JUDITH, *Antigone's Claim: Kinship between Life & Death* (New York: Columbia University Press, 2000)

——— *Bodies that Matter: On the Discursive Limits of 'Sex'* (New York: Routledge, 1993)

——— *Gender Trouble: Feminism and the Subversion of Identity* (New York: Routledge, 1990)

CAMPBELL, EMMA, 'Homo Sacer: Power, Life, and the Sexual Body in Old French Saints' Lives', *Exemplaria*, 18 (2006), 233–73

——— *Medieval Saints' Lives: The Gift, Kinship and Community in Old French Hagiography*, Gallica, 12 (Cambridge: Brewer, 2008)

CARLONE, AUGUSTIN, 'Études historiques sur l'ancien comté de Nice, III: Le troubadour Raymond Féraud, son temps, sa vie, ses œuvres', *Annales de la Société des lettres, sciences et arts des Alpes-Maritimes*, 2 (1873), 5–68

CAWSEY, KATHY, 'Disorienting Orientalism: Finding Saracens in Strange Places in Late Medieval English Manuscripts', *Exemplaria*, 21 (2009), 380–97

CERDÀ SUBIRACHS, JORDI, 'La leyenda de santa Margarita de Antioquía en Cataluña', in *Medioevo y literatura I-IV: Actas del V Congreso de la Asociación Hispánica de Literatura Medieval (Granada, 27 septiembre-1 octubre 1993)*, ed. by Juan Salvador Paredes Núñez, 2 vols (Granada: Universidad de Granada, 1995), II, 23–32

CHAMBERLAIN, GEOFFREY, *From Witchcraft to Wisdom: A History of Obstetrics & Gynaecology in the British Isles* (London: Royal College of Obstetricians and Gynaecologists, 2007)

COHEN, JEFFREY JEROME, 'Hybrids, Monsters, Borderlands: The Bodies of Gerald of Wales', in *The Postcolonial Middle Ages*, ed. by Cohen (Basingstoke: Macmillan, 2000), pp. 85–104

——— 'Monster Culture (Seven Theses)', in *Monster Theory: Reading Culture*, ed. by Cohen (Minneapolis: University of Minnesota Press, 1996), pp. 3–25

CONSTABLE, GILES, 'The Place of the Crusader in Medieval Society', *Viator*, 29 (1998), 377–403

DAY, ELIZABETH, 'Holy Comic Books! Saints Are the Latest Superheroes!', *Sunday Telegraph*, 26 March 2006, <http://telegraph.co.uk/news/uknews/1513978/Holy-comic-books-Saints-are-the-latest-superheroes.html> [accessed 29 September 2015]

DELANY, SHEILA, *Impolitic Bodies: Poetry, Saints, and Society in Fifteenth-Century England: The Work of Osbern Bokenham* (Oxford: Oxford University Press, 1998)

DERRIDA, JACQUES, *De l'hospitalité*, with Anne Dufourmantelle (Paris: Calmann-Levy, 1997)

—— *L'Autre Cap, suivi de La Démocratie ajournée* (Paris: Minuit, 1991)

—— *Le Monolinguisme de l'autre, ou, La Prothèse d'origine* (Paris: Galilée, 1996)

—— *Politiques de l'amitié, suivi de L'oreille de Heidegger* (Paris: Galilée, 1994)

—— *Spectres de Marx: l'état de la dette, le travail du deuil et la nouvelle Internationale* (Paris: Galilée, 1993)

—— *The Other Heading: Reflections on Today's Europe*, trans. by Pascale-Anne Brault and Michael B. Naas (Bloomington: Indiana University Press, 1992)

DINSHAW, CAROLYN, 'Chaucer's Queer Touches / A Queer Touches Chaucer', *Exemplaria*, 7 (1995), 75–92

—— *How Soon is Now? Medieval Texts, Amateur Readers, and the Queerness of Time* (Durham, NC: Duke University Press, 2012)

DISDIER, JEAN-BAPTISTE, *Recherches historiques sur saint Leonce, évêque de Fréjus et patron du diocèse* (Draguignan: Gimbert, 1864)

DOAN, LAURA, *Disturbing Practices: History, Sexuality, and Women's Experience of Modern War* (Chicago, University of Chicago Press, 2013)

DOUGLAS, MARY, *Purity and Danger: An Analysis of Concepts of Pollution and Taboo* (London: Routledge & Kegan Paul, 1966)

EDELMAN, LEE, *No Future: Queer Theory and the Death Drive* (Durham, NC: Duke University Press, 2004)

ENGEL, PÁL, *The Realm of St. Stephen: A History of Medieval Hungary, 895–1526*, trans. by Tamás Pálosfalvi, ed. by Andrew Ayton (London: Tauris, 2001)

FISHER, JOHN H., *The Emergence of Standard English* (Lexington: University Press of Kentucky, 1996)

FLACHAIRE DE ROUSTAN, RENÉE, 'Les manuscrits du poème de Raimon Féraut sur la vie de saint Honorat de Lérins', *Le Moyen Âge*, 35 (1924–1925), 255–84

FOSTER, HAL, 'Obscene, Abject, Traumatic', *October*, 78 (1996), 106–24

FOUCAULT, MICHEL, 'Nietzsche, Genealogy, History', in *Language, Counter-Memory, Practice: Selected Essays and Interviews*, ed. and trans. by Donald F. Bouchard, trans. by Simon Sherry (Ithaca, NY: Cornell University Press, 1977), pp. 139–64

—— 'Nietzsche, la généalogie, l'histoire', in Suzanne Bachelard, and others, *Hommage à Jean Hyppolite* (Paris: Presses universitaires de France, 1971), pp. 145–72

—— 'Qu'est-ce que les Lumières?', in *Dits et écrits, 1954–1988*, ed. by Daniel Defert and François Ewald, with the assistance of Jacques Lagrange, 4 vols (Paris: Gallimard, 1994), IV, 679–88

FREEMAN, ELIZABETH, *Time Binds: Queer Temporalities, Queer Histories* (Durham, NC: Duke University Press, 2010)

FREUD, SIGMUND, *Das Unbehagen in der Kultur* (Vienna: Internationaler psychoanalytischer Verlag, 1930)

FROMAGE, HENRI, 'Sainte Énimie et le drac', *Bulletin de la Société de mythologie française*, 65 (1967), 1–18

GAUNT, SIMON, *Gender and Genre in Medieval French Literature*, Cambridge Studies in French, 53 (Cambridge: Cambridge University Press, 1995)

—— *Love and Death in Medieval French and Occitan Courtly Literature: Martyrs to Love* (Oxford: Oxford University Press, 2006)

—— 'Straight Minds/"Queer" Wishes in Old French Hagiography: *La Vie de sainte Euphrosine*', in *Premodern Sexualities*, ed. by Louise Fradenburg and Carla Freccero, with the assistance of Kathy Lavezzo (New York: Routledge, 1996), pp. 155–73

GEARY, PATRICK J., *Living with the Dead in the Middle Ages* (Ithaca, NY: Cornell University Press, 1994)

GILBERT, JANE, *Living Death in Medieval French and English Literature*, Cambridge Studies in Medieval Literature, 84 (Cambridge: Cambridge University Press, 2011)

GIRARD, RENÉ, *Le Bouc émissaire* (Paris: Grasset, 1982)

GOOD, JONATHAN, *The Cult of Saint George in Medieval England* (Woodbridge: Boydell, 2009)

GÖRLACH, M., 'Middle English Legends, 1220–1530', in *Hagiographies* (see Bonnassie above), I, 429–85

GOUIRAN, GÉRARD, 'Le regard sur l'autochtone: sainte Énimie en Gévaudan', *Perspectives médiévales*, 22 (1996), 105–17

GRANGE, HUW, 'Fraudsters or Patriots? The Authors of the Lives of St Honorat', *Romania*, 133 (2015), 201–18

GRIFFIN, MIRANDA, *The Object and the Cause in the Vulgate Cycle* (Oxford: Legenda, 2005)

GRIMAUD, ALBERT, and MARIUS BALMELLE, *Précis d'histoire du Gévaudan rattachée à l'histoire de France* (Mende: Planchon, 1925)

GROSZ, ELIZABETH, *Volatile Bodies: Toward a Corporeal Feminism* (Bloomington: Indiana University Press, 1994)

GUPTON AKHAVEIN, KARENA, '*Reman say in aquesta terra*: The Function of *translatio* in the Occitan *vita* of Saint Enimie' (unpublished doctoral thesis, Columbia University, 2002)

HALBERSTAM, JUDITH, *In a Queer Time and Place: Transgender Bodies, Subcultural Lives* (New York: New York University Press, 2005)

HALPERIN, DAVID, *How to Do the History of Homosexuality* (Chicago: University of Chicago Press, 2002)

HERRING, SCOTT, *Queering the Underworld: Slumming, Literature, and the Undoing of Lesbian and Gay History* (Chicago: University of Chicago Press, 2007)

HILL, CAROLE, ' "Here Be Dragons": The Cult of St Margaret of Antioch and Strategies for Survival', in *Art, Faith and Place in East Anglia: From Prehistory to the Present*, ed. by T. A. Heslop, Elizabeth Mellings, and Margit Thøfner (Woodbridge: Boydell, 2012), pp. 105–16

—— *Women and Religion in Late Medieval Norwich* (Woodbridge: Boydell, 2010)

HUOT, SYLVIA, *Madness in Medieval French Literature: Identities Found and Lost* (Oxford: Oxford University Press, 2003)

HUTCHESON, GREGORY S., 'The Sodomitic Moor: Queerness in the Narrative of *Reconquista*', in *Queering the Middle Ages* (see Burger & Kruger above), pp. 99–122

IOGNA-PRAT, DOMINIQUE, 'La femme dans la perspective pénitentielle des ermites du Bas-Maine (fin XIᵉ- XIIᵉ siècles)', *Revue d'histoire de la spiritualité*, 53 (1977), 47–64

JORY, EUGÈNE, *Histoire de sainte Énimie: vierge mérovingienne, fondatrice d'un monastère royal en Gévaudan au commencement du VIIᵉ siècle* (Mende: Masseguin, 1873)

KANIUK, ROSS, 'PC Crazes: St George Now Black', *Daily Star*, 21 December 2010 <http://daily star.co.uk/posts/view/168380/PC-crazes-St-George-now-black> [accessed 3 April 2016]

KANT, IMMANUEL, *Kritik der Urteilskraft*, ed. by Karl Vorländer, 6ᵗʰ edn (Leipzig: Meiner, 1948)

KAY, SARAH, *Courtly Contradictions: The Emergence of the Literary Object in the Twelfth Century* (Stanford: Stanford University Press, 2001)

—— 'The Sublime Body of the Martyr: Violence in Early Romance Saints' Lives', in *Violence in Medieval Society*, ed. by Richard W. Kaeuper (Woodbridge: Boydell, 2000), pp. 3–20

KRETTEK, ADOLF, 'Die Ortsnamen der *Vida de sant Honorat* von Raimon Feraut, und ihrer lateinischen Quelle', in *Vita sancti Honorati* (see Munke, above), pp. 163–204

KRISTEVA, JULIA, *Étrangers à nous-mêmes* (Paris: Fayard, 1988)

—— 'Héréthique de l'amour', *Tel Quel*, 74 (1977), 30–49

—— 'Maternité selon Giovanni Bellini', in Kristeva, *Polylogue* (Paris: Seuil, 1977), pp. 409–35

—— *Pouvoirs de l'horreur: essai sur l'abjection* (Paris: Seuil, 1980)

—— *Powers of Horror: An Essay on Abjection*, trans. by Leon S. Roudiez (New York: Columbia University Press, 1982)

—— *Soleil noir: dépression et mélancolie* (Paris: Gallimard, 1987)

—— 'Stabat mater', in *Histoires d'amour* (Paris: Denoël, 1983), pp. 225–47

—— *Strangers to Ourselves*, trans. by Leon S. Roudiez (New York: Columbia University Press, 1991)

LACAN, JACQUES, *Le Séminaire. Livre 7: L'Éthique de la psychanalyse, 1959–1960*, ed. by Jacques-Alain Miller (Paris: Seuil, 1986)

—— *The Seminar of Jacques Lacan. Book 7: The Ethics of Psychoanalysis, 1959–1960*, ed. by Jacques-Alain Miller, trans. by Dennis Porter (London: Tavistock/Routledge, 1992)

LAMBERT, GUSTAVE, *Histoire de Toulon*, 4 vols (Toulon: Le Var, 1886–1892)

LARSON, WENDY R., 'The Role of Patronage and Audience in the Cults of Sts Margaret and Marina of Antioch', in *Gender and Holiness: Men, Women and Saints in Late Medieval Europe*, ed. by Samantha J. E. Riches and Sarah Salih, Routledge Studies in Medieval Religion and Culture, 1 (London: Routledge, 2002), pp. 23–35

LE GOFF, JACQUES, 'Au Moyen Âge: temps de l'Église et temps du marchand', in *Pour un autre Moyen Âge: temps, travail et culture en Occident* (Paris: Gallimard, 1977), pp. 46–65

LECLERCQ, ARMELLE, *Portraits croisés: l'image des Francs et des Musulmans dans les textes sur la Première Croisade*, Nouvelle bibliothèque du Moyen Âge, 96 (Paris: Champion, 2010)

LÉONARD, ÉMILE G., *Les Angevins de Naples* (Paris: Presses universitaires de France, 1954)

LOCHRIE, KARMA, 'Desiring Foucault', *Journal of Medieval and Early Modern Studies*, 27 (1997), 3–16

MADDOCKS, HILARY, 'Pictures for Aristocrats: The Manuscripts of the *Légende dorée*', in *Medieval Texts and Images: Studies of Manuscripts from the Middle Ages*, ed. by Margaret M. Manion and Bernard J. Muir (Reading: Harwood Academic, 1991), pp. 1–23

MAITLAND, SARA, and WENDY MULFORD, *Virtuous Magic: Women Saints and their Meanings* (London: Mowbray, 1998)

MARINONI, MARIA CARLA, 'Il drago e la principessa: considerazioni su una *Vita di S. Giorgio* occitanica', *ACME*, 57 (2004), 161–82

MATZKE, JOHN E., 'Contributions to the History of the Legend of Saint George, with Special Reference to the Sources of the French, German and Anglo-Saxon Metrical Versions', in *Publications of the Modern Language Association of America*, 17 (1902), 464–535; and 18 (1903), 99–171

MAYNARD, STEVEN, '"Respect Your Elders, Know Your Past": History and the Queer Theorists', *Radical History Review*, 75 (1999), 56–78

MCAFEE, NOËLLE, 'Abject Strangers: Towards an Ethics of Respect', in *Ethics, Politics, and Difference in Julia Kristeva's Writings*, ed. by Kelly Oliver (London: Routledge, 1993), pp. 116–34

MENNINGHAUS, WINFRIED, *Ekel: Theorie und Geschichte einer starken Empfindung* (Frankfurt a. M.: Suhrkamp, 1999)

MEYER, PAUL, 'La Vie latine de saint Honorat et Raimon Féraut', *Romania*, 8 (1879), 481–508

—— 'Notice du ms. Sloane 1611 du Musée britannique', *Romania*, 40 (1911), 532–58

MILLS, ROBERT, *Suspended Animation: Pain, Pleasure and Punishment in Medieval Culture* (London: Reaktion, 2005)

—— 'Violence, Community and the Materialisation of Belief', in *A Companion to Middle English Hagiography*, ed. by Sarah Salih (Cambridge: Brewer, 2006), pp. 87–103

—— ' "Whatever You Do is a Delight to Me!" Masculinity, Masochism, and Queer Play in Representations of Male Martyrdom', *Exemplaria*, 13 (2001), 1–37

MORGAN, DAVID A. L., 'The Cult of St George *c.* 1500: National and International Connotations', in *L'Angleterre et les pays bourguignons: relations et comparaisons XVe-XVIe siècles*, ed. by Jean-Marie Cauchies (Neuchâtel: Centre européen d'études bourguignonnes (XIVe-XVIe s.), 1995), pp. 151–62

MORUZZI, NORMA CLAIRE, 'National Abjects: Julia Kristeva on the Process of Political Self-Identification', in *Ethics, Politics, and Difference* (see McAfee, 'Abject Strangers', above), pp. 135–49

NANCY, JEAN-LUC, *Être singulier pluriel* (Paris: Galilée, 1996)

—— *La Communauté désœuvrée* (Paris: Bourgois, 1986)

OLIVER, KELLY, *Reading Kristeva: Unravelling the Double-Bind* (Bloomington: Indiana University Press, 1993)

PARIS, GASTON, *Histoire poétique de Charlemagne* (Paris: Franck, 1865)

PORÉE, CHARLES, *Études historiques sur le Gévaudan* (Paris: Picard, 1919)

QURESHI, YAKUB, 'Church Calls Up "Black St George" to Fight Racism', *Manchester Evening News*, 20 December 2010 <http://menmedia.co.uk/manchestereveningnews/news/s/1400368_church_calls_up_black_st_george_to_fight_racism> [accessed 3 April 2016]

—— 'Manchester Cathedral Event Depicting St George as Black Goes Ahead Despite Hate Mail', *Manchester Evening News*, 7 May 2011 <http://menmedia.co.uk/manchestereveningnews/news/s/1420106_manchester-cathedral-event-depicting-st-george-as-black-goes-ahead-despite-hate-mail> [accessed 3 April 2016]

REINEKE, MARTHA J., ' "This Is My Body": Reflections on Abjection, Anorexia, and Medieval Women Mystics', *Journal of the American Academy of Religion*, 58 (1990), 245–65

RICHES, SAMANTHA, *St George: Hero, Martyr and Myth* (Stroud: Sutton, 2000)

ROBERTSON, DUNCAN, 'Authority and Anonymity: The Twelfth-Century French Life of St. Mary the Egyptian', in *Translatio studii: Essays by his Students in Honor of Karl D. Uitti for his Sixty-Fifth Birthday*, ed. by Renate Blumenfeld-Kosinski and others, Faux titre, 179 (Amsterdam: Rodopi, 2000), pp. 245–59

—— *The Medieval Saints' Lives: Spiritual Renewal and Old French Literature*, Edward C. Armstrong Monographs on Medieval Literature, 8 (Lexington, KY: French Forum, 1995)

—— 'Writing in the Textual Community: Clemence of Barking's *Life of St Catherine*', *French Forum*, 21 (1996), 5–28

SALIH, SARAH, *Versions of Virginity in Late Medieval England* (Cambridge: Brewer, 2001)

SAMUELS, ROBERT, 'Žižek's Rhetorical Matrix: The Symptomatic Enjoyment of Postmodern Academic Writing', *JAC*, 22 (2002), 327–54

SANOK, CATHERINE, *Her Life Historical: Exemplarity and Female Saints' Lives in Late Medieval England* (Philadelphia: Pennsylvania University Press, 2007)

SCHÄFER, WILHELM, 'Das Verhältnis von Raimon Ferauts Gedicht *La Vida de sant Honorat* zu der *Vita Sancti Honorati*', in *Vita sancti Honorati* (see Munke, above), pp. 134–62

SCHULENBURG, JANE TIBBETTS, *Forgetful of their Sex: Female Sanctity and Society, ca. 500–1100* (Chicago: University of Chicago Press, 1998)

SÉNAC, PHILIPPE, *L'Image de l'autre: l'Occident médiéval face à l'islam* (Paris: Flammarion, 1983)

SETTON, KENNETH M., 'Saint George's Head', *Speculum*, 48 (1973), 1–12

SKEMER, DON C., *Binding Words: Textual Amulets in the Middle Ages* (University Park: Pennsylvania State University Press, 2006)

SMITH, KAREN P., 'Serpent-Damsels and Dragon-Slayers: Overlapping Divinities in a Medieval Tradition', in *Christian Demonology and Popular Mythology*, ed. by Gábor Klaniczay and Éva Pócs, Demons, Spirits, Witches, 2 (Budapest: Central European University Press, 2006), pp. 121–38

SOUTHERN, R. W., *Western Views of Islam in the Middle Ages* (Cambridge, MA: Harvard University Press, 1962)

SPIEGEL, GABRIELLE M., 'Genealogy: Form and Function in Medieval Historical Narrative', *History and Theory*, 22 (1983), 45–53

STOCK, BRIAN, *The Implications of Literacy: Written Language and Models of Interpretation in the Eleventh and Twelfth Centuries* (Princeton: Princeton University Press, 1983)

STRICKLAND, DEBRA HIGGS, *Saracens, Demons, & Jews: Making Monsters in Medieval Art* (Princeton: Princeton University Press, 2003)

SUNDERLAND, LUKE, *Old French Narrative Cycles: Heroism between Ethics and Morality*, Gallica, 15 (Cambridge: Brewer, 2010)

TOLAN, JOHN V., *Saracens: Islam in the Medieval European Imagination* (New York: Columbia University Press, 2002)

TOUATI, FRANÇOIS-OLIVIER, *Maladie et société au Moyen Âge: la lèpre, les lépreux et les léproseries dans la province ecclésiastique de Sens jusqu'au milieu du XIVe siècle*, Bibliothèque du Moyen Âge, 11 (Brussels: De Boeck, 1998)

TREHARNE, ELAINE M., ' "They Shall Not Worship Devils... Which Neither Can See, Nor Hear, Nor Walk": The Sensibility of the Virtues and *The Life of St Margaret*', in *Proceedings of the Patristic, Medieval, and Renaissance Conference*, 15 (1990), pp. 221–36

VAUCHEZ, ANDRÉ, '*Beata stirps*: sainteté et lignage en Occident aux XIIIe et XIVe siècles', in *Famille et parenté dans l'Occident médiéval: actes du Colloque de Paris (6–8 juin 1974)*, ed. by Georges Duby and Jacques Le Goff (Rome: École française de Rome, 1977), pp. 397–406

WALTER, CHRISTOPHER, 'The Origins of the Cult of Saint George', *Revue des études byzantines*, 53 (1995), 295–326

WIENCKE, HELMUT, *Die Sprache Caxtons* (Leipzig: Tauchnitz, 1930)

WOGAN-BROWNE, JOCELYN, 'The Apple's Message: Some Post-Conquest Hagiographic Accounts of Textual Transmission', in *Late-Medieval Religious Texts and their Transmission: Essays in Honour of A. I. Doyle*, ed. by A. J. Minnis (Woodbridge: Brewer, 1994), pp. 39–53

WOLF, KENNETH BAXTER, *The Life and Afterlife of St. Elizabeth of Hungary: Testimony from her Canonization Hearings* (Oxford: Oxford University Press, 2011)

ŽIŽEK, SLAVOJ, *Enjoy Your Symptom! Jacques Lacan In Holywood and Out* (London: Routledge, 1992)

—— *Looking Awry: An Introduction to Jacques Lacan through Popular Culture* (Cambridge, MA: The MIT Press, 1991)

—— *The Metastases of Enjoyment: Six Essays on Women and Causality* (London: Verso, 1994)

—— *The Sublime Object of Ideology* (London: Verso, 1989)

INDEX OF MEDIEVAL MANUSCRIPTS

❖

GENERAL INDEX

❖

www.ingramcontent.com/pod-product-compliance
Lightning Source LLC
LaVergne TN
LVHW061327060426
835511LV00012B/1903